QUESTIONS IN THE PHILOSOPHY OF MIND

QUESTIONS IN THE PHILOSOPHY OF MIND

David Pears

Duckworth

First published 1975 by
Gerald Duckworth & Co. Ltd.
The Old Piano Factory
43 Gloucester Crescent, London NW1.

ISBN 0 7156 0688 3

Printed in Great Britain by
The Anchor Press Ltd, and bound by
Wm Brendon & Son Ltd, both of Tiptree, Essex

To Anne

Contents

	Preface	9
1	Predicting and Deciding	13
2	Wanting and Intending	39
3	Causes and Objects of Some Feelings and Psychological Reactions	56
4	The Paradoxes of Self-Deception	80
5	Sketch for a Causal Theory of Wanting and Doing	97
6	Ifs and Cans	142
7	Hume's Empiricism and Modern Empiricism	193
8	Hume's Account of Personal Identity	208
9	Russell's Theories of Memory	224
10	Russell's Theory of Desire	251
11	Wittgenstein's Treatment of Solipsism in the *Tractatus*	272
	Index	293

Preface

The first five papers in this collection are concerned with a group of connected problems in the philosophy of mind. A human agent often knows what he is going to do, because he already intends to do it. But what sort of knowledge is that? Like memory, it is immediate or non-inferential. But immediate knowledge would be miraculous if it were not causally connected with its object. For if there were no such causal connection, how could the mind generate so many accurate accounts of the remembered past or the intended future? In the case of memory, the causal connection runs from the past experience, which is the object, to the present knowledge of that object. But if the agent's knowledge of his own future action is connected causally with that action, the pattern of the connections between these two things must be more complicated. Obviously the future action, which is the object, does not cause the present knowledge of itself. But perhaps both are caused by the desire to perform the future action.

This suggestion is defended against various objections and alternative theories. The issue belongs to a general controversy of some importance. Can the achievements of the human mind be explained as complex exploitations of simple causal connections, or are they unlike anything else in nature? The dispute about the agent's knowledge of his own future actions is a small part of this controversy, but it raises some intricate questions about deliberation and about the lack of symmetry between this kind of foreknowledge and memory. It also raises the question whether it is possible to make mistakes about one's own intentions, and this leads into an investigation of self-deception, which is located somewhere along the line between pure insincerity and downright mistake.

These problems are connected with the question whether an agent's account of his reason for an action is like a report of a causal process observed in the physical world. There are striking dissimilarities between these two kinds of statement and between the two types of knowledge that they express. But underneath the dissimilarities there ought to be a common structure. For if the desires mentioned by the agent in his account of his motivation had no general tendency to produce the same outcome when the same circumstances recurred, they would not explain his action. On the other hand, we can seldom use the underlying structure in order to falsify agents' accounts of their motivation, whereas we can often use it in order to falsify reports of causal processes in the physical world. I argue that this difference is attributable to the peculiar complexity of the mind rather than to any fundamental difference in the pattern of its operations.

The sixth paper, 'Ifs and cans', is also concerned with actions. It is an inquiry into the basis of the distinction between conditional sentences and other hypothetical sentences which J. L. Austin drew in his celebrated lecture on this topic.[1] He used the distinction in his analysis of the statement, 'I can if I choose', and he argued that here the 'if' is not conditional, and that ascriptions of ability are not dispositional. I argue that both theses need some modification.

The remaining five papers are historical. Those on Hume and Russell are connected in a general way with the first five papers. For both Hume and Russell tried to construct their philosophies of mind on causal foundations. It is generally agreed that the causal foundations used by them are too simple, and that they neglected the intentionality ('directedness') of the mental. The two papers on Russell explore the effect of this neglect on his symmetrical theories of memory and desire in *The Analysis of Mind*. I suggest that, when intentionality is put back into his theories, the causal foundations need to be modified, but not abandoned. This is in line with the argument of the first five papers.

The last paper, 'Wittgenstein's treatment of solipsism in the *Tractatus*', belongs to a different part of the philosophy of mind. It is an attempt to detach Wittgenstein's transcendental solipsism from the solipsism of his middle period, and to

1. British Academy Lecture, 1956, reprinted in *Philosophical Papers*, Oxford, 1961.

connect it with both Russell's and Schopenhauer's theories about the ego.

The paper on Hume's account of personal identity is not due to be published elsewhere. Four other papers are new only in that they have not yet appeared elsewhere. These are 'The paradoxes of self-deception' (4), 'Russell's theories of memory' (9), 'Russell's theory of desire' (10), and 'Wittgenstein's treatment of solipsism in the *Tractatus*' (11). Of the remaining six papers two are new in other ways. 'Predicting and deciding' (1) remains unaltered in its first half, but its second half has been rewritten. 'Sketch for a causal theory of wanting and doing' (5) is a rewritten version of four articles on this topic which overlapped one another. The four articles are, 'Are reasons for actions causes?', 'Desires as causes of actions', 'Two problems about reasons for actions', and 'Rational explanation of actions and psychological determinism'. 'Russell's theories of memory' (9) is the only other paper that is reprinted with substantial alterations. All changes in the rest are minor.

The paper on 'Wanting and intending' (2) was written in reply to some criticisms of 'Predicting and deciding' made by Professor R. M. Hare. His criticisms are quoted extensively, and the issues should be clear.

I am grateful to the original editors and publishers for permission to reprint. Details of publication are as follows.

1. Revised version of 'Predicting and deciding'. British Academy annual philosophical lecture 1964. Published by Oxford University Press. Reprinted in *Studies in the Philosophy of Thought and Action*, ed. P. F. Strawson, London, 1968. The first half is unaltered, but the second half is rewritten.

2. Reprint of 'Comments on Professor Hare's "Wanting: some pitfalls" ', in *Agent, Action and Reason*, papers given to the fourth philosophy colloquium, University of Western Ontario, 1968; Toronto 1971.

3. Reprint of article under same title in *Ratio* 4, No. 2, December 1962, also published in *Philosophy of Mind*, ed. Stuart Hampshire, Harper and Row, 1966.

4. Reprint of paper read at a symposium on Knowledge and Belief at the University of Valencia in April 1973; forthcoming in *Teorema*, 1974, and also published in *Freud*, ed. R. A. Wollheim, New York, 1974.

5. Revised version of a thesis developed in four articles: 'Are reasons for actions causes?' in *Epistemology*, ed. Avrum Stroll, New York, 1967; 'Desires as causes of actions', in *Royal Institute of Philosophy Lectures*, I, ed. G. N. A. Vesey, London, 1968; 'Two problems about reasons for actions', in *Agent, Action and Reason* (see 2); and 'Rational explanation of actions and psychological determinism', in *Essays on Freedom and Determinism*, ed. Ted Honderich, London, 1973.

6. Reprint of article under same title in *Canadian Journal of Philosophy* I, No. 2, December 1971, and I, No. 3, March 1972; also published in *Essays on J. L. Austin*, ed. G. J. Warnock, London, 1973.

7. Reprint of article under same title in *David Hume: a Symposium*, ed. D. F. Pears, London, 1963.

8. Paper read to the Eighteenth Century Society, McMaster University, in November 1973, not previously published.

9. Revised version of a paper read at a centenary symposium on Bertrand Russell at the University of Indiana, March 1972, also published in *Bertrand Russell's Philosophy*, ed. George Nakhnikian, London, 1974.

10. Paper read at a centenary symposium on Bertrand Russell at McMaster University in October 1972, forthcoming in *Russell in Review*, ed. John E. Thomas, Toronto.

11. Reprint of article under same title forthcoming in *Critica*, published by Instituto de Investigaciones Filosóficas, Universidad Nacional Autónoma de México.

Oxford
September 1974

D.P.

1 Predicting and Deciding

Other people's decisions can be predicted inductively. But can anyone treat his own decisions in this way? It has been claimed[1] that the answer to this question would be a step towards the solution of the problem of free will. But my aim is at something closer. I ask the question because it opens a way to a problem about the nature of deliberation. How is one person's deliberation related to another person's prediction of its result?

If someone tries to make an inductive prediction of the result of his own deliberation, it looks as if he is trying to see the matter as another person would see it. But can he really take a spectator's seat? Certainly he can, when what he predicts is that, even if, after deliberation, he decided on an action, and never changed his mind, he still would not perform it. But that is not the point. The point that some philosophers[2] want to make is that, when he thinks that his action will depend on his decision, he cannot predict it inductively, because he cannot predict his own decision inductively. They maintain that, in such cases, what he will do must remain an open question for him until he has made his decision. It would follow that an inductive prediction, made by him, of his own decision could never come true, since his prior certainty would exclude the possibility of his subsequent decision. It is admitted that the decision would be possible if he forgot, or ceased to believe, his inductive prediction after he had made it; and that, when he seems to be making an inductive prediction of his own future decision, he may really be making a present decision, expressed in a mis-

1. By Professor Hampshire in *Thought and Action*, London, 1959, Chs. 2 and 3.

2. e.g. ibid.; Hart and Hampshire in 'Decision, intention and certainty', *Mind* 1958; and D. M. Mackay in 'On the logical indeterminacy of a free choice', *Mind* 1960.

leading way. But, it is contended, a prediction of a decision which is genuinely inductive, and made, remembered, and still believed by the agent, is strictly self-frustrating. He may take a spectator's seat in such cases, but, so long as he stays in it, he cannot play the whole of his predicted part as agent.

There are two things which make it difficult to assess this answer to my question. First, deciding and acting may be almost simultaneous, and, even when they are not, deciding need not be a definite event. It is no accident that the present tense of the verb 'to decide' leads a very marginal life outside subordinate clauses. Secondly, it is not always clear when the agent's prediction of his own decision is properly called 'inductive'.

In order to circumvent the first difficulty, I shall begin by considering cases in which the agent would naturally and easily make his decision at a definite moment which precedes the moment of action. What I shall say about these cases can be generalised, without much modification, to cover similar cases where, although the decision does not occur at a definite moment, there would be a time before the action at which he could say that he had decided. Later, I shall say something about the very different situation where he finds it hard to make up his mind before the moment of action. In that kind of situation the best way to secure examples where a decision, or something like a decision, might naturally be expected before the moment of action is to assume that there is some special consideration which makes this necessary. For instance, there might be other decisions which he could not postpone, and which depended on his decision about the matter in question: or other people might require him to make up his mind, perhaps for a similar reason. But, as I said, I shall begin with simpler cases.

In order to circumvent the second difficulty, I shall confine the initial scope of my inquiry even further. My first cases will all be ones in which the agent's prediction of his own decision will be obviously inductive. I shall leave the more dubious cases, where we should hesitate to call it 'inductive', until later. That will make it possible to isolate one problem, the compatibility or incompatibility of deciding with inductively predicting the decision, and to deal with it first.

One way of securing cases where the agent's prediction of his own decision is obviously inductive is to assume that he does not know all the relevant details of the situation in which he will make his decision. Then there might be special circumstances which made it possible for him to predict it inductively in spite of this gap in his knowledge. In a matter of taste, for example, he might predict that in a certain shop he would decide to buy what a friend of his, with similar tastes, had just bought, even if he did not yet know what the shop offered. Or, to take a more calculative example, he might predict that in a game of chess, confronted by the same simple position as a friend of similar skill, he would decide to make the same move, even if he did not yet know what the position was. In both these examples his prediction would be obviously inductive. Moreover, so long as he remained unaware what his friend's purchase or move specifically were, there is no doubt that, confronted by the situation – shop-counter or chess-board – he could make each of the predicted decisions. For there is not even an appearance of incompatibility between predicting one's own decision under one description and making it under another description, provided that one does not know in advance that the two descriptions are uniquely satisfied by the same decision. But suppose that the agent, before he makes his decision, does find out what article his friend bought, or what move he made, so that he can predict his decision under the description under which it will be made. Then, when he is confronted by the situation, can he still make his decision without giving up his prediction of it? This is the controversial question.

When I ask it, I am, of course, assuming that the agent really does begin by making an inductive prediction, and does not begin by deciding to do whatever his friend does. I am also assuming that he maintains his prediction, neither forgetting it later, nor abandoning it, nor modifying it in any way. However, within these limitations, the question can be generalised a little. The agent might begin by predicting that he would decide to do what his friend advised, or what his friend predicted, on the evidence of his (the agent's) past decisions, that he would decide to do. The only restriction on the descriptions in the agent's original prediction is that they must be descriptions from which, given additional information available *before* the decision is made, it would be possible to deduce the description under which it will be made. So the description in his prediction must not be 'what my friend will imitate', if the friend will imitate whatever he does. Of course, if the agent is going to make his decision under a rationalising description, the matter becomes more complex. But I shall ignore that complexity, and confine myself to cases where he makes his decision under a description which connects it with the desires from which it issues.

What is the answer to the controversial question? Consider first the more calculative case where the agent asks himself what move he will make when he is handed the chess-board, and predicts that it will be the same move as his friend's, and then discovers what the move was. Here, provided that the position is simple, a fairly high degree of certainty is often justifiable. For this kind of practical problem is not merely like a theoretical one: it actually contains a theoretical one. Now, whether the agent's problem is only theoretical – what move would lead to the swiftest certain checkmate –, or practical – what move to make –, there are things which remain to be done after he has predicted the result inductively, and which cannot be done before he sees the board. The question is what ought we to call those things. Had he not made a confident prediction of the result, we should say that he solved the theoretical problem, and, if there were also a practical one, that he deliberated and decided. But, since he has made the prediction, we cannot say that he solves the theoretical problem, because solving is discovering the solution by working it out. Nor can we even say that he is checking the solution. For, given his initial inductive certainty, he will be working it out from the position in order to see how it fits, rather than that it fits. Still, this is something that is related to solving. It is what is left when initial uncertainty is subtracted from solving.

If his problem is practical, what he does will be slightly more complex. For he will start not from the position alone, but from the position and his desire for the swiftest certain checkmate, and he will work forward from these two to the project. However, as before, he will be seeing how the project fits rather than that it fits. But this time that will not be all that he is doing. Something that is not purely intellectual will be happening simultaneously. His desire will be directed on to the project. And there is a great difference between knowing that this will happen and actually feeling it happen. Can we call this deliberating and deciding? Perhaps not. But, if we do not, it is important to see that this time more that is the same is left when the initial uncertainty is taken away. For, though he may not be making the decision, nevertheless, when he sees how the project fits his desire and the position, and when he feels the direction of his desire, he is making the decision his own. No such essential part is played by desire when the problem is theoretical, since, though he may want to solve a theoretical problem, the solution does not depend on his desires. So if, in my example, he makes the solution of the theoretical problem his own, the sense in which he makes it his own will not be so strong as the sense in which he makes the decision his own when the problem is practical. Hence the subtraction of initial uncertainty from normal deciding leaves more that is the same. What about deliberating? There too, I think, the same considerations apply. But we should add that, since deliberation is a sort of working out, if we refuse to allow that an agent can deliberate with prior certainty, this refusal ought to be even more qualified.

The other example, where a choice between available articles is a matter of taste, is different in several ways. Desires that may vary from person to person play a larger part, and calculation plays a smaller part. Consequently, it would often be artificial to try to extract a theoretical problem from the practical one: exposure to the articles is almost inevitably followed by the process which has a claim to be called deliberating; and prior certainty is more rarely attainable. Still there are cases of this kind where a high degree of prior certainty is attained, and, if we ask whether the agent deliberates and decides in such cases, the answer will be much the same as before, except that, since competing desires play a larger part here, a negative answer would need to be qualified even further.

It has been suggested[3] that the idea, that there is anything like a contradiction concealed in the phrase 'deciding to do A with prior inductive certainty that one will decide to do A', is an illusion; an illusion which comes from thinking that the agent decides to do A in order to achieve certainty that he will in fact do A. For if we think this, we shall naturally regard his inductive certainty that he will decide to do A and his actually

3. By J. W. Roxbee Cox in 'Can I know beforehand what I am going to decide?', *Philosophical Review* 1963.

deciding to do A as two competing, and therefore, possibly, incompatible ways of achieving certainty that he will in fact do A. But, it is contended, people decide in order to achieve certainty about what to do, and not in order to achieve certainty about what they will do. And to those who realise this, it is suggested, the phrase will no longer even appear to be contradictory.

If this is correct, my treatment of the two examples is too cautious and qualified. But I do not think that it is correct: not just because people do sometimes decide to do A with the primary purpose of achieving certainty that they will in fact do A, and then building on it; but for the more important reason that, whatever the primary purpose of a decision may be, after it has been made, the agent will be certain what he will in fact do, and so the apparent contradiction cannot be removed in this way. In any case another apparent contradiction confronts us when we consider certainty about what to do. For in my two examples, if the agent assumes that his friend made the right choice, he will be inductively certain about what to do: and it is equally plausible to maintain that there is another contradiction concealed in the phrase 'deliberating and deciding with prior inductive certainty about what to do'. But, as I have been arguing, even in my two examples there is room for important elements of deliberating and deciding. However, it is true that in unusual cases, such as these, the agent, before he is confronted with the actual situation, will not have the feeling that normally accompanies certainty about what to do. He cannot have it until he makes the decision his own by seeing how it fits the situation and his desires, and by feeling the final direction of his desires. These are the elements of deliberating and deciding that come later.

I hope that a fairly general truth is beginning to emerge. To put it negatively, if an action depends on a decision, it is an exaggeration to say that the two things which yield certainty about it, deciding and predicting the decision inductively, are independent and uncombinable. To say that they are independent is exaggerated, because the description under which the decision is predicted must be one from which, given additional information available before the decision is made, it would be possible to deduce the description under which it will be made (unless the description under which it will be made is a rationalisation). To say that they are uncombinable is exaggerated, because one of them, unmodified, can be combined with a modified form of the other. Even if the agent maintains the so-called spectator's viewpoint, he will not be prevented from playing his part as agent: he will only play it rather differently (unless, of course, he has a desire to falsify the prediction as such: but I am assuming that he has not).

It might be admitted that the two things that yield certainty about an action that depends on a decision can be combined, after some modification of one of them, in unusual cases where the agent predicts his decision under the description under which it will be made before he discovers the relevant features of the situation of choice. For when he discovers them, he does something very like deliberating and deciding, and, even if he does not make his prediction come absolutely true, at least he catches up with it. But in the more usual cases, where he already knows the relevant features of the situation of choice, it is not so easy to see how his prediction can outstrip his deliberating and deciding and yet come almost true. However, this often seems to happen. How can it happen? This time there is an additional difficulty. For how can his prediction keep its inductive character, in spite of the fact that it goes through his own desires and knowledge of the situation of choice? How can it avoid becoming a decision made in advance?

I think that it is clear that we cannot go very far towards answering this question without examining the deeper operations of induction, and unearthing contingent facts which are taken for granted in everyday life and built into the structure of our concepts. However, I shall begin, as before, by taking cases in which the agent's prediction is obviously inductive, and I shall assume that naturally, and without the pressure of any special consideration, he would make, or at least would have made, his decision before the moment of action. Now where the deliberation is largely calculative it will be difficult to find such cases. For the more calculative the deliberation, the more unlikely it will be that the agent's prediction will outstrip his decision and still keep its inductive character. For instance, if his desire to checkmate swiftly is firm, and, if he sees the position, and, after calculating, appears to predict with complete certainty that he will decide to make a particular move, there are strong reasons for saying that he has already decided, but is expressing his decision misleadingly. For it is irrelevant that he has not yet made the move or touched the piece, and any behavioural confirmation of the hypothesis that he has not yet made the decision would be very likely to undermine the hypothesis that he is certain that he would make it. So I shall choose examples where the deliberation is far from being purely calculative, and involves the weighing of desires that may change.[4] In such cases there will be more than an analogy between predicting one's decision before it is made and predicting one's emotion before it is felt.

In this area there seem to be two types of case where the agent's inductive prediction outstrips his decision. First, there is the radical type of case where he predicts that the general pattern of his desires will change, and that after it has changed he will make a particular decision. For instance, he predicts that it will change after physical or psychological treatment, conversion, or some other cardinal experience. Secondly, there is the less radical, and far more frequent type of case, where he predicts only that, in some particular matter, his present desire[5] or favour will change, and that he will make a different decision in the end. Everyone would agree that this happens in matters of taste and in cases where pleasure is the avowed aim. But it also happens in other kinds of delicately balanced predicament. If we were interested only in the nature of desire, the difference between the two types of case, the more and the less radical, could be presented as simply a difference of degree. For even a desire about a particular matter contributes something to the general pattern, and a change in it might be part of a larger rearrangement. But, since we are also interested in the agent's ability to predict the change inductively, the difference is, perhaps, more than one of degree. For he can often predict from his own past record that his desire in a particular matter will change, but the prediction of a change in the general pattern would usually be based on a striking external cause.

4. Even the desire to win a game of chess may come and go. But usually its constancy is taken for granted in deliberation about one's next move.

5. I use the word 'desire' in an inclusive way. Contrast the exclusive use of the verb 'to want' in 'deciding to do what one does not want to do'.

What the two types of case have in common is that the agent predicts a change in his desires. He considers the possible projects, favours one of them most, and then predicts that he will decide on a different one. In the radical type of case the prediction which is based on an external cause is obviously inductive, and it will sometimes yield a high degree of prior certainty. If it does, will the agent be able to make the prediction come true by deliberating and deciding? I think that he will, but not quite in the way that he could in my first two examples. For in those examples, when he made the predictions, he did not know the situations: but in this case, when he made the prediction, he already knew the situation and saw how the project would fit it and the pattern of his desires, if that pattern changed. What happens later is that it does change, and the direction of his desires, which he then feels, is new. The general character of this group of examples is that, in the triangle formed by situation, desire, and project, either the first point is not known by the agent when he makes his prediction, or the second point is not fixed.

The usual objection to this answer is that the agent decides, or ought to decide, before the change comes about. But ought he? Surely the idea that beneath such changes there is an unchanging source of decisions is a moralising fiction. How can he make a decision in advance? Perhaps it will be suggested that he can decide in advance to do whatever he feels like doing later. But when a decision is expressed in that way, there is an implied contrast between one's own momentary feelings and other considerations, and the decision, which issues from the present pattern of desires, is a decision to exclude those other considerations. Our case, however, is quite different. In it the implied contrast is lacking, because the later feelings will not be momentary, and so that way of expressing a decision in advance would be deprived of its usual point. If there were a decision in advance, it could only issue from a higher desire, which could not compete with the others, the desire to be true to oneself, but such a decision would not be necessary.

In the less radical cases, where the agent claims that in a particular matter his desire will change, it might be doubted whether the claim is really inductive. As before, he knows what the possible projects are, favours one most at the moment, but predicts that in the end he will decide on a different one. But this time there is no suggestion that the general pattern of his desires will change, and the prediction is based on the outcome of his own previous deliberations in similar situations. So his reasoning is very closely connected with the usual operation of the pattern of his desires. However, it can still be called inductive. If he had waited for his desires to point in their final direction, his reasoning would not have been inductive. But he does not wait. His prediction outstrips his decision, and so, though it is closely connected with the usual operation of the pattern of his desires, the connection is not the kind of connection that would deprive his reasoning of its inductive character.

Can he, in this kind of case, make his prediction come true by deliberating and deciding? The answer seems to be that, even if he is quite certain of his prediction, he can, in much the same way that he could when the change was more radical. However, in this kind of case he would seldom feel very certain about his prediction. So I ought also to ask my question about cases where his prediction is more tentative.

Tentative predictions introduce complications which are off my route. So I shall deal with their effect briefly and schematically. When the agent predicts confidently that he will decide to do A, let us suppose that he would assign the probability $1/x$ to the proposition that he will decide to do A. When he predicts his decision tentatively, the probability that he would assign to it would be smaller, say $1/(x+w)$. Now nobody would claim that it is absolutely certain that, if he decided to do A, he would do it, even if the moment of action were very close. For, even if nothing else changed in the interval, his desire might change. Of course, there are cases where any change would be enormously improbable, particularly if the interval were short. Let us say that in such cases the agent's decision to do A would give the proposition that he will do A the probability $1/z$. I pointed out earlier that often deciding and acting will be almost simultaneous. When this is so, $1/z$ will be almost indistinguishable from 1.

There is another complication which ought to be mentioned at this point. There is something else, which is very like a decision, but less firm. It may be that decisions are, by definition, firm. If so, the other thing ought to be called 'a tentative intention'. The noun 'intention', and the verb 'to intend', even when they are not qualified, often have this suggestion of tentativeness. Now suppose that an agent predicts inductively that he will form a tentative intention to do A.[6] Then the formation of this intention would give the proposition that he will do A a probability less than $1/z$, say $1(z+y)$. These two assessments of probability can be made by anybody, but I am assuming that they are made by the agent.

Now, if we hear him predict that he will decide to do A, or that he will form the tentative intention of doing A, we may inquire what probability he would assign to the proposition that he will in fact do A. So far, I have only taken cases where the prediction is confident and what is predicted is a decision, and in such cases he would assign the high probability $1/xz$. But there are also three other theoretically possible types of case. He can confidently predict the formation of a tentative intention, and then the probability that he would assign would be $1/x(z+y)$: or tentatively predict a decision, and assign the probability $1/z(x+w)$: or tentatively predict the formation of a tentative intention, and assign the probability $1/(x+w)(z+y)$.

This fourfold schema generalises the problem, and my original question can now be put in its most general form: can the agent make a decision or form an intention which, in his estimation, gives the proposition that he will perform the action a probability scarcely greater than the probability which he had already implicitly assigned to it when he inductively predicted the decision or the formation of the intention? I have been arguing for a qualified affirmative answer in some cases where the prediction is confident and what is predicted is a decision. Exactly the same arguments apply when the prediction is confident and what is predicted is the formation of a tentative intention. But in the other two types of case, where the prediction is tentative, the situation is quite different. For here, when the predicted decision is actually made, or the predicted tentative intention is actually formed, it will give the proposition that the agent will

6. No doubt, the prediction that one will form a tentative intention is often a prediction not of a definite event but only of the gradual emergence of a preference. But sometimes there is a special consideration which forces one to crystallise one's desires, however inadequately, before the moment for action arrives.

perform the action a probability substantially greater than the probability which he had already implicitly assigned to it when he made the inductive prediction. Consequently, in these cases, the agent's prior certainty is not great enough to modify the nature of his deliberation and decision, or the formation of his tentative intention. This explains why people find nothing puzzling in the very frequent cases where an agent predicts with less than complete certainty that in a particular matter his desire will change, and that he will make a different decision or form a different intention in the end.

The existence of these cases, which is hardly in dispute, is enough to dispel two very common prejudices. The first is the idea that an agent cannot really make an inductive prediction of his own future decision, since, if he did, that could only be because between the moment of prediction and the moment of decision there was going to be such a change in him that the decision would not be, in the full sense, his own. The second is the idea that, if he considers the possible projects and favours one most, he cannot help deciding on it. The first is connected with the moralising fiction mentioned just now.[7] Against the second it is enough to point out that, even when the result of deliberation is a very strong preference for a particular project, the preference need not amount to a decision. Everyone would agree that it need not in cases where the agent thinks that the circumstances may change, or that the matter may be taken out of his hands. What is less obvious is the thesis for which I have been arguing, that, even if there are no considerations of this sort in his mind, his preference still will not amount to a decision if he has inductive reasons for thinking that it will change.

If the spectator's viewpoint can be combined with the agent's viewpoint in many cases and in various ways without any radical modification of either of them, there ought to be a general explanation of their compatibility. Such an explanation would either take the form of a neutral theory into which both viewpoints could be fitted on an equal footing, or it would use one of the two to explain the other. The chief difficulty is that the agent's immediate knowledge of his future actions is so different from inductive knowledge. Memory of our past ex-

7. It is the other horn of the dilemma: 'Either there is an unchanging source of decisions, or they will not really belong to the same person.'

periences is similarly immediate, but there is also a difference which makes this analogy inadequate. We form intentions and make decisions, but memories merely occur to us. It is true that we can try to remember our previous experiences, but recollection is not a stepwise process of building up memories, whereas deliberation is related in that way to decisions. So the compatibility of the spectator's viewpoint with the viewpoint of the person who remembers is easier to explain than its compatibility with the agent's viewpoint. When I decide to perform a certain action, I know immediately that I shall perform it, but it also seems that there must be some contemporary fact about me – if not the fact of my decision, then some more basic fact – from which I could predict my action inductively. If the preceding arguments are correct there will also have been earlier facts about me from which I could have predicted my decision without preventing myself from making it. The problem is to explain how my life as an agent is combinable with my life as a spectator of my own agency, and this problem is more difficult than the parallel problem about memory, because the two viewpoints intersect at two quite different stages in the origination of actions, the first of which leads up to the making of a decision, while the second leads on from the decision to the action.

It is sometimes a good policy to start with a very simple solution to a problem and to modify it later when modifications are required. So I shall merely suggest two simple points which seem to me to provide the only possible basis for explaining the compatibility of immediate and inductive knowledge of one's own future actions. The first point is that, if desires are dispositions, they are manifested in the inner life of the agent as well as in his behaviour. The second is that it is a contingent fact that the desires of a normal person are sufficiently constant for all their manifestations to exhibit a regular pattern. The inner manifestations put the agent in a position to make claims to knowledge of his own future decisions and actions, and the regularity of the pattern of all the manifestations explains why most of his claims are correct.

This explanation does not give the two viewpoints parity, because it uses the spectator's viewpoint to explain the agent's. It is a very simple explanation, which obviously needs a lot of elaboration and some modification. However, I shall not attempt such a large task in the remainder of this paper. Instead, I shall confine myself to criticising two lines of thought which would undermine the explanation if they were valid. This is a negative procedure, but it will strengthen the foundations for more constructive developments later.

The first of the two lines of thought is to assimilate 'I will do A' to a command. The suggestion is either that it is a command rather than a statement, or at least, that it is more like a command than a statement. If it were a command, it could not express the agent's knowledge, however special, of a future fact, and even the more cautious assimilation to a command would make it difficult to construe it as a claim to such knowledge. But the explanation of the compatibility of the two viewpoints that has just been put forward requires that, whatever else 'I will do A' may be, it is at least some kind of claim to knowledge of a future fact. So either that line of thought must be rejected, or the explanation must be abandoned.

Let us open the bidding at the top, and ask whether 'I will do A' actually is some kind of command. This question has recently been answered in the affirmative.[8] It is said that an expression of intention, like 'I will do A', may be regarded as a kind of command addressed to oneself, and that the utterance 'I intend to do A', when it is a genuine report of a state of mind, is tantamount to the statement 'I have said in my heart "Let me do A" '. The kind of command that is meant must be self-exhortation, which, according to this theory, in the latter case, is said by the agent to have been done by himself in the past, and, in the former case, is actually being done by him audibly at the moment. But how can the theory allow for the fact that he might be insincere in what he says? When he says what he has done, he may, of course, be lying. But that is not possible in the other case, in which he does not make a statement at all. Nor does the possibility of a lie completely cover the possibilities of insincerity when he reports his past self-exhortation. For his past self-exhortation may itself have been 'insincere'.

8. By A. Kenny in *Action, Emotion and Will*, London, 1963, pp. 216–27. However, his thesis, that an intention is a species of command, may be only an emphatic way of saying that the two things are similar to one another. It ought to mean that intentions possess the generic properties of commands and certain specific properties of their own.

The solution proposed[9] is that an insincere expression of intention is a piece of overheard self-exhortation which the speaker does not mean, just as an ordinary 'insincere' command is an exhortation to another person which he does not mean, whereas an insincere statement is one which he does not believe. Similarly, the past self-exhortation, even when he reports it correctly later, may not have been meant by him at the time.

There are many obscurities in this theory, but the points that I shall make against it are simple. To exhort oneself to do something is a way of getting oneself to decide to do it, or else a way of keeping oneself up to the mark after one has decided to do it, but to form an intention to do something is neither of these things. If someone exhorts himself to do A in order to get himself to decide to do it, he has not yet fully formed the intention to do it. Consequently, in this case, though it is true that, if he does not really mean his self-exhortation, and if he knows that he is overheard by another person, then that would be a devious kind of insincerity, nevertheless he would not be deceiving the other about his intention to do A, but only about his intention to get himself to decide to do A. If, on the other hand, he exhorts himself in order to keep himself up to the mark after deciding to do A, this piece of self-exhortation comes too late to express the intention to do A at the moment when it is formed. Consequently, in this case, though it is true that, if he believed that the self-exhortation was necessary, and if he did not mean it and knew that it was overheard, then that too would be a devious kind of insincerity, nevertheless he would be deceiving the other not about the present formation of an intention to do A, but, rather, about the reinforcement of that intention, after it had been formed: for he would be implying that it needed reinforcing, and yet he would only be pretending to reinforce it. Therefore, when 'I will do A' expresses an intention that is formed at the moment of utterance, it cannot be right to regard it as a piece of self-exhortation. It follows that the other half of the theory, which analyses the formation of an intention in the past in a similar way, cannot be right either.

Moreover, even if the thing about which the speaker might deceive his audience when he says 'I will do A' or 'I intend to

9. ibid.

do A' had been the thing about which he might deceive them when he produces what the theory regards as the equivalent of these utterances, it is also important that the method of deception suggested by the theory is too devious. For conveying information is not the primary purpose of self-exhortation, whereas it is the primary purpose of the two utterances.

So it looks as if we ought not to expect more than an analogy between intentions and commands. Now the most important point of analogy that has been suggested concerns their direction of fit. It has been said that, when an action does not fit what the agent said that he would do, it is the action that is mistaken and not what he said,[10] and this direction of fit is characteristic of commands, whereas the opposite direction of fit is characteristic of statements. Let us signalise this by calling commands and intentions 'dominant partners', and statements 'subordinate partners'. Then another point of similarity that has been suggested is that intentions, like commands, produce the subordinate partners that fit them.[11] But already it is not clear exactly what the dominant partner here is supposed to be. Commands can be heard or seen, but in the case of intentions many of the candidates for the position of dominant partner are not perceptible. Is the dominant partner the announcement that one will perform the action, or the decision to perform it, or the knowledge that one will perform it, or, perhaps, the intention itself? A third point of analogy that has been suggested[12] is that, if someone says that he will do something, the contradictory rejoinder would not be that he will not, because he never does such things, but, rather, that he will not, because you, the speaker, are going to stop him; just as the contradictory of a command is not the prediction that for some reason the thing will not be done, but, rather, another command, not to do it.

In these suggestions too there are many obscurities. My discussion of them will be aimed at establishing only one thing: that, whatever the exact analogy between intentions and commands, it ceases at the point where my problem begins, since it contributes nothing to an account of the agent's knowledge that

10. By Professor E. Anscombe, in *Intention*, Oxford, 1957, pp. 55–7. Kenny agrees with this—*Action, Emotion and Will*, p. 216.

11. Anscombe, *Intention*, p. 87.

12. ibid., p. 55.

he will in fact do A.[13] Indeed, if it is exaggerated, it actually makes any account of this knowledge impossible.

First, it is true that an action which does not conform to an unchanged intention is often a mistake. But it does not follow that the agent did not make another mistake when he said what he would do. He did. Admittedly, if what he said turned out to be mistaken because he changed his mind later, there would not also be a mistake in his action. But it does not follow that the two kinds of mistake are incompatible; nor, of course, if it did, could it follow from this that there never could be a mistake in what he said. The idea that the two kinds of mistake are incompatible comes from assuming that there can be only one direction of fit here. But why? What fits what? Certainly the action (subordinate) should fit the intention (dominant). But also, if the agent says that he will perform the action, his statement (subordinate) should fit the action (dominant), and so, if he does not perform the action, it is mistaken.

Admittedly, in such a situation we are at least reluctant to call what he said 'false', or even 'not true'. For these predicates, used by themselves, home on to a different target, viz. the agent's implication[14] that he intended to perform the action. There seems to be a very reasonable feeling that the front-line target for truth and falsity is the thing that the agent has the best chance of getting right. So I prefer to say that his statement, that he will perform the action, may come out true, or may possess eventual truth. But, whatever semantic phrases are used, the pejorative one will imply that a mistake has been made. Why should a mistake have to be signalised by the word 'False', or by the phrase 'Not true'?

13. Anscombe herself makes this point, ibid., p. 55. 'But, returning to the order and the description by the agent of his own intentional action, is there not a point at which the parallelism ceases: namely, just where we begin to speak of knowledge? For we say that the agent's description is a piece of knowledge, but an order is not a piece of knowledge. So though the parallelism is interesting and illuminates the periphery of the problem, it fails at the centre and leaves that in the darkness that we have found ourselves in.' The point on which I disagree with her is that it seems to me that she exaggerates the analogy between intentions and commands, and that this exaggeration makes any account of the agent's knowledge impossible.

14. It is difficult to determine the logical character of this implication, and in what follows I make no attempt to do so.

To say 'I will do A' is, on any view, to hold up a rather complex target. If someone retorts 'You will not in fact do A (although you intend to)', that will hit the target. If he retorts 'You do not intend to do A', that too will hit the target. How should we characterise these two impacts? The simplest answer to this question is that the target is a conjunction, and that each retort is the contradictory of one of its members. If that answer were right, the contradictory rejoinder would be the disjunction of the two retorts, and the complete denial would be the conjunction of them. However, there are reasons for regarding this simple answer as too crude. I shall not explore those reasons, or try to refine on the answer. But, if what I have been saying is right, any refinement of it must allow the first retort to be characterised as the imputation of some kind of mistake in what was said. This does not require that the first retort should be the contradictory rejoinder.[15]

But at least, it will be said, intentions, like commands, produce actions. But what exactly produces an action? Certainly not the agent's statement, nor even his knowledge that he will perform it. And, in order to see what a small fraction of truth there is in the idea that the decision produces the action, it is only necessary to reflect how much its efficacy would be reduced if one remembered it without remembering one's reasons for it. The efficacy of an intention would be similarly reduced if one remembered only that one had formed it, and not why. If, on the other hand, the thesis, that decisions or intentions produce actions, means that desires produce actions through decisions or intentions, there is much more truth in it, but, correspondingly, less room for the analogy with commands.

So, though the analogy between intentions and commands may well be worth exploring further, it clearly does not account for the agent's knowledge that he will in fact do A. Indeed, if the analogy is exaggerated and if the similarity between 'I will

15. The idea that the contradictory rejoinder is 'You will not because I am going to stop you' seems to be produced by the requirement that a contradictory rejoinder must be the same kind of utterance as its target, and yet must be produced by another speaker. But if this exceedingly stiff requirement has to be met as well as the usual requirement for contradictories, how can there be such a thing as the contradictory rejoinder to 'I will do A'?

do A' and 'It will rain' is underestimated, it will be impossible to account for his knowledge.

The second line of thought which is opposed to the suggested explanation of the compatibility of the two viewpoints is to argue that there are ways in which inductive predictions can be mistaken but in which 'I will do A' can not be mistaken. Suppose that I see a toy mouse moving up an inclined plane and I predict that it will reach the top. I may be mistaken because some obstacle stops it, or because the clockwork runs down, or because I over-estimated its speed. But, it is argued, 'I will do A' can be mistaken only in the first of these three ways: if it is false, that will be my mistake only when my non-performance is attributable to external circumstances. Of course, this possibility takes more forms for a human agent than it does for a simple clockwork mouse. For there is not only the possibility that I may be prevented by circumstances, but also the possibility that a change in the situation, or at least in my view of the situation, may alter or remove my desire to do A. But the point is that I am supposed not to be liable to errors of the other two kinds. It would follow that, if I exaggerated the present strength or constancy of my desire, that could not be my mistake and so could only be my insincerity.

This line of thought is less radically opposed than the other to the suggested explanation of the compatibility of the two viewpoints. For it allows that 'I will do A' may be false, and that, when its falsity is attributable to external circumstances, I may have been in error. But the refusal to allow that its falsity can ever be counted as my mistake when it is attributable to my internal state, unless that state is altered by some change in external circumstances, is something which cannot be reconciled with the explanation. For according to the explanation 'I will do A' is partly based on the following two things – my assessment of the strength of the present inner manifestation of my desire to do A and my extrapolation of the general regularity of the manifestations of my desires to this particular case. But this account of the way in which my internal state supports 'I will do A' implies that the falsity of the statement may be counted as my mistake even when it is attributable to this part of its basis. So it appears that either this explanation of the compatibility of the two viewpoints must be rejected or the proposed line between insincerity and error must be redrawn.

Now there is some room for manoeuvre here. For it is possible to detach the thesis that a statement has an inductive basis from the thesis that the speaker must have argued for it inductively from that basis. This move will usually increase the plausibility of any thesis of the first kind and allow a reconciliation between the fact, that the speaker jumped the gap between his internal state and the statement based on it, and the theory, that his leap could have been replaced by a series of shorter stages. Thus in the case under consideration the agent's internal state normally produces in him the immediate certainty that he will do A, and the statement 'I will do A' is sometimes the only contemporary manifestation of his desire to do A. But these facts can be reconciled with the theory that in all such cases he could have paused to reflect, and then his desire to do A would have produced an inner manifestation which he could have assessed for strength and constancy.

However, this reconciliation still leaves much unexplained. For though it suggests a plausible way of dealing with the constancy of the agent's desires, there are special difficulties about their strength which remain untouched. But it is something that his attitude to their constancy can be explained. The explanation would be that he assumes that his desire to do A will remain constant unless it is altered by some change in external circumstances. This assumption is inductive, and he could defend it by appealing either quite generally to average human nature, or, if he is different, to his own record, and if A is the kind of project that characteristically produces unusually fluctuating reactions, he can take that too into account. Whatever the basis of the assumption that underpins his immediate certainty, he can always extract it, scrutinise it, and, if necessary, modify it. On the other hand, he may fail to modify it when modification is needed. In such cases the falsity of 'I will do A' will sometimes indicate insincerity on his part. But there is no plausibility in the suggestion that it will always indicate insincerity in such cases, and never a mistake. For insincerity is a kind of avoidable falsity, and nobody has sufficient foreknowledge of his own psychological development to ensure that he could always avoid falsity attributable to inconstancy of desire.

So at this point the proposed line between insincerity and error must be redrawn.

It might be objected that it is artificial to isolate the agent's psychological development from any further influence by external circumstances after he has made his decision. For even the fact that he has announced his decision to do A might reinforce his desire to do it, because he might want to avoid disappointing other people who counted on his doing it. Even if he did not announce his decision, he himself might build on it, and then his original desire to do A would be reinforced by his desire not to upset his own further plans. So it might be argued that it is artificial to abstract the agent's inner history not only from the effect of independent changes in his circumstances but also from internal repercussions which are intrinsically probable. But the answer to this objection is that to focus on one factor is not to deny the existence of others. It is essential to distinguish between keeping to a stated intention and keeping to a statement of intention close to what one would have done even if one had not made it, and between keeping to an intention because it has been built into a further plan and keeping to an intention because of the desire which originally led to its formation. Everything is what it is and not another thing. The reason for focussing on the isolated history of the agent's desire to do A, or rather on what it would have been if it had been isolated, is simply that it is one of the things that is a source of the truth or falsity of 'I will do A'.

A more telling objection would be that, if the agent does wonder whether he will change his mind in this purely spontaneous way, he will not adopt the spectator's point of view or ask himself whether his desire to do A belongs to a class of desires that usually remain constant. He will remain in the agent's seat and go over in his mind his reasons for doing A, in order to see whether they still strike him as cogent. Of course, even if he remains persuaded by them, he may still doubt whether their ascendancy will last. But this doubt too should be interpreted not as a doubt about the constancy of the force exerted on him by the desire to do A, but rather as a suspicion that later he might see the matter in a different light, because he might analyse it into different elements, or because he might attach different weights to the same elements.

This objection owes much of its persuasiveness to the difference already noted between remembering and deciding. An agent makes up his mind about a project, but there is something wrong with a witness who has to make up his mind about what he saw. But this is only the tip of the iceberg, and below it there is a mass of connected differences. The agent wants to know whether the desires which led up to his decision will also lead on to the action which would match his decision. So he goes back over the deliberation that terminated in his decision, analysing his final desire to do A into its elements and resynthesising them in order to see if he gets the same result again. Much of the force of the objection comes from the fact that this kind of rehearsal seems to have no connection with any inductive argument about the constancy of his final desire to do A.

Contrast the witness who wonders whether his memory-impression is accurate. He will start from his memory-impression, which is the effect, and he will want to know whether it matches the experience which he believes to have been its cause. This is one difference. Another is that the causal line leading to the memory-impression starts from a single cause, whereas in the case of agency described by the objector several causal lines, each starting from a different desire, converge on his decision. A third difference is that the witness is concerned with only two nodal points, the original experience and the memory-impression, whereas in the case of agency there are three, the original desire (or, in the case described, desires), the decision, and the action. As a result of these three differences the witness can only adopt the spectator's point of view and assess on inductive grounds the probability that his original experience produced a matching memory-impression, whereas the agent can do something which seems to be independent of the inductive argument that his final desire to do A will persist and produce the action that matches it.

However, a closer look at the three differences might lead to a verdict against the objection. The first point that needs to be made is that not all decisions are reached by combining and balancing a number of desires. There are also simple cases where someone decides to do A merely because he wants to do it under the description 'A'. In a case of this kind he can review his decision by asking himself whether he really does want to do A. Perhaps he will even imagine himself doing A. But that is as close as he can get to projecting himself into the future, and it still leaves a gap, because what he imagines himself doing in the future is brought before his present desire for assessment. If he made no assumption about the constancy of this desire, his rehearsal would not give him any indication of his future action. But it does give him an indication and often a reliable one. Therefore, his rehearsal presupposes the correctness of the assumption. The assumption itself is very seldom questioned, and so if he has any doubts about his decision, he will nearly always resolve them by going over his deliberation again. But that does not show that this kind of rehearsal is an independent substitute for an inductive review of the assumption. It could not be an independent substitute, because, if he suspected that he might change his mind after deciding to do A, he could not reassure himself by deciding not to change his mind.

The first difference between the agency-line and the memory-line was that the former leads from present cause to future effect, while the latter leads from present effect to past cause. Let us now inquire how this difference works out for the simple case in which the agent decides to do A merely because he wants to do it under the description 'A'. Just as this agent has to rely in the last resort on an inductive estimate of the probability that his desire will remain constant and produce a matching action, because he is unable to project himself into the future, so too the witness has to rely on an inductive estimate of the probability that his original experience produced a constantly matching memory-impression, because he is unable to project himself into the past. The difference is that the agent can always carry out a check on the agency-line at the point of time which he happens to occupy at the moment, whereas all points on the memory-line are now in the past, so that the witness cannot check what his memory-impression would have been, had he recalled the original experience at some earlier point of time. Thus the witness can only make a single inductive estimate of the probability of constancy, which he applies to the whole of the memory-line, whereas the agent can try to resolve his doubts again and again as he travels down the agency-line towards the moment for action, and each time, whatever else he does, he will inevitably rely in the last resort on an inductive estimate of constancy.

The third difference was concerned with the number of nodal points on the two lines. On the memory-line there are only two, the original experience and the memory-impression, but on the agency-line there are three, the original desire, the decision and the action. This difference can now be seen to be connected with the first difference. For the reason why there is a third nodal point on the agency-line between the other two is that the agent can carry out a kind of check that is not available to the witness. However, this is an incomplete analysis of the third difference, and it would be misleading not to complete it. It is nothing but the truth that, when the agent checks the agency-line by deciding in advance or by reviewing his decision, one result is that he knows, or knows with greater certainty, what he will do. But there are several ways in which this falls short of the whole truth. People do not make or review decisions merely in order to find out what they will do. Their primary goal is usually to make up their minds what to do. Naturally, knowledge of their own future actions will be a by-product, because, if A continues to seem to the agent to be the thing to do, he will very probably do it. Now sometimes his primary goal in making up his mind is to attain knowledge of that future fact. But even in such cases, in order to attain it, he still has to make up his mind what to do. So deciding is in part a creative process and not just a way of discovering what one will in fact do, and even the reviewing of decisions should be regarded in this light. These processes are creative, not merely because they terminate with the drawing of a conclusion, but because the conclusion is practical and so it is always possible that it will alter the agent's future behaviour. It need not be the case that he discovers what he was going to do anyway.

However, when a decision is creative, it is not creation *ex nihilo*. For the difference that it makes might merely be attributable to the fact that, before he deliberated, his desires determined the thing for him to do, but he did not know what it was, because the issue was so complicated. Even when the difference made by deliberation cannot be attributed to his previous inability to draw an objectively determined practical conclusion, his decision still must not deviate from the basic pattern of his desires, because, if it does, it will not endure. No doubt, in such cases his desires hold his decisions on a loose and subjective rein, which cannot be formalised as any kind of logical inference. But the constraint is none the less real, and it comes from a source that cannot be altered at will. His certainty that he will do what he has decided to do is not based on the assumption that his future self is a zombie entirely dependent on the instructions of his present self, as is implied by the close assimilation of statements of intention to commands. The creativity of deliberating and deciding is limited by the agent's antecedent desires, and the certainty that his future action will match his decision is limited by the proviso that those desires do not change. So, though this creativity is important, its effects should not be exaggerated. Certainly, the intermediate points on the agency-line are more than check-points. Certainly too, they sometimes make a difference to the outcome. But this is compatible with the thesis that an important by-product of deciding is knowledge of one's own future actions, which would be unattainable if the constraints that limit the creativity of one's decisions were not constant.

There is, finally, the second difference, that the memory-line starts from a single cause, while the agency-line may start from several independent causes, *viz.*, the various desires that the agent synthesises as the desire to do A. This difference appears at first sight to be the most important of the three, because, when we think about reviewing decisions, it is natural to take a complex case, where the review would involve an analysis of the project A into its elements and the attachment of different weights to the elements. However, none of these complications make any difference to the fact that the rehearsal would give the agent no indication of his future action unless he relied in the last resort on an inductive estimate of the probability that his desires would remain constant. The only peculiarity of the complex case, from this point of view, is that the estimate can be made not only for the desire to do A but also for each of its component desires, and this introduces the possibility of systematising the agent's desires and actions in a way that would sometimes allow the spectator to reject his account of his motivation for a particular action. The point that destroys the objection is that there is the same necessity for inductive estimation of the probability of constancy in complex cases as in simple cases.

Perhaps these arguments provide enough support for one half of the suggested explanation of the compatibility of the two viewpoints. For they show that the gap between deciding and acting cannot be spanned without the aid of inductive argument even when it is only the agent's contribution to the outcome that is in question. So everything that the agent does in order to reassure himself that he will do A presupposes the correctness of an assumption about the constancy of his desire to do A, which can only rest in the last resort on induction. If he suspects that he may change his mind after deciding to do A, he cannot reassure himself by deciding not to change his mind.

But the other half of the explanation, which deals with the strength of his present desire to do A is more difficult to defend, and there is no space left for its defence in this paper. So perhaps it would be best to end with a brief analysis of the difficulty.

The suggested explanation allows that the agent's internal state normally produces in him the immediate certainty that he will do A, and that the statement 'I will do A' is sometimes the only contemporary manifestation of his desire to do A. But it claims that in all such cases he could have paused to reflect, and then his desire to do A would have produced an inner manifestation which he could assess for strength. But how is this assessment carried out? Does he assess his desire as strong enough to produce the action other things being equal? If so, is this a causal property of the desire about which he might be mistaken? And does the desire have other properties in addition to this causal one? There is a case for saying that it must have some other property, if it is the cause of the action other things being equal. But what can this other property be? There are problems about the concept of the strength of a desire, and no attempt to solve them has been made in this paper. So the defence of the explanation of the compatibility of the two viewpoints that has been offered remains incomplete.[16]

16. An attempt to complete it is made in 'Sketch for a causal theory of wanting and doing'. See pages 97–141.

2 Wanting and Intending

Professor Hare has argued[1] that in my criticism[2] of Anthony Kenny's[3] assimilation of expressions of intention to commands I slipped into one of the pitfalls that await philosophers who deviate from the true account of intending. I do not agree with this description of my present position, and I shall try to show that it is not even precarious. I shall also do two other things in this paper. I shall put Kenny's theory back where it belongs in the wider setting in which he presented it in his book *Action, Emotion and Will*, and I shall say more about the larger issue which he raises there.

First, I have to deal with the so-called pitfall. Let 'A' be the specification of a particular action. Then I would like to consider the following four sentences:

S1 I really want to do A (all things considered).
S2 I intend to do A.
S3 I will do A.
S4 I shall do A.

The part of Kenny's theory which I criticised in the lecture to which Hare refers is concerned with the analysis of S2 and S3. Kenny says that, when S2 'is a genuine report of a state of mind', it 'is tantamount to the statement "I have said in my heart 'Let me do A'" ' (p. 218). Hare protests that 'this is not a very fair statement of the theory' (I repeated it in my lecture) 'for it ex-

1. R. M. Hare, 'Wanting: some pitfalls', in *Agent, Action and Reason* (papers and commentaries presented at the Fourth Philosophy Colloquium held at the University of Western Ontario in November 1968), Toronto, 1971; reprinted in R. M. Hare, *Practical Inferences*, London, 1971.

2. D. F. Pears, 'Predicting and Deciding', *Proceedings of the British Academy* 50 (London, 1964); reprinted in this volume, pp. 13–38.

3. Kenny, *Action, Emotion and Will*.

poses it gratuitously to the objection that a man might have said in his heart "Let me do A", and then, afterwards, changed his mind and said (also in his heart) "No, let me not do A after all". Such a man would have said in his heart "Let me do A", but would not now intend to do A' (p. 91). I agree that Kenny ought to have added a caveat about change of mind, but I did not make this criticism in 1964, because it seemed to me then, as it does now, that he took the addition for granted.

Kenny then offers an analysis of S3 and (I believe, but I am not sure of this: see p. 218, lines 11–15) of S2 when S2 is the expression of an intention. It is not clear to me how to determine when S2 is a genuine report of a state of mind and when it is the expression of an intention. So in my discussion of the analysis which he offers – which is simply 'Let me do A' – I shall concentrate on S3 as he himself does.

Now the sentence 'Let me do A' is (if one is not too strict about grammatical categories) in the imperative mood. In Kenny's theory is it supposed to be a command addressed to oneself? It is, I think, clear that, in order to get an answer to this question, we need examine only his analysis of S3. For, whatever force the imperative sentence has in the analysis of S3, it will also have when it is quoted in the analysis of S2 when S2 is a genuine report of a state of mind.

But, unfortunately, the question is ambiguous, at least in the context of this discussion. For Hare distinguishes two different senses of the word 'command', a generic sense and a specific sense. In its generic sense it is supposed to apply to anything expressed by a sentence in the imperative mood, and in its specific sense it applies only to what would ordinarily be called 'a command' (see Hare, pp. 95–6). In what follows, when I use the word 'command' without qualification, I shall always mean 'what would ordinarily be called "a command"'. As far as I can see, Kenny too always used the word in this way in his book. Occasionally, in order to make my meaning absolutely plain, I shall insert a reminder that I am using the word in this way. On the few occasions when I use the word in what is supposed to be its other sense, I shall always say that this is what I am doing.

Let me now repeat my question. In Kenny's theory is the sentence 'Let me do A' supposed to be a command addressed to oneself? I did not find this question of interpretation easy to answer in 1964, and I do not find it any easier now. On the one hand he says that his analysis of S3 is justified by the analogy between S3 and a command (p. 216), and this suggests that the answer to my question is negative, because the sentence 'Let me do A' would only be *like* a command. But on the other hand he says, 'The insincere expression of intention may be regarded as giving oneself an order in the presence of one's listener, which one does not mean oneself to obey. It is as if a superior, having received a complaint against a subordinate, should summon the subordinate and tell him in the complainer's presence "Put this matter right", though both superior and subordinate know that the command is not meant seriously and is issued merely to satisfy the complainer' (p. 220). This suggests an affirmative answer to my question.

Notice that this difficulty of interpretation is not produced by any doubt about the sense of the word 'command'. In the passage which has just been quoted Kenny uses the word 'order', and in any case, as I have already pointed out, he seems always to use the word 'command' in its specific sense. The difficulty is that it is not clear whether it is supposed that the analysis of S3 is a command, or only that S3 is in some way like a command.

My reaction to this difficulty in 1964 was to try out both interpretations of Kenny's theory. First, in the section of my lecture to which Hare refers,[4] I criticised the theory on the assumption that S3 was supposed to be a command. Then I criticised it on the assumption that S3 was supposed only to be like a command.[5] Hare does not mention the second of these two pieces of criticism. If he had noticed it, he would have realised that I did not confuse the thesis that S3 is like a command with the thesis that it is a command (in any case, this confusion would not be the same as the confusion between the supposed generic sense of the word 'command' and its specific sense).

The reason why Hare does not notice the second of my two pieces of criticism may be that I directed it against Anscombe's version of the thesis that S3 is like a command,[6] merely observ-

4. 'Predicting and deciding', pp. 206–8; this volume, pp. 26–8.
5. ibid., pp. 208–10; this volume, pp. 28–31.
6. Anscombe, *Intention*, pp. 55–7.

ing in a footnote that Kenny agreed with Anscombe that the two are alike. This was, as I now see, unfair to Kenny. For it might well leave the impression that Kenny's theory has to be interpreted to mean that S3 is a command. This is far from true. For the main drift of his arguments supports the other version of his theory, and as far as I can see, there is only one passage (p. 220; already quoted) which implies that S3 is a command.

However, before I move on to the other version of the theory, which seems to me to be the more interesting of the two, I would like to make two points about the version which implies that S3 is a command.

First, there is the question why, in interpreting this version of Kenny's theory, I substituted self-exhortation for self-addressed command. My reason was that there are obvious objections to taking commanding to be the speech-act which is, as it were, internalised when S3 is analysed as 'Let me do A'. I chose self-exhortation instead, because it seemed to me to be the least inappropriate speech-act for the drama which, according to this version of the theory, would be enacted *in foro interno* every time that a person utters S3. Of course, with the other version of the theory it is not clear that there is a specific speech-act to be internalised. Certainly, there would be no need to internalise any of the speech-acts which are closely associated with the imperative mood. But I shall say more about that later, when I examine the other version of the theory.

Second, there is Hare's objection to a criticism which I directed against Kenny's analyses of S2 and S3. I think that I ought to quote rather more of my criticism than Hare does before I deal with his objection to it: 'Moreover, even if the thing about which the speaker might deceive his audience when he says "I will do A" or "I intend to do A" had been the thing about which he might deceive them when he produces what the theory regards as the equivalent of these two utterances, it is also important that the method of deception suggested by the theory is too devious. For conveying information is not the primary purpose of self-exhortation, whereas it is the primary purpose of the two utterances.'[7] Hare's comment on this is: 'It seems to me that this lacks even the appearance of cogency as

7. 'Predicting and deciding', pp. 207–8; this volume, pp. 27–8.

an argument against Kenny's view; for, on Kenny's view, "I intend to do A" *would* have the primary purpose of informing (*viz.*, of the fact that I subscribe to the self-addressed command to do A); and, on the other hand, "I will do A", which is on Kenny's view not primarily informative, is indeed not primarily informative, but rather an expression of intention or resolve' (p. 95).

Here, as at all other points, Hare is defending the thesis that S3 is like a self-addressed command against a criticism directed at the thesis that S3 is a self-addressed command, or, at least, a piece of self-exhortation. For in the preceding paragraph of my lecture I had argued that a person who exhorts himself to do A, but who does not really mean the self-exhortation, is not deceiving his audience about his intention to do A, but rather about his intention to get himself to decide to do A; or, alternatively, if he has already decided to do A, but needs to keep himself up to the mark, he is deceiving his audience by pretending to reinforce his infirm intention. Therefore, I suggested, the theory makes the speaker deceive his audience about the wrong thing. I then argued, in the passage which I have just quoted, that the theory makes the speaker's method of deception too indirect. So the version of the theory which I was attacking is not the version which Hare is defending, and it might appear that no more need be said about this particular skirmish.

But there are two points in Hare's objection which I would like to take up. First, it is surely wrong to say that S3, when it is uttered by one person to another, is not primarily informative. In such a case its primary function is to convey two pieces of information to the hearer – that the speaker is determined to do A, and that he will in fact do A. There is of course, the problem of characterising the way in which these two pieces of information are conveyed, and Hare's thesis, that the speaker's determination (he says 'intention or resolve') is expressed, is a small contribution to half of this problem. It is also difficult to decide which of the two pieces of information is the main burden of the communication (S4 treats the first piece of information more lightly, but how much more weight does S3 put on it?). But there can surely be no doubt that the primary function of S3, when it is said by one person to another, is to convey these two pieces of information. My argument – a valid one – was simply that, if overheard self-exhortation conveys information, it conveys it indirectly and as a side-line, and therefore, S3 cannot be analysed as a piece of self-exhortation.

The second feature of this objection of Hare's on which I would like to comment is his assumption that I did not notice that, according to Kenny, S2 'when it is a genuine report of a state of mind' (Hare omits this qualification, and I think that the omission is probably an error of interpretation) is primarily informative – it conveys the information that the speaker has said in his heart, 'Let me do A' (and has not subsequently unsaid this in his heart). In fact I had noticed this.[8] But, of course, even if the speaker of S2 did convey this piece of information, he would not thereby convey the information which is in fact conveyed by S2, unless, at the very least, the self-exhortation 'Let me do A' itself conveyed the information conveyed by S3. Here I intended the same two criticisms to be applied again – first, the criticism (in the passage preceding Hare's quotation from my lecture) that the self-exhortation does not convey this information, and, second, the criticism (in the passage which he quotes) that the self-exhortation does not convey any information in the direct way in which S3 conveys information. But I did not set this argument out in detail in my lecture, and I must admit that what I said could give the impression that it might depend on the false assumption that Kenny did not regard S2 as primarily informative 'when it is a genuine report of a state of mind'.

It is tedious to rehearse all this, particularly when the main drift of Kenny's arguments supports the other version of his theory. But perhaps it has been worth it. For, as I shall show in a moment, it is very easy to slide from the version which says that S3 is like a command to the version which says that it is a command (or a piece of self-exhortation).

I now turn to the more interesting thesis that S3 is like a command – so like a command that an imperative sentence is a suitable form of words to express an intention. According to Hare an imperative sentence is also a suitable form of words to express a desire to perform an action (p. 92). So he would

8. ibid., p. 206; this volume, p. 26.

say that at least the first three of my four sentences, S1–S3, could be appropriately expressed in the imperative mood, or in a form which included a quoted sentence in the imperative mood (a complication introduced by S2). He also puts wishes in the imperative camp.

Kenny gives a more detailed account of the route by which he arrives at the thesis that S3 is like a command. He believes that the auxiliary verb in S3 should be classified with other affective verbs and verbal phrases – e.g. 'to intend', 'to prefer', 'to want', 'to choose', 'to desire', 'to be glad', 'to hope', and, negatively, 'to regret', 'to be ashamed', 'to fear'. According to him the members of this class all have something in common, something which makes it appropriate to use the language of wishes or commands in their analyses – i.e., to use the imperative mood, or one of the tenses which in English sometimes play the role of the imperative mood.

But why should anyone suppose that an imperative sentence is a suitable form of words to express what is expressed by S1 or by S3, or that a paraphrase of S2 would contain a quoted imperative sentence? And what about S4? Is it insufficiently vehement for this treatment? In his reply David Gauthier complains that Hare offers little positive argument for casting imperatives in this role.[9] In the subsequent open discussion Hare relied on an argument which makes a brief appearance in the part of his paper which is devoted to me. 'Actually, as Kenny, I think, points out, it is very plausible to say that, when Hannibal orders his troops to march on Rome, he is not merely commanding them to do so, but expressing the intention that they should do so: and this lends some plausibility to the thesis that, when I form the intention to go to Rome, I have that in my mind which would, if it were expressed in words, naturally be expressed by saying "Let me go to Rome", or, if I were to address myself in military style in the mood which I was taught in the army to call the future imperative, "Hare will go to Rome", or "I will go to Rome"' (p. 94).

This is a very weak argument. If the verb 'to express' is used, as Hare uses it here, to signify a loose bond, there are all sorts of locutions which might express the intention that another, or

9. David Gauthier, 'Comments' (on Hare, 'Wanting: some pitfalls'), in *Agent, Action and Reason*, p. 98.

others should do A. Why pick on imperative sentences for this role? Why, as Professor Davidson asked in the discussion, assume that there is any single locution (other than 'I intend that you should do A') to which this role ought to be assigned on the ground that it is generally and pre-eminently suited to it? Of course, in the particular case chosen by Hare, Hannibal's position makes it especially appropriate for him to use an imperative sentence. For he is in a position to secure the achievement of his intention by issuing a command (specific sense) to his troops. But this is not true in general of people who have such intentions.

Even if it were generally true that a person who intended that another should do something was in a position to issue a command (specific sense), or to use the imperative mood in one of the milder speech-acts that are closely associated with it, that would not support Hare's thesis. For, as he insists in his paper, his thesis is not that intentions are (or find expression in) internalised commands (specific sense). Nor, as far as I can see, does he think that any of the other speech-acts which are closely associated with the imperative mood would be a better candidate for internalisation (see Gauthier's 'Comments', p. 103). His point is, rather, that what is internalised is the essence of the imperative mood when it has been extracted from the different speech-acts which are closely associated with it.

But, though this is his point, it is, I think, significant that in the passage just quoted he flirts with the other version of the theory, which I dealt with in the first part of this paper: '. . . or, if I were to address myself in military style in the mood which I was taught in the army to call the future imperative, "Hare will go to Rome", or "I will go to Rome".' This suggests that, when Hare substitutes 'I' for 'Hare', a command (specific sense) is internalised. Naturally, he would not endorse this suggestion, but its presence is revealing. It fills an uncomfortable vacuum, and makes us feel that we understand what is supposed to be going on when Hare says 'Let me go to Rome'. But, since, according to Hare's and Kenny's preferred version of the theory, the internalisation of this locution does not carry with it the internalisation of any of the speech-acts which are closely associated with the imperative mood, I doubt if we do understand what is supposed to be going on.

It is merely an expository device to skate as close as possible to the other version of the theory, but it can be taken too far. On one occasion, as I have already shown, Kenny actually slides into a defence of the other version. In *The Language of Morals* Hare is more circumspect. In Chapter 2 he introduces the concepts of affirming and assenting to a command (generic sense). In cases which involve two people, to affirm is to address it to the other person, and, at the receiving end, to assent to it is to agree to carry it out. But, when a person addresses a command (generic sense) to himself, Hare says that 'affirmation and assent are identical. It is logically impossible for a man to dissent from what he himself is affirming (though of course he may not be sincere in affirming it).'[10] Here, too, if we allow our minds to slide over to the other version of the theory, as is only too easy, we shall feel that we understand what is supposed to be going on. For the other version would allow some distinction *in foro interno* between the issuing end of a first person command (specific sense) and the receiving end, and the thesis would be that it is logically necessary that sincere affirmation of such a command should be accompanied by sincere assent to it (i.e., by sincere agreement to carry it out). No doubt, this thesis is vulnerable to objections, but it is intelligible, and it owes its intelligibility to the idea that one of the speech-acts which are closely associated with the imperative mood is internalised. But if there is no distinction *in foro interno* between the issuing and receiving ends of a first person command (generic sense), and if there is no internalised speech-act closely associated with the imperative mood, what is supposed to be going on?

This question is not unanswerable. The answer to it is simply that Hare is expressing his intention to himself. So we must not put any emphasis on the fact that Hannibal was issuing a command (specific sense) to his troops. All our emphasis must be on the fact that he was expressing his intention. But if we take this line, we must abandon the thesis that an imperative sentence is a generally and pre-eminently suitable form of words to express an intention. For the bond between an intention and an imperative sentence is loose and one-many [it just happened that Hannibal was in a position to express (loose sense

10. *The Language of Morals*, Oxford, 1952, p. 20.

of this word) his intention by commanding (specific sense) his troops to march on Rome]. Moreover this particular case does not even support the less ambitious thesis that an imperative sentence is *a* suitable form of words to express an intention. For the thing which made it appropriate for Hannibal to express (loose sense) his intention by issuing a command (generic sense) was precisely that he was in a position to issue a command (specific sense). But the appropriateness of a command (specific sense) absolutely depended on the fact that what he was expressing (loose sense) was his intention *that they should march on Rome*. So how does this case lend any plausibility to the thesis that an imperative sentence is a suitable form of words to express the speaker's intention *to do something himself*? When this version of the theory is argued for in this way, it is not surprising that we get an uncomfortable feeling which vanishes only when we add a rider which is no part of the theory – the rider that one of the speech-acts which is closely associated with the imperative mood (unlike expressing an intention) is internalised.

But there is an argument which, if it were valid, would provide appropriate support for the thesis that an imperative sentence is a suitable form of words (but not pre-eminently suitable) to express an intention. Hare alludes to the argument, and Kenny actually gives it. The argument is that, if we extract the essence of the imperative mood from the different speech-acts which are closely associated with it [not loosely associated with it, like 'expressing' in the sentence 'Hannibal's command (specific sense) expressed his intention that his army should march on Rome'], we shall find that this same essence is shared by S1, S2, and S3 (but not, apparently, by S4). In fact, according to Kenny, the same essence is shared by all the affective words and verbal phrases which would be included in a complete list governed by a principle of selection which is sufficiently determined by his examples ('to intend', 'to prefer', 'to want', etc.). Now it would help us in logic if a single form of words were chosen to express the essential feature of all these different locutions.[11] So *we might as well choose* the imperative mood for this role.

11. Hare, 'Wanting: some pitfalls', p. 89; Kenny, *Action, Emotion and Will*, pp. 213–15.

This argument cuts a path through the jungle of English usage (Hare, Hannibal, and the British Army), and goes straight to the heart of the matter. But what is the heart of the matter? What is the essential feature of all these different locutions? The surprising thing is that, though Hare shows a strong feeling for the genus, he does not tell us what he supposes the generic property to be. It is the great merit of Kenny's treatment of this subject that he does tell us what he supposes the generic property to be.

At this point in my 1964 lecture I switched attention from Kenny's account of what is common to these different locutions to Anscombe's account of what is common to intentions and commands (specific sense here and hereafter). I had two reasons for doing this. First, the central point in Kenny's more far-reaching theory is the analogy between intentions and commands, and, second, Anscombe's account of this analogy, which Kenny largely adopts and develops over a wider field, contains a more detailed list of the supposed points of similarity. However, as I have already admitted, when I switched attention to Anscombe's account of this analogy, I gave the impression that Kenny confined himself to the thesis that S2 and S3 actually are commands (or pieces of self-exhortation), and that he did not develop the thesis that they are like commands. But in fact he spent most of his time developing the thesis that they are like commands, and I shall now concentrate on what he says in support of that thesis, quoting Anscombe's views only when Kenny quotes them.

The thesis that there is an analogy between S3 (or any of my other three sentences) and a command is of little interest unless the point of analogy is specified. Kenny's first specification of what he regards as the central point of analogy is the following:

> There is, in fact, an important logical feature common to commands [*sc.* specific sense], wishes, and expressions of intention, which distinguishes them from statements. If a man sincerely utters a statement which fails to accord with the facts, then he is mistaken; if he utters a command, a wish, or an expression of intention, then he is not mistaken merely because the facts do not accord with his utterances (p. 216).

The footnote which Kenny attaches to his text at this point contains the following quotation from Anscombe's book *Intention*:

> There is a difference between the types of ground on which we call an order and an estimate of the future sound. The reasons justifying an order are not ones suggesting what is probable or likely to happen, but, e.g., ones suggesting what it would be good to make happen with a view to an objective, or with a view to a sound objective. In this regard, commands and expressions of intention are similar . . .
>
> Let us consider a man going round a town with a shopping list in his hand. Now it is clear that the relation of this list to the things he actually buys is one and the same whether his wife gave him the list or it is his own list; and that there is a different relation when a list is made by a detective following him about. If he made the list himself, it was an expression of intention; if his wife gave it to him, it has the role of an order. What then is the identical relation to what happens, in the order and the intention, which is not shared by the record? It is precisely this: if the list and the things that the man actually buys do not agree, and if this and this alone constitutes a *mistake*, then the mistake is not in the list but in the man's performance; whereas if the detective's record and what the man actually buys do not agree, then the mistake is in the record.[12]

Kenny then endorses this last point of Anscombe's, and goes on to disagree with something else that she says, *viz.*, 'that there is no reason other than a dispensable usage why we should not call commands true and false according as they were obeyed and disobeyed'.

Since I have now moved outside the area of the discussion at the Colloquium, my comments on this text will be sketchy, although it is of central importance.

Consider, first, the question whether the suggested analogy holds between a command and S4. Of course, the claim that it does not would not be a direct criticism of this version of

12. Anscombe, *Intention*, pp. 55–6.

Kenny's theory. For, as far as I can see, if we asked which of my four sentences are, according to him, expressions of intention, his answer would be S3 and S2, when S2 is not a genuine report of a state of mind, but not S4. But a theory which claims to isolate the essential feature of the genus to which intentions belong surely ought to apply to S4. So, if the suggested analogy does not hold between a command and S4, that would be a damaging limitation.

Now anyone who utters S4 to someone else, whatever else he does, conveys two pieces of information, the information that he intends to do A, and the information that he will in fact do A. It is true that the exact analysis of S4 is a difficult matter. But, fortunately, it is not necessary for me to try to determine which of the two pieces of information is the main burden of the communication, e.g., whether both facts are asserted, or one is in some way implied, etc. The only point that I need to make here is that the second piece of information is not cancellable – e.g., the speaker of S4 could not cancel it by continuing '. . . but, in fact, A is impossible'. He could not even mitigate it by reducing the categorical force of this part of his communication, e.g. by the continuation '. . . but, as a matter of fact, I probably shall not be able to do A'. So it seems to me that, whenever someone utters S4, it will not be correct unless it fits his future performance.

If the Anscombe-Kenny argument were applied to S4 (and, as I said, Kenny does not apply it to S4), it might appear to undermine this conclusion. For S4 expresses (in some sense) an intention, and, if the speaker fails to carry out his intention (through inefficiency, let us suppose), the mistake would appear to be in his performance (assuming that he has not changed his mind in the meantime). But this is a very weak argument. It depends on a tendentious use of the phrase 'the mistake'. Why must we assume that, in the circumstances described, the speaker has made only one mistake, a mistake in his performance? It is surely obvious that he has made two mistakes, one in his performance (which failed to fit his intention), and one in his earlier utterance (which failed to fit his performance).

I made this criticism of the suggested analogy between intentions and commands in 'Predicting and deciding' (p. 209, this volume, p. 29). As far as S4 is concerned (and Kenny does not bring S4 into the discussion), it seems to me to be a sufficient criticism. It is true that it does not take any notice of a third type of mistake which is mentioned by Anscombe in the passage quoted by Kenny (and taken up by Kenny in a later passage in his book, which I shall quote at the end of this note), the mistake made by an agent who intentionally performs a wrong action (in some sense of this vague adjective), or (derivatively) the mistake made by an agent who forms a wrong intention, or by someone else who commands him to act wrongly. But I think that it is obvious that the possibility of this kind of mistake has no effect whatsoever on the *general* question whether S4 ought to fit the agent's future action, or his future action ought to fit the intention, which in some loose sense S4, whatever else it does, expresses, or both.

Now let us look at S3 in order to see whether there is a better case for maintaining, as Anscombe and Kenny actually do maintain, that the suggested analogy holds between S3 and a command. It seems to me that the case for the analogy between these two is no better than the case for the analogy between S4 and a command. It is true that S3 expresses a greater degree of determination than S4, but this is entirely compatible with its conveying the second of the two pieces of information – *viz.*, that the speaker will in fact do A. And it does convey this piece of information. For the cancellation and the mitigation, which were found to be impossible for S4 are also impossible for S3.

I think it probable that the reason why supporters of the version of the theory which I am now criticising usually concentrate on S3 to the neglect of S4 is that the use of S3 suggests that there may have been, or may be, quite a lot of warming up of the engine before the agent actually moves off; and this may seem to require a self-addressed command, or at least a piece of self-exhortation. But I hope that I have shown that this version of the theory cannot get any support from that quarter.

If we take the facts conveyed by S3, and subtract from them the fact that the speaker will actually do A, what is left is only the fact that he is determined to do A but will not do it. Here we have to use the third person, because S3 cannot be cancelled by the continuation '. . . but I shall not do it'. In the cases of S1 and S2 straightforward changes to the third person, with the supplementary statement that he will not do A, will give us the residual fact. S4, like S3, needs a further transformation: we must say that he intends to do A, but will not do it.

There are complications here, but they do not affect my simple criticism of the thesis that the suggested analogy holds between S3 and a command. As I have already pointed out, Kenny's analysis of S2, when it is a genuine report of a state of mind, contains his analysis of S3, and, since this does not convey the information which is, in fact, conveyed by S3, his analysis of S2 must be incorrect.

There are three final points that I would like to make.

First, I do not claim to have dealt with all Anscombe's further developments of the basic idea which I have been criticising.[13]

Second, it would be fair to Kenny to point out that, when he is explaining what he supposes all the various items on his list have in common, he often gives pride of place to wishes alongside intentions – e.g. he does this in the first sentence of my last quotation from his book. I am not sure how important this is. Perhaps the explanation is that on his list the verb 'to wish' is the only one which sometimes signifies a speech-act which is closely associated with the imperative mood (or with something which might be classified as the imperative mood); and that the verb 'to wish' is substitutable for the verb 'to want' in S1 without change of sense. This might make it look as if this verb could be used as the central span of a bridge connecting S1 directly with a speech-act closely associated with the imperative mood, and so indirectly connecting all the affective verbs and verbal phrases on Kenny's list with the whole family of speech-acts which are closely associated with the imperative mood. But, as Kenny points out (pp. 215–16), a wish (expressed in the imperative mood, or in something like it) is appropriate only when what is wished for is not that the wisher himself should perform some action (cf. my point about Hannibal's intention and the imperative mood). In any case the version of the theory which I am now criticising does not require the construction of this kind of bridge between usages even if it could be satisfactorily completed. For according to this version, the reason why wishes are assigned to the same genus as commands is not that they are associated with any of the same speech-acts.

13. See *Intention*, passim.

Finally, I would like to emphasise that the thesis that an intention is like a command is only a small part of this version of Kenny's theory, and so my criticism of the theory has been developed on a narrow front – e.g. I have not argued that wishes expressed in the imperative mood are unlike commands. My point has been that the particular analogy which Kenny sees between a command and S3 does not exist, and that this analogy does not hold between a command and S4 either (and he does not claim that it does hold here). About his analysis of S2, when S2 is a genuine report of a state of mind, I have said little more than that it contains his analysis of S3, with which it fails. These arguments of mine are more restricted in scope than his total theory. I shall end this note with a final quotation from his book which will show how much more restricted in scope my arguments are:

> Despite, therefore, the varied constructions which follow affective verbs, it seems that the one distinction of logical importance is between two modes of speech which we may call the indicative and the optative. In the first mode, the facts, or what happens, sets the standard by which the utterance is judged and found true or false; in the second mode, the utterance sets the standard by which the facts, or what happens, is judged and found good or bad. *Verum et falsum in mente, bonum et malum in rebus.* That is to say, whether a statement or a belief is true or false depends on what the facts are; the facts are the standard by which statements and beliefs are judged. On the other hand, whether an agent makes a mistake in what he does depends on what his intentions are; whether a subject's actions are obedient or disobedient depends on what his master's commands were; whether a citizen acts legally or illegally depends on what the laws are; whether a particular state of affairs is good or bad depends on what somebody wants. In all these cases, a Volition[14] is the standard by which what happens is judged. (pp. 220–1)

14. 'Volition' is his name for what is common to all the items on his list (pp. 214–15). So in this passage he calls the mode of speech to which they all belong 'the optative mode'. His thesis is that we might as well use the imperative mood to express what is common to them all.

I do not share this view of the great watershed dividing the two modes of speech. Perhaps the terrain looks like this when it is viewed from a great height, and perhaps it is a good thing to begin by trying to draw this line right across the map. But, if we try to relate intentions to this line, the most plausible thing that we can say is that it cuts through them, and splits the sentences which express them into two elements, one concerned with the speaker's future performance, the other concerned with his state at the moment. But then it is at least an over-simplification to characterise the second of these two elements as 'the imperative (or optative) element'. For its characterisation is a much more complex matter than the use of these grammatical terms suggests.

3 Causes and Objects of some Feelings and Psychological Reactions

There are many statements that a person can make about his own feelings and psychological reactions which seem to be causal or at least partly causal, and yet which seem to be incorrigible, or at least not corrigible in the light of parallel negative instances, as Hume's account of causation requires that they should be. For example:

'I was pleased by the publication of my letter.'

In this case it is arguable that I must know what pleased me, or at least that, if I am mistaken, this will not be established by my indifference when newspapers have rejected other letters of mine: and yet the statement seems to be partly causal. The same might be said of other statements which mention feelings that usually last longer, such as:

'His behaviour made me angry.'
and 'I am depressed by my lack of money.'

There are also statements that raise this problem at the opposite end of the scale, where the psychological reaction is almost too brief and superficial to be classified as a feeling. For example:

'I was amused by his remark.'
and 'The explosion made me jump.'

This last example may look rather out of place on the list, but I think that it usually implies that there was a psychological reaction, namely surprise or shock.

These statements seem to force us to make a difficult choice between three alternatives. Either they are not causal: or they are corrigible in the Humean way; or Hume's account of causation is not universally true. Ought we to accept one of these three alternatives? Or should we look for a fourth solution, perhaps a compromise?

Before this problem is discussed, it needs to be made more precise, in two ways. First, it must be separated from another problem, the problem whether the person's knowledge of the truth of these statements is immediate. And secondly, the type of corrigibility that is in question must be specified.

First, statements of this kind have often been said to possess the following peculiarity: the person himself does not come to make them by considering evidence and he does not use observation and inference because for him, at least, they are not hypotheses but immediate. This is obviously a very plausible thesis, and some version of it is almost certainly true of typical utterances of the statements that I have listed. But I am not going to discuss this thesis. For although the question whether a person makes a certain kind of statement immediately is connected with the question whether that statement is incorrigible, the two questions are not identical, and can be separated. Many ordinary causal statements are made immediately and yet they are corrigible, indeed corrigible in the Humean way. Therefore I shall separate the two questions, ignore the question of immediacy, and discuss only the question of corrigibility.

But at this point the second preliminary question has to be answered. What feature of the listed statements is supposed to be incorrigible, and what sort of correction is being ruled out? I shall not be concerned with the question whether the description of the feeling or psychological reaction is incorrigible, though that is an interesting question. I shall restrict myself to the question whether it might be incorrect for a person to say that it was his lack of money that depressed him, or that it was a particular person's behaviour that made him angry, etc. Also I shall not be concerned with cases where the incorrectness is the result of untruthfulness, but only with cases where it is the result of a mistake made by the person himself. Given the previous restriction, this means that the mistakes in question will be mistaken identifications, made by the person himself, of what depressed him, what made him angry, etc.

But even this question is rather wider than the question that I want to ask. For it covers some borderline cases of mistaken identifications, which raise special difficulties irrelevant to my problem. This comes about in the following way. Someone might know what it was that depressed him, in that he could produce a sufficiently individuating true description of what it was. Then it might be the case that there was another description, which he also believed to be true of it, although, in fact, unlike the first, it was not. In this situation he might produce the second description instead of the first. Suppose that he did this, and suppose that he did it not merely because he expressed something that he really knew in the wrong words (which would be the sort of mistake that he could instantly correct for himself). Then he would have mistakenly identified what depressed him, and the mistake would be substantial. Yet *ex hypothesi* he would know what depressed him, since he could also produce the first, true description of it. Would this put him in a position to correct his substantial mistake? It might, since, on reflection, he might realise that the two descriptions did not apply to the same thing, and he might opt for the first one. Alternatively, there might be some other outcome. It would depend on the nature of the particular case. There are all sorts of interesting complications in these borderline examples, but I want to avoid them, because they are irrelevant to my problem. So I shall confine myself to the extreme case in which there is a substantially mistaken identification and no knowledge in reserve that might lead the person to correct his mistake. My question is whether it is possible for a person to make this kind of mistake about what depressed him, what made him angry, etc. From now on, when I ask whether one of the statements on my list is corrigible or might be mistaken, this will always be the kind of mistake that I mean.

The problem that I have posed is how, if at all, we should choose between three alternatives: that the statements listed are not causal; that they are liable to the kind of mistake that is revealed by parallel negative instances – e.g. by similar situations in which I am not angry; and that Hume's account of causation is not universally true. I shall begin by examining some of the ways in which others have dealt with this problem, or with part of it.

It is clear from what Professor Anscombe (as she now is) says in her book *Intention* that her view about all the statements on my list except the last one would be that they report that something is both the cause and the object of the feeling in question.[1] But does she think, that, in so far as they report causes, they are immune from mistakes? Her rejection of Hume's account of causation for such cases suggests that she does think this, since the main point of Hume's account is that causal statements are liable to mistakes revealed by parallel negative instances, and it does not seem likely that her view is that they are liable to mistakes revealed in some other way. Moreover, she will not allow that such causal connections are known,[2] and according to her usage the verb 'to know' is admissible only if there is some possibility of mistake.[3] But even if she were right in rejecting Hume's main point, that causal statements are always vulnerable to parallel negative instances, it would not be enough to do this. For if there are causal statements that are not liable to this kind of correction, we need to understand why this is so. We need to know what the other peculiarities of these causal statements are, and how much they still retain in common with Humean examples. We cannot just accept a large, unexplained gap between two types of causal statements. So this solution is, at best, incomplete.

Is it, then, possible to defend the first of the three solutions that I mentioned, the one that denies that the statements are causal? If they are not causal, what are they? The most plausible suggestion is that they report the object of the feeling or reaction, that and nothing more. Professor Williams (as he now is), in his article 'Pleasure and belief',[4] makes this suggestion about one group of cases, *viz.* statements beginning 'I am pleased by –' 'I am pleased that –' and 'I am pleased because –'. His article also contains a theory about the nature of the connection between being pleased and its objects,[5] and an attempt to extend the theory to cover certain causal statements.[6] I shall examine this theory later. At the moment I am only concerned with his denial that statements in the group that he examines are causal. The point that I want to make about it is that, even if it is true

1. *Intention*, p. 16, cf. Wittgenstein, *Philosophical Investigations*, §476.
2. *Intention*, p. 15.
3. ibid., p. 14.
4. *Proceedings of the Aristotelian Society*, Supp. Vol. XXXIII, 1959, p. 59.
5. ibid., p. 61 ff.
6. ibid., p. 65.

that none of the statements in his group are causal (I shall argue later that it is not true), this is certainly not true of some of my other examples. For instance, the statement that I am depressed by my lack of money is obviously partly causal. Moreover, one of his reasons for denying that the statements in his group are causal is that they are immune from mistakes.[7] But I shall argue later that some of my other examples are not immune from mistakes, and that perhaps even the statements in his group are not immune from mistakes. (Here, as always, I mean mistakes of the kind specified above.)

Ought we, then, to adopt the only remaining solution of the three that I mentioned, and say that the statements on my list are liable to the kind of mistake that is revealed by parallel negative instances? But this alternative will not work for all the examples. For there does not seem to be any possibility of mistake about the fact that I was amused by a remark. And where there is some possibility of mistake, as I shall argue that there is about depression, it seems that the mistake would not always be revealed by parallel negative instances.

So it seems certain that we cannot solve the problem by simply choosing one of the three alternatives and applying it to all the statements on my list. It also seems probable that those statements lie in the intersection of two different conceptual schemes, the conceptual scheme of ordinary causation, and the conceptual scheme of feeling and object. This is the possibility that I shall explore.

There are two reasons why it is likely that this possibility is realised. First, a statement that something is the object of a feeling does not seem to be reducible to a causal statement. Secondly, in all the examples given, the high degree of certainty that the person himself would have, whether or not it amounts to immunity from mistake, always seems to depend on the identification of the object of the feeling. I shall now expand these two points.

First, suppose that we say that the object of a feeling or reaction is what it is about. This will hardly do as a definition, since other prepositions and even entirely different forms of words are capable of conveying the idea of being about some-

7. ibid., pp. 65–8.

thing in this particular sense. But it does roughly demarcate the concept of the object of a feeling or reaction. Given this explanation of the concept, it is immediately clear that, although the object of a feeling or reaction may cause it, and although one and the same statement may imply that it is both the object and the cause, nevertheless the statement that it is the object is not reducible to a causal statement. The reason why this is so is not that object-statements, unlike causal statements, are immune from mistakes. For I shall argue later that at least some object-statements are not immune from mistakes. The reason is simply that there is an obvious divergence between the meanings of the two types of statement. For instance, someone might say that his depression was caused by too much aspirin, and this would not mean that he was depressed about his excessive consumption of aspirin. Or, to take a non-physiological example, depression is sometimes the sequel to a period of excessive excitement, but, if someone gives this as the cause of his depression, he will not mean that this is what he is depressed about.

It might be objected, at this point, that a general argument for the irreducibility of object-statements to causal statements ought not to be based on the solitary example of depression. For depression belongs to the class of feelings or reactions that need not have an object, although presumably, they always have causes: i.e., a person can be depressed without being depressed about anything in particular, although his depression will have a cause. And it might be thought that this is the only reason why object-statements cannot be reduced to causal statements in this case. But this is not so. For if we take an example from the other class of feelings and reactions, which must have an object, for instance being pleased, we still get the same result: i.e., we still find that, if a person says that something is the cause of his being pleased, he will not mean that he is pleased about it; for example, he may be asked why he is pleased about some trifling thing, and he may reply that it is because he is in a good mood, itself produced by a satisfying meal or an enjoyable opera, and yet this reply will not mean that he is pleased about any of these other things. So it seems that object-statements are not reducible to causal statements, because causal statements do not imply object-statements. (In spite of this it may be the case that object-statements imply causal statements: i.e., it may be that, if something is the object of a feeling, it follows that it, or at least some thought or belief about it, is the cause of the feeling. I shall examine this possibility later.)

The second point that I was going to expand is the suggestion that the high degree of certainty that the person himself would have about the statements on my list would depend on the identification of the object of his feeling or reaction. The argument for this is that, if we consider a feeling like depression, and if we take cases where the person does not know what he is depressed about, perhaps because there is nothing in particular that he is depressed about, or perhaps because, though there is, he does not know what it is, then he will not be so certain what made him depressed, unless he offers a remote cause, such as too much aspirin or too much previous excitement. That is, if we subtract the identification of the object, then his certainty about any residual proximate causal statement will be diminished.

It might be objected that the argument is weak because this subtraction is not possible with the class of feelings and reactions that must have an object. For example, the concept of amusement does not allow the minimal knowledge that I am just amused, and perhaps the concept of being pleased does not allow the minimal knowledge that I am just pleased. But in many of these cases it is possible to take a related concept, for instance being in a good mood instead of being pleased, and to make the same point about the proximate causal statement in this case. Perhaps we can extend the conclusion reached about these cases to the other cases in which we cannot find a related concept which makes the subtraction possible. If so, the identification of the cause in the latter cases too would depend on the identification of the object, although the dependence could not be verified by any thought experiment.

The only example on the list that looks as if it might be a counter-example to the suggestion that is being defended, is the last one, 'The explosion made me jump'. For at first sight it does not look as if this statement implies that there is any psychological reaction to an object, and so it seems that the person's certainty about it cannot depend on his identification of an object. In fact, this is how Anscombe interprets a similar example in her book, welcoming the conclusion that it is a purely causal statement which refutes Hume's account of causation.[8] But this is unconvincing if it means that the example refutes the thesis that all purely causal statements are liable to the kind of mistake that is revealed by parallel negative instances. For if the statement simply reported a reflex movement, it would be vulnerable to parallel negative instances, and if, on the other hand, we regard it as immune from parallel negative instances, and so credit the person himself with a high degree of certainty about it, it seems that this can only be because it carries the implication that the explosion was the object of his reaction of shock.

So it seems likely that the statements on my list are grouped around the point of intersection of the conceptual scheme of ordinary causation and the conceptual scheme of feeling and object. What effect would this have on their analysis? This is a large and complex question. Perhaps the simplest way of approaching it is to begin by describing the conceptual scheme of feeling and object. So what I shall do next is to offer, without much argument, a general picture of the logic of object-statements. Then I shall try to defend this picture by dealing with two objections to it. And finally, I shall offer a solution of the problem posed at the beginning. These three tasks will occupy the remainder of this paper.

The first of them can be completed more quickly than the other two. For the important question about the logic of object-statements is whether the person himself can make a mistaken identification, and the general lines of the answer to this question are fairly clear. Two, at least, of my examples are not liable to mistakes in the identification of the object, 'I was amused by his remark' and 'The explosion made me jump'. For suppose that someone tried to persuade me that the object of my amusement was really something else. For instance, he might point out that a great many factors had predisposed me to laugh at a not very amusing remark, and that among those factors were other excellent jokes made by the same speaker, which had, in fact, greatly amused me. Then he would necessarily fail, because this sort of mistake is not allowed for by the concept of amusement. The most that could be conceded to him would be that

8. *Intention*, pp. 15–16.

the object of my amusement played an unusually small part in causing it, but this would not debar it from being its object. Similarly, if the statement about the explosion implies that I was startled, I cannot have made a mistake in identifying it as the object of my reaction, although it may have played an unusually small part in causing it.

But these two statements seem to lie at one end of a spectrum whose other end is quite different. For at least one of my examples is liable to a mistake in the identification of the object. Someone who says 'I am depressed by my lack of money' might well be led to change this identification of the object of his depression. For instance, he might be contemplating a journey when he made the statement, and he might later be brought to admit that what he was really depressed about was some aspect of his relationship with the people whom he was going to visit. If this happened, he would see that the thing that he had originally given as the object of his feeling was a kind of symbol, representing but concealing its real object. Perhaps it is also possible to be mistaken in identifying what one is angry about, or even what one is pleased about. But I do not want at the moment to extend this thesis towards the middle of the spectrum. I simply want to use the concept of depression to fix its extreme point.

How would it be established that someone had mistakenly identified the object of his depression? There seem to be three different ways, which are sometimes used together, and sometimes separately. First, he might cease to feel depressed about the stated object as soon as his attention was drawn to the rival object, about which he would immediately begin to feel depressed. Of course, in this situation he might say that one bout of depression had been replaced by another. But he would not have to say this, as he would have to say the parallel thing about amusement. For in certain circumstances he would use a different criterion of identity for bouts of depression and he would say that he had discovered that the bout of depression which, according to the first statement, had one object, really had another.

The second way in which the mistake might be established is quite different. The person might come to realise that the stated object of his depression was not a sufficiently important part of its cause, and that something else, which might well be its object (unlike the excessive excitement in the earlier example), was a much more important part of its cause. In fact, he might come to realise this in an ordinary Humean way: for instance, he might remember that he had not felt depressed on other occasions when he was even more short of money, and that he had felt depressed on other occasions when he was about to visit those people.

The third thing that might establish that a mistake had been made is behaviour. For example, either the person himself or other people might notice that he kept postponing the date of his departure and that this decreased his depression, and that he went on spending money on other things without increasing it. This method of correction is related to the second one, but differs from it in that the observations are confined to the history of the particular case, and do not range over other parallel cases in the person's life. I shall not discuss this way of establishing that an identification of an object is mistaken, but only the first and second ways.

It is sometimes said that the second way can never be used alone, as the first way can: or at least that, though it may be used alone in psychoanalytic case-histories, it never is in everyday life. But this seems to be incorrect. For if the possibility of mistake and the relevance of Humean evidence are admitted, there cannot be any good reason for maintaining that Humean evidence alone, however strong, is never sufficient to establish a mistake. However, this kind of evidence is often very inconclusive, since the causation of human feelings is so complex that it is seldom possible to be sure that there is no relevant difference between the particular case that is under scrutiny and the supposedly parallel negative instances that are cited.

Much more ought to be said in defence of the thesis that a person can make a mistaken identification of the object of his depression and of other similar feelings. For example, an account is needed of the way in which his behaviour might lead him to admit that he had made such a mistake, and it should be added that he might be forced back to an intermediate position, in which he knew that he was depressed, but did not know what he was depressed about.

But that will have to do as a general picture. My second task is to defend it by dealing with two objections to it. The first objection is simply that it is false that there are any mistaken identifications of the objects of feelings and psychological reactions except in psychoanalytic case-histories. The second objection is that, even if my description of the logic of object-statements is correct, it is inadequate. For we need to understand the nature of the connection between feeling and object, and, in particular, we need to know why mistakes are possible at one end of the spectrum, but not at the other.

First consider the objection that mistaken identifications of objects do not occur outside psychoanalytic case-histories. What lies behind this objection is the notion that psychoanalytic accounts of such mistaken identification are either false, or else contain conceptual innovations that are so extreme that the use of ordinary words is illegitimate. I shall counter this objection by trying to show that our ordinary conceptual scheme really does allow that objects may be mistakenly identified, though perhaps it would not allow some of the more extreme examples that occur in psychoanalytic case-histories (but here it is by now difficult to draw a line between ordinary and technical concepts), and though it certainly does not presuppose any psychoanalytic theory about the nature of the difference between appearance and reality, or about the nature of the screen that divides them.

First, it is worth reiterating that the mistakes in question are in one way fairly extreme. For they are made by the person himself, and there is going to be no knowledge in reserve that might lead him to correct them on reflection. But in another way they are not so extreme as they might appear at first. For his original identification of the object need not be totally mistaken, and perhaps never would be. There are various reasons for this. One is that there is a very weak sense of the word 'about', according to which, if a person is depressed, he is depressed about everything that he thinks about in a depressed way. This is what people mean when they say that they are depressed about everything. I call this sense of the word 'about' weak because it is very non-selective, and does not pick out one thing that is thought about in a depressed way rather than another. But though it is a weak sense, it is an important one, because, as we shall see later, it is a much larger part of the normal meaning of the word 'about' when it is used with phrases from the other end of the spectrum, like 'being pleased' and 'being amused'. Anyway, in this weak sense of the word it would almost certainly be true that the person was depressed about the object that he identified first, even if he later admitted that he was really depressed about something else, this time using a more selective sense of the word. This is one reason for not regarding the original identification as totally mistaken.

Another, related reason is that, even when the word 'about' picks out one thing that is thought about in a depressed way rather than another, it might be that it did not pick out the most important thing. In such a case, if the person corrected his original identification and made a more judicious selection from the possible factors, much more might be left unretracted. For it might still be true that he was depressed about what he originally said that he was depressed about, in a sense of that word that is selective, but insufficiently selective.

These variations in the selectivity of the word 'about' give a certain flexibility to the concept of 'the object'. Consequently, there is no need to insist that a person's original identification of the object of a feeling or psychological reaction must be totally mistaken if it is mistaken at all. This may remove one ground of objection to the thesis that I am defending. For objection to it is sometimes based on the false assumption that, if mistakes are possible at all, total mistakes must be possible, as they are with analogous statements about physical objects – for instance, it is possible to be totally mistaken about the direction in which an arrow is pointing. But if this analogy has a bad effect on philosophers who find it too attractive, it has an equally bad effect on those who are too averse from it. In general, it is unnecessary to assume that analogies between psychological reports in the first person and statements about physical objects are either total or null, so that there is no need to accept this artificial dilemma.

In spite of this qualification the thesis might still be found objectionable, and the interpretation of the example that I gave just now and of others like it might be challenged. For it might be argued that nobody could be ignorant even of the most highly selected object of his depression, and that what is interpreted as lack of knowledge is really self-deception. It would be admitted that a person might turn his depression loose on other things, allowing himself to dwell on them in a gloomy and destructive way: or – to take a more familiar example, where thought is more closely connected with action – it would be admitted that he might allow his anger to colour his thinking about perfectly innocent things. But it would be argued that, if he appeared not to know the true object of his feeling, this could only be because he was deceiving himself.

Here it ought to be reiterated that the impossibility of lack of knowledge that is being alleged is supposed to be conceptual, and the conceptual scheme that is in question is non-technical. Given this, is the objection valid? Is self-deception the extreme limit of what is possible here, or is it on the borderline between knowledge and lack of knowledge? The question is made difficult by the complexity of the concept of self-deception. For self-deception sometimes involves a kind of partial, intermittent lack of knowledge. The person half-realises at times what the object of his feeling is, but he suppresses the fact, or allows it to slide from his mind, or at least from the centre of his attention. But in other cases the lack of knowledge is complete and uninterrupted, because he simply will not raise the question whether the object of his feeling might really be something different from what he takes it to be, or, if he does raise it, he will not reach the correct answer, that it is. Now do all examples of the sort that I cited belong to one of these two kinds of self-deception? Certainly they do not all belong to the first kind, where the correct answer to the question is actually suppressed, and the suppression comes close to being a deliberate action. This is important, because people who make the objection that is being examined are usually thinking of this kind of self-deception.

But the line between the second kind of self-deception and simple lack of knowledge is exceedingly hard to draw. Some genuine surprise at the correct answer seems to be necessary in order to establish simple lack of knowledge, and certainly it sometimes occurs. But is it sufficient? Would it not have been possible for the person to have reached the correct answer if he had really tried? So is not the lack of knowledge still to some extent self-induced? In many cases it will be hard to tell, because the whole idea of making the best possible use of one's available psychological resources in such matters is an extremely vague one. But in some cases the statement, that one could have reached the correct answer if one had really tried, surely degenerates into a form of encouragement or blame. In any case, this kind of self-deception is not an alternative to uninterrupted lack of knowledge, but, rather, uninterrupted lack of knowledge maintained by a certain mechanism. So the objection could not be sustained by an appeal to it.

Another form which the objection might take is this. It might be argued that this so-called lack of knowledge of the object of a feeling, which, as I said at the beginning, is a necessary condition of the kind of mistake that I am investigating, appears to exist only when the question that the person is required to answer is very specific. For instance, he is able to say what he is depressed about, but unable to answer the more specific question, what aspect of that thing he is depressed about. But, it might be argued, this inability should not be called lack of knowledge of the object of the feeling, but, rather, lack of knowledge of the precise aspect of the object that arouses the feeling, and this is something different.

There seems to be some force in this form of the objection, but not enough to make its point. There is some force in it, because, if we move in the direction of greater specificity, we often find something which should not be called the object of the feeling or reaction, but, rather, an aspect of the object. For instance, it is sometimes possible to give an undoubtedly correct account of the precise elements in a joke that made another person find it so amusing, although he himself could not give such an account, because it was too recondite, involving an analysis of the associations of certain words that produced their effect on him without his realising how they produced it. But this would not show that he did not know the precise object of his amusement, because we, the theorists, would have crossed the line that divides identifications of objects from identifications of those aspects of them that explain the ways in which people feel about them or react to them.

However, I do not think that the objection makes its point. For often the aspect of a thing that arouses a feeling can be regarded as its precise object. And, if we confine ourselves to such cases, it is not enough for the objector to say that lack of knowledge at a more specific level is always compensated by knowledge at a less specific level: for instance, it is not enough for him to say that, if a person does not know exactly what aspect of a conversation depressed him, this is compensated by his knowledge that at least it was the conversation that depressed him. For the thesis I am defending is that it is possible to make mistaken identifications of objects without any reserve of knowledge that might enable one to correct them, and, if such mistaken identifications of objects occur at any level of specificity, that is enough to establish the thesis. The fact, if it is a fact, that at a less specific level the person can identify the object, is irrelevant. The objector might as well argue that mistakes about the apparent colours of physical objects are impossible, and, when he is confronted by counter-examples, fall back on the defence that there will always be a less specific colour-word about which there will be no mistake. In any case, it is not true that a person can always give a correct generic identification of the object of his depression.

According to the second objection that has to be answered, even if my description of the logic of object-statements is correct, it is inadequate. For we need to understand the nature of the connection between feeling and object, and in particular, we need to know why mistakes are possible at one end of the spectrum, but not at the other.

Let us begin with the question about the nature of the connection. Obviously it is no good just calling it 'intentional', since that leaves everything unexplained. What we need is a detailed, explanatory description of it. Perhaps the best way to discover such a description would be to begin by looking at statements like 'I was pleased by the publication of my letter' and 'I was amused by his remark', since statements at this end of the spectrum seem to exhibit the connection in its purest form. Now the second of these two statements is, as I said earlier, quite immune from mistakes in the identification of the object. For it is clear that I could not be completely mistaken about the object of my amusement, and it does not even seem to be possible that, if I considered the matter more selectively, I would realise that its preponderant object was really something else. But in the case of being pleased it is not so clear that there is immunity from such mistakes. For though there are many cases, like the one that I mentioned earlier, where the statement that I am pleased about something resists all attempts to undermine it by extraneous explanations, there seem to be other cases where this concept lies closer to the concept of a good mood; for instance, if what I say is not that I am pleased about something momentarily, but that I continue to be pleased about it – a steady state – then a mistaken identification of the object does seem to be possible. So perhaps the report of amusement occupies the extreme limit of the spectrum in this direction, and would be the best example to start with.

What, then, is the nature of the connection between amusement and its object? I shall approach this question like an auctioneer, starting the bidding at a low point, in order to see how much it is necessary to raise it later. First, if I am amused about something, it is clearly necessary, even if it is not sufficient, that I should hear it with amusement, think about it with amusement, etc. That is, it is necessary that I should be amused about it in the weak sense of the word 'about' that I introduced earlier. But how ought we to characterise this element in the connection between amusement and its object? Williams's theory is that being pleased is a mode of attention.[9] Perhaps this theory could be generalised to cover amusement and other feelings and psychological reactions. For it seems to be a successful characterisation of the connection marked by the weak sense of the word 'about', since it brings out the fact that, even if feelings and reactions are effects, they are not separate effects, but colour one's perception of the object and determine the tone of one's thoughts about it.

But is this opening bid sufficiently high? Certainly it gives a necessary element in the connection between feeling and object, but is it all that is involved? Even for the concept of amusement it does not seem to be all that is involved. For when someone says that he is amused about a remark, he means more than that this is true in the weak sense of the word 'about'. He also means that the remark caused his amusement. (In other cases, as I pointed out earlier, it may not be the object itself but rather some thought or belief about it that causes the feeling or reaction.) It may not be so obvious that this causal implication is carried by the report of amusement as it is that it is carried

9. 'Pleasure and belief', pp. 70–1.

by the report of depression. Nevertheless it is a fact that it is carried by the report of amusement. For, if it were not, that report would mean no more than that he merely happened to feel amused when he heard, or thought about, the remark. But this would understate its meaning. So here we have the problem that was posed at the beginning of this paper: an object-statement that is immune from mistakes implies a causal statement, which must, therefore, itself be immune from mistakes.

If we consider statements that lie further along the spectrum, it is more obvious that my opening bid is not sufficiently high. For when the implied causal statement can be mistaken, it makes a much more noticeable addition to the meaning of the statement: i.e. it adds something much more conspicuous to the minimal connection signified by the weak sense of the word 'about'. Thus this addition is very obvious in the case of depression which lies at the far end of the spectrum. But even when a person says that he is pleased about something the addition ought sometimes to be fairly noticeable. For if what was suggested just now is correct, in cases where this statement refers to a steady state it can be mistaken. But mistakes are not possible with the weak sense of the word 'about'. Therefore when a mistake is possible, it is clear that more is meant by the statement. And since one method of correction is to show that the stated object is not the cause of the feeling, or at least not a sufficiently important part of its cause, it is evident that the extra element in its meaning is partly causal.

It must be emphasised that this thesis does not depend on this particular argument. For the causal implication can be demonstrated in all these cases without appeal to the possibility of mistake. Where the appeal can be made, it merely helps to make the point clear. Incidentally, it ought also to make it clear that being pleased is sometimes more than a mode of attention. For Williams intended the word 'mode' to denote something that could not conceivably belong to anything but the person's attention to a particular thing, as, for instance, the care with which he attends to it cannot conceivably be concerned with anything else (which explains why his theory exactly fits my weak sense of the word 'about'). But if so, it is probable that the word 'mode' cannot properly be applied to all cases of being pleased about something, since, when this feeling is a steady state, it seems that it might be concerned with something other than what the person is attending to with pleasure.

If even a person's statement that he is amused about a remark carries a causal implication, this confronts us inescapably with the problem that was posed at the beginning of this paper: How can the implied causal statement be known to be true unmistakably? For this problem can be evaded only when it can be shown that the identification of the object is liable to be mistaken. When it is not, as it is not in this case, it is impossible to evade the problem. Nor is it any good saying that hearing the remark or thinking about it cannot be regarded as causes of the person's amusement because his amusement cannot be separated from these events. For it is only necessary to describe his amusement in a more abstract, general way that makes no reference to these events, and then it can be regarded as their contingent effect. I shall try to solve this problem in the last part of this paper.

I think that Williams was aware of the possibility that being pleased about something might carry a causal implication. For he also puts forward another theory, which is related to the first one but different from it. He also says that being pleased is a mode of having one's attention drawn to something.[10] This is avowedly an attempt to do justice to the fact that being pleased is something that happens to one, like an effect, rather than something that one does, and to admit the causal implication without losing the immunity from mistake. Suppose that we substitute being amused for being pleased, in order to get a more convincing case of immunity from mistake. Then does this new theory work? It seems not. For, in general, it is possible to give a mistaken answer to the question, what drew one's attention to something, and amusement does not colour the way in which one is brought to listen to it, so that the theory puts the causation in the wrong place.

The account given so far of the connection between feeling and object, though it is fairly detailed, is still insufficiently explanatory. It says that object-statements imply causal statements at both ends of the spectrum and that this raises the familiar problem only at the end where object-statements are incorrigible. But it does not explain why the two ends of the

10. ibid., pp. 64–5.

spectrum differ in this way. Why should there be two such very different kinds of object-statements? This is puzzling.

If what is puzzling is the strangeness of the facts of human psychology, I do not see how this can be mitigated. But if it is the apparent isolation of the factor, corrigibility and incorrigibility, that varies along the spectrum, something can be done to mitigate it. For that variable is not really as isolated as it appears to be. Other connected things vary with it, and the connection can be explained. So the philosopher's task is not restricted to placing different statements at various points along the spectrum of corrigibility and incorrigibility.

The most important of the connected variables was mentioned at the beginning of this paper. It is duration. Depression lasts longer than amusement, and this gives it a stronger claim to be called a feeling, whereas amusement is more of a reaction. It is a fact that there are such variations in duration, and this fact is then made part of the logic of the concepts that lie at various points along the spectrum. Some feelings or reactions are momentary, like amusement, and these tend to be individuated together with their objects. For there is simply no question whether the amusement that someone is feeling at this particular moment might be identical with an earlier feeling of amusement which had, or seemed to have, a different object. Contrast the other end of the spectrum, where a feeling like depression or anxiety is persistent, so that the person himself at the time when he is feeling it can sometimes individuate it in a minimal way that involves no reference to its object (i.e. it can be free-floating). In such cases one can ask oneself questions of identity that are in many ways analogous to questions of identity about physical objects. For instance, is the anxiety that I am feeling today still yesterday's anxiety about a task that I rashly undertook? And the answer to this question can even be tested. The analogy with things in the external world, which is part of the concept of introspection, may not be perfect, but it certainly exists.

But what is the connection between duration and corrigibility? Perhaps it is something like this. Amusement, which is a momentary reaction, is never free-floating, because the person himself can always claim to identify its object, and the same is true of nearly all momentary reactions and feelings. This, in itself, would not be enough to lead us to regard the connection with the particular object as unmistakable in such cases. An additional inducement is provided by the fact that a momentary feeling or reaction does not get any chance to collect other things on other occasions which the person would then be equally ready to identify as its object. Contrast a persistent feeling, like depression, which does collect other things in this way. Now these other things are candidates for the position of the object of the feeling or reaction. Therefore a momentary feeling or reaction, unlike a persistent one, lacks alternative candidates for this position. However, this still does not really explain why we should regard a person's identification of the object of his momentary feeling or reaction as immune from mistakes. For why should it not be possible for him to make a mistaken identification of the object, and to retract it without being able to produce an alternative candidate? Perhaps the final step in the explanation is to appeal again to the fact mentioned just now, that momentary feelings and reactions are never free-floating: i.e. the person himself is never unable to make a claim to identify the object. For this fact conditions the logic of such concepts by inducing us not to regard it as an open possibility that he should retract his original claim to identify the object, and not produce an alternative candidate, but leave the position unoccupied. That is, the first candidate is not allowed to vacate the position, when it is impossible to find another candidate because this would leave the position empty.

This explanation is rough and insecure, and may well be open to the charge of circularity. For it is exceedingly difficult to isolate the facts that underlie the logic of concepts. There is always the besetting danger that the concepts that need to be explained might themselves colour the supposedly independent facts that are adduced in explanation.

My third task is to deal with the problem posed at the beginning of this paper: How can an object-statement that is immune from mistakes imply a causal statement? Perhaps it would be more accurate to call this the residue of the problem posed at the beginning, since it has now been both narrowed and sharpened: narrowed because it is only when the object-statement really is immune from mistakes that the problem persists, and sharpened, because something has been done to explain the component elements in the meaning of such object-statements.

But why not just abandon Hume at this point, and so dissolve the problem? I said at the beginning that this would be inadequate, because some explanation of the non-Humean sense of the word 'cause' would have to be given. For otherwise both its points of difference from the ordinary sense of the word, and its points of resemblance would be left obscure. But that was really an understatement. For, if the word 'cause' here does not at least mean 'sufficient condition' or 'sufficient condition in similar circumstances', what can it mean? And, if it does mean this, how can it be invulnerable to parallel negative instances? Here it is no use saying that the fact that a person is amused about a remark in the weak sense of the word 'about' is exceedingly strong evidence that the remark caused his amusement. For if this were so, it still ought to be conceivable that the causal statement should be mistaken, and mistaken not just because he had misheard the remark, but because, although he heard it as it was made and was amused about it in the weak sense of that word, nevertheless it did not cause his amusement. But this does not seem to be conceivable.

But what sort of inconceivability is this? I have said all along that a mistaken identification of the object is not allowed for by the concept of amusement. But it might still be the case that this particular inconceivability has a very firm contingent fact as its basis. After all, it is unlikely that the inconceivability was generated spontaneously out of nothing. And now that we have dissected the concept of being amused about something into two component elements, being amused about it in the weak sense of the word 'about', and having one's amusement caused by it, we do not have to look far for the contingent fact that might serve as the basis of the inconceivability. For it is plausible to suggest that it is the contingent fact that at one end of the spectrum the thing to which the feeling or reaction is linked by the connection signified by the weak sense of 'about' is always its cause. If this suggestion is correct, then, though the possibility of a mistaken identification of the object is not allowed for by the conceptual scheme at this end of the spectrum, it still exists in the substructure of the conceptual scheme. We avert our eyes from it because the concepts would be radically changed if it were realised, and in particular because the change would be a change in human nature, and the sort of change that is well known to make us uneasy. For though the possibility of a mistaken identification of the object at this end of the spectrum is not contained in our conceptual scheme, it lies only just outside it. Perhaps we could say that the possibility of the possibility is contained in it.

If this suggestion is correct, we ought to be able to describe a contingency that would split the concept of being amused about something into its two components. I shall end by describing two such contingencies, both of which would upset our conceptual scheme, but in slightly different ways. The first contingency is this. It might have been the case that when a person said that he was amused about something, it could be demonstrated quite often that this was true only in the weak sense of the word 'about'. The demonstration would take the usual form of pointing out that something else that had happened to him previously was the kind of thing that was sufficient to cause his amusement, and that the thing about which he said he was amused was not the kind of thing that was sufficient to cause his amusement. There might be a special difficulty in establishing this for amusement, but that would not affect the general validity of such a speculation about this end of the spectrum. It is, of course, an essential feature of this speculation that the thing that is offered as the real object is something that the person himself has experienced.

It is no objection to this speculation to say that the contingency is not admitted by the concept of amusement. It certainly is not admitted by our full concept of amusement, but the point is that it is admitted by the attenuated concept that merely uses the weak sense of the word 'about'. If it were realised, it would be upsetting in the following way. Amusement would have to become a persistent feeling like depression, colouring our reactions to many things for long periods at a time. So telling someone a joke would be a serious step to take. Also the reasons that people gave for their amusement would be regarded as rationalisations far more often than they are now (or, at least, half-rationalisations).

However, it is arguable that, though individual concepts might have been shifted to the other end of the spectrum in this way, it would not be possible for this to have happened to all concepts, because steady psychological states presuppose momentary psychological reactions. If this is so, the part of the spectrum to which momentary reactions belong could not have been obliterated altogether, unless the rest of it had ceased to exist too. It is also arguable that, even if we confine ourselves to a single concept, like amusement, it could not have happened that everybody's first spontaneous identifications of objects were always mistaken. For, as things are now, most of these identifications are intelligible, reasons can be given for them, and some kind of systematisation of the laughable seems to be possible, and these extremely important facts constitute an immovable obstacle that stands in the way of a progressive extension of the concept of a rationalisation, which anyway could not cover the whole area because it is logically dependent on the concept of a true reason. So the speculation, in the form in which I am putting it forward, is restricted in two ways: it does not apply to all concepts at this end of the spectrum, and it does not apply to all cases, or even to the majority of cases of any one concept. Of course, it does not include a breakdown of the general connection between amusement and laughter.

It is, perhaps, worth emphasising that these two restrictions on the speculation are very different in strength. For it may be possible to imagine a situation in which the first would be removed. There is, as has just been pointed out, an obstacle. For if momentary reactions never occurred, steady psychological states would have a different character. But perhaps that too can be imagined, and the obstacle is not insuperable. But if we tried to circumvent the second restriction by imagining an alteration in the facts, we should encounter an insuperable difficulty. For we should have to suppose the facts altered in such a way that there would be no such thing as understanding why people found some things amusing and not others. But, since the intelligibility of such reactions depends on their regularity and on the possibility of systematising them, we could get rid of intelligibility only by getting rid of regularity. But, if there were no regularity in people's reactions of amusement, it would be impossible to assign them causes. That would undermine the very concept of a reaction. So the obstacle here consists not only in the fact that rationalisations presuppose reasons, but also in the fact that all reasons of this kind are causes (though, of course, many causes are not even capable of functioning as reasons of this kind).

The second speculation includes the first, but goes beyond it. The additional element is this. Suppose that a drug, secretly administered, always made people feel amused about everything that happened in the following hour, even if none of those things would have amused them had they not taken the drug. Suppose too that it is discovered that the drug works by producing a secretion in the blood-stream, and that this same secretion is sometimes found for short periods in the blood of people who have not taken the drug, and that its effect is then the same. If all this happened, we should regard the reasons that both these classes of people gave for their amusement during these periods as rationalisations, in exactly the same way that we now regard the irrelevant reasons that people give for physically induced depression as rationalisations. What distinguishes this speculation from the first one is that the real cause does not also function as the real object. Consequently, the feeling of amusement, in this contingency, would not really have an object (except in the weak sense). In short, this second speculation, if it were realised, would completely assimilate amusement to depression. So it is not necessary to make the real cause of amusement physical, like the excessive consumption of aspirins in the earlier example of depression: it could equally well be made psychological, like the excessive excitement in the other earlier example.

This solution of the problem with which I began this paper is very sketchy. Much more ought to be said about the various stages in the assimilation of a concept like amusement to a concept like depression. I have imagined this assimilation occurring suddenly and completely. For in my speculation a feeling of amusement simply acquires an entirely different principle of individuation, which is exactly like the principle of individuation of a bout of depression. But this is probably too sudden, and the change ought to be broken down into its separate stages.

But some such solution ought to be correct. For the immunity from mistakes possessed by some of the statements that I have been examinining ought to be based on some statable contingent fact about human nature. How could it be an ultimate fact that statements as complex as these are immune from mistakes?

4 The Paradoxes of Self-Deception

There is an air of paradox about an unconscious desire and an unconscious interpretation of a situation, and especially about an unconscious formulation of a plan. These concepts flout the natural assumptions that the contents of a mind all interact freely with one another, and that they can be surveyed from a single vantage point, consciousness. One way of trying to dispel the air of paradox would be to investigate the theory of the unconscious. Another way, which I shall take in this paper, is to examine some ordinary concepts whose use does not depend on the theory, in order to see if the two natural assumptions are entirely valid in their case. If they are not, the transition to the theory will not be so sudden and there will not be such a startling break in continuity.

The concept of self-deception seems to be the most suitable object of such an enquiry. It is the most prominent member of a family of pre-theoretical concepts – wishful thinking is another – and it has generated several much discussed paradoxes. For it can hardly combine in one mind everything that is distributed between two minds in a case of ordinary deception. Yet this is what the name 'self-deception' seems to imply. In order to avoid this difficulty, some recent accounts[1] have reduced the similarity between the two kinds of deception to a point which deprives the name 'self-deception' of its appropriateness. Certainly the thing takes many forms, and perhaps some of them do not quite deserve the name, with its suggestion of deliberateness. But others are more properly so called, and in their case the idea behind the name really does produce the paradoxes.

1. e.g. by J. V. Canfield and D. F. Gustafson, 'Self-deception', *Analysis* 23, 1962, and by T. Penelhum, 'Pleasure and falsity', in *Philosophy of Mind*, ed. Stuart Hampshire, New York, 1966. Both these accounts are criticised by H. Fingarette, *Self-deception*, London, 1969.

The paradoxes of self-deception mark dubious similarities between self-deception and ordinary deception. Since ordinary deception is complex, there are several dimensions of possible similarity. They may be pictured as lines radiating from a centre which would represent complete assimilation to ordinary deception. What the paradoxes seem to establish is that on some of these lines self-deception cannot reach the centre. It would follow that no type of self-deception could achieve complete assimilation to ordinary deception. But it would still be possible for certain types to approach very close to the centre along the disputed lines, and even to reach it along the others.

I shall enquire whether these possibilities are realised. My strategy will be to resist the conclusions that are commonly drawn from the paradoxes until I have reduced them to an irresistible residue. Self-deception may not be very like ordinary deception, but let us not conclude that it cannot be at all like it until this has been proved. Let us not be stampeded by the paradoxes.

There are four distinct paradoxes which have been discussed in recent accounts of self-deception.

(1) If I have deceived myself that *p*, I believe *p*, but at the same time I really know, or believe, or suspect that *not-p*. These combinations of attitudes seem to be impossible, whatever their cause.

(2) If the cause is a process properly called 'self-deception', that process seems to involve another, consequential impossibility: if I am aware that the combination of attitudes is impossible, I cannot intend to produce it in myself.

(3) If it is suggested that my fundamental belief that *not-p* is somehow screened from the rest of my thoughts and feelings, the process becomes unintelligible. For awareness of the belief is needed to motivate the process and to guide its strategy: it is, as Sartre says, part of the 'unitary structure of a single project'.[2]

(4) Perhaps, then, what is screened is the whole plan, together with everything mental that it requires for its existence. But that merely shifts the previous paradox to a different point, where it remains unresolved. If an internally incoherent plan is impossible, it will not be made possible simply by my being unaware of it and not identifying myself with it.

2. *Being and Nothingness*, tr. Hazel Barnes, London, 1957, p. 49.

These four paradoxes arise because structures that are subject to the demands of rationality do not meet them fully in cases of self-deception. The claim made by (1) is that 'being self-deceived' is a state which does not conform to the requirements of rational belief. The immediate answer to this is that in fact people do hold incompatible beliefs, and that, when this happens, the requirements are flouted. But this is hardly a sufficient answer, because the explanation of 'being self-deceived' is not that the person himself is unaware of the incompatibility – in simple cases he could not be – nor that his judgment is equally split between the two alternatives, as might happen if he witnessed an immensely improbable event. Moreover, the name of the state implies an identification of its cause, which runs into the more interesting difficulties raised by (2), (3) and (4). These paradoxes invoke the requirements of rational planning, and their strategy differs from that of (1). (1) claims, in the spirit of Zeno, that the thing cannot happen at all, but the argument of (2), (3) and (4) is that it cannot happen in the way that the name suggests. Here the implied account of the process brings down the requirements of rationality on its own head.

My strategy is to concede to these arguments no more than has to be conceded. So I shall look for ways of evading the requirements of rationality, hoping that they will allow the thing to happen without depriving the name of its appropriateness. Naturally, it is not to be expected that the name will be equally appropriate to every type of the thing. But if the argument from the paradoxes is valid, there could not be a type to which it would be at all appropriate. It is this conclusion that I shall resist, if it can be resisted.

(1) exploits the fact that a person's beliefs ought to form a system which does not violate the laws of nature or logic. (2), (3) and (4) apply a similar requirement to the contents of the parts of a rational plan: you cannot intend to do what you know that you cannot do, and you cannot execute an intention to eliminate something from consciousness if the intention is partly motivated, and perhaps also guided, by continuing awareness of that very thing. In each case the obstacle is the need for coherence between the elements of a complex structure, and in the second case the obstacle is put there by the implied account of the process of self-deception.

Perhaps we might be able to evade this obstacle if the complexity of the structure of a plan could be reduced a little. This is a possibility worth exploring. But let us first ask how we could make such a large reduction in complexity that the result would scarcely count as a plan at all. When this question has been answered, we shall have a clearer view of the zone within which small reductions might be found.

The phenomenon of wishful thinking offers an instructive example of a large reduction in complexity. Suppose that your wish to believe *p* produces the belief, in spite of the fact that it is not beyond your intellectual powers to realise that your evidence for *p* is insufficient, and perhaps even points to the conclusion that *not-p*. Here the idea would be that the wish, by its very nature, tends to produce not only satisfaction that *p*, when *p* is believed, but also the belief itself unless it is held in check by the rational assessment of evidence.

There is no need to complicate this theory by supposing that behind some screen the wish is associated with the suspicion that *not-p*, and that because of this suspicion it develops into the intention to make yourself believe *p*, and even works out a suitable strategy. All that we have to suppose is that the wish directly produces the ill-founded belief that *p*, in much the same way that it would have needlessly reinforced it, had it been well-founded. The distinctive mark of wishful thinking is only that the contribution made by the wish to the production of the belief is needed. Naturally, you must be unaware that it is needed, and so there must also be some uncharacteristic distortion in your intellectual processes: perhaps you uncharacteristically over-estimate the strength of your evidence for *p*, or – to take a case where your belief is not based on evidence – your memory-impression that *p* is stronger than it would have been without the wish. But you do not have to be unaware of the wish or of its two general tendencies. For the tendency to produce the belief that *p* can be held in check, and the tendency to produce satisfaction that *p*, when *p* is already believed, is innocent. You can even identify yourself with the wish.

So in a case of wishful thinking only two facts have to be screened: the fact that the contribution made by the wish is needed, and the fact that therefore there is some uncharacteristic distortion in your mental processes.

But what is the screen? In order to determine its nature, various theories would have to be tested against the evidence. But my concern is only with the minimum conditions that have to be met by any explanation of wishful thinking, and it is worth emphasising how little has to be screened, because it is so easy to exaggerate the amount. We imagine that the wish itself has to be screened, because in fact it often is. But it need not be screened. Moreover, when it is, we have to guard against another exaggeration: we must not suppose that behind the screen the wish is incorporated in a complex structure exactly like a plan. It is naive to assume that we are bound to explain wishful thinking by reduplicating every detail in the pattern of deliberate agency. We do not even have to suppose that the screen is impervious in both directions. If you are unaware of your wish and do not identify yourself with it, it does not follow that it is no more closely connected with your conscious thoughts and feelings than the altruistic wish of another person who deceives you for your own comfort. To draw that conclusion would be to produce a fifth paradox, sometimes presented in treatments of this topic: wishful thinking and self-deception are interpreted as extraordinary cases of ordinary altruistic deception, but then it is unintelligible how the deceiving agent knows what to do.

But I am still confining the discussion to wishful thinking, and at this point it might be objected that I have reduced its necessary conditions too far. For if you have to be unaware that the contribution made by the wish was needed, will there not necessarily be behind the screen a second associated wish, that your unawareness of the first wish be maintained? And does not that association amount to a plan?

But we do not have to regard even this rudimentary structure as a necessary feature of wishful thinking. For there is another way of explaining your unawareness of the fact that the contribution made by the wish to believe *p* was needed. It might merely be a further intellectual distortion produced directly by that wish. For if that wish has a natural tendency to produce any distortion in your intellectual processes that is required for the manufacture and maintenance of the belief that *p*, why should the distortions not include the inhibition of any normal mental process that would conflict with the belief? If we choose this explanation of the success of a piece of wishful thinking, we shall be multiplying the effects of a single wish; whereas if we choose the other explanation we shall be multiplying wishes behind the screen.

Neither of the two explanations leads to an infinite regress. For according to the second one the extra effect, that you are unaware that the contribution made by the original wish was needed, may well be the last effect to occur in the series. There need not be anything prompting you to ask yourself why you do not believe that it was needed. Perhaps you do not even ask yourself whether it was needed. All that is required is that the original wish should produce the wrong answer to this question, if you ask it, and also to any later question in the series, if, improbably, you persist in your self-examination.

The objection, that the other explanation leads to an infinite regress of associated wishes, may be answered in a parallel way. Instead of multiplying wishes behind the screen, we should put generality into the original wish. We should represent it as the wish to produce the belief that *p*, and to produce unawareness that its contribution to producing the belief was needed, and to produce unawareness that its contribution to producing *that* unawareness was needed, and so on for any later unawareness in the series. But since the first unawareness will usually be the only one that actually has to be produced, your wish need not reach very far into this potentially infinite series.

It is not clear how we should choose between the two explanations, because it is not clear whether there is a real difference between them. But that does not affect the point that I want to make, which is that it is possible to explain the secondary effects of wishful thinking without postulating a plan behind the screen. If it is objected that no such explanation can work, because the complexity of the manoeuvres requires foresight and calculation, it should be remembered that their so-called 'complex' pattern is governed by a single, simple principle.

If this is the basic structure of wishful thinking, two questions may now be asked about it. Is it sufficiently complex to count as self-deception? And if not, can we add enough further elements to transform it into self-deception without falling foul of the paradoxes?

The first question does not deserve a lengthy answer. It will be agreed that, if these minimal cases of wishful thinking do count as self-deception, they certainly do not achieve the maximum possible assimilation to ordinary deception. But it is less important to allocate the name than to discover what these cases lack by seeking an answer to the second question. We should not even assume that the commonest cases of self-deception will be those that come closest to ordinary deception. For it may be that the connotation of the name is not carried over without loss to its most prevalent application. But if that is so, we would expect to find that it has other applications forming a bridge between ordinary deception and minimal wishful thinking.

In fact, there is one very familiar kind of case in which we can add all the elements required for a plan without falling foul of the paradoxes. Suppose that you begin to suspect that someone whom you had assumed to be honest is defrauding you in some minor way, and then you refuse to take any steps to ascertain whether he is or not, and so you maintain your ailing belief in his honesty. Here paradoxes (1) and (2) hardly make themselves felt. For this kind of belief that *p* is not incompatible with the suspicion that possibly *not-p*, and so there is no incoherence in what you plan. If it is irrational to foster the belief that *p* in such circumstances, that is only because you refrain from using your best available method for reaching the truth, and that kind of irrationality is not incoherence. In any case, truth is not a paramount goal, and so your plan might not even exhibit that kind of irrationality. For your motive might be not merely your own ease of mind but the sort of visible faith in him that might put a stop to his thefts, if he was thieving, and you might well regard that goal as more worthwhile than truth.

It is not quite so easy to dispose of (3). The trouble is that your suspicion that possibly *not-p* is, as Sartre says, 'part of the unitary structure of a single plan'. But we must not exaggerate the problem in this kind of case. The reason why you need to be aware of your suspicion that possibly *not-p* is not that, in order to neutralise it, you have to work out an elaborate plan. For in this case your plan is a simple one. The reason why it might be held that you need to be aware of your suspicion that possibly *not-p* would only be that a typical plan can be reviewed when it is being carried out. But, the objector will ask, can you in this case reflect that your motive for not seeking more evidence is that you wish to maintain your belief that *p*?

The first step towards answering this question is to realise that in this case the wish does not get between your evidence and your conclusion. For you have not collected the evidence, and you do not intend to collect it. So there is no intellectual distortion of the sort that occurs in the kind of wishful thinking that has just been described. There does not need to be, because here the wish does not emerge as a deliberate plan to flout the precept, 'Accommodate your beliefs to your evidence'. It flouts the different precept of reason, 'Get all the available evidence that you need'. Once this is realised, paradox (3) vanishes. For there is no incoherence in the structure of the plan, and so no need for any distortion in order to fit its elements together. If the plan is irrational its irrationality is of the other kind.

That disposes of (3) in this kind of case, and (4) does not arise. The case is a simple one, and it is common. Its importance is that it provides one clear and fairly complete bridge between wishful thinking and the kind of deception of another person that works by depriving him of access to a source of evidence which, you realise, would be likely to lead him to abandon his belief that *p*. In this kind of self-deception you deprive yourself of the evidence.

Next let us consider a different kind of case, which raises the paradoxes in a sharper form. I shall describe this case in extreme terms which are unlikely to be fully exemplified in real life. The point of the description will be to show what can happen, even if it seldom does happen, whereas the previous case was presented exactly as it frequently occurs.

p is a proposition about yourself which you would like to be true. But you have sufficient evidence to convince you of *not-p*, if the proposition were about another person. However, it is about yourself, and you don't like it, and so you set about producing in yourself the contradictory belief that *p*. Here all the paradoxes are sharper. For in this case your original attitude to *not-p* is belief, rather than suspicion, and you have to produce in yourself the belief that *p* instead of merely maintaining it, and you actually set about producing it. This is an extreme case, which will seldom be completely exemplified in real life.

Even so, (1) is not too difficult to deal with. In time your belief that *not-p* will undergo a change, after which, if you are aware of it, it will be weaker, and if it retains its strength you will not be aware of it. But *does* it retain its strength behind a screen? One answer to this question is that it does, if and only if it regains it in front of the screen when the wish is removed or its operation neutralised, without any new supply of evidence or new instruction in the assessment of the old evidence. The idea underlying this answer is that new data which affect the belief in a rational way do not disclose its hidden strength. There might also be forms of non-rational treatment which we would prefer to regard as creating a new strong belief rather than disclosing an old one. Here the precise details depend on theoretical considerations. But all that I need is the outline of a way of dealing with (1) which is used in our everyday judgments about people.

If (1) can be dealt with in this kind of case, so too can (2). For if the project is feasible, then, as far as this point goes, you can plan it. But (3) is more difficult and interesting. Two quotations from Sartre's discussion of this topic will serve to bring out the difficulty.

> *A*. I must know the truth very exactly *in order* to conceal it more carefully – and this not at two different moments, which at a pinch would allow us to establish a semblance of duality – but in the unitary structure of a single project. How then can the lie subsist if the duality which constitutes it is suppressed?
>
> *B*. To this difficulty is added another which is derived from the total translucency of consciousness. . . . the lie falls back and collapses beneath my look; it is ruined *from behind* by the consciousness of lying to myself which pitilessly constitutes itself well within my project as its very condition. We have here an *evanescent* phenomenon . . .[3]

In *B* the word 'lie' makes us look in the wrong direction. It is obvious that if you say to yourself something which you believe to be false, that will not persuade you that it is true.

3. ibid., p. 49.

But straightforward lying is not the only way of deceiving another person, and so there is no need to suppose that it must be the way in which you deceive yourself.

It is, however, an interesting fact that if we do want to find something analogous to lying in your dealings with yourself, it would have to be something of which your mind delivers itself without reflecting on evidence, such as a memory, or an impression of your motivation for an action. But though you receive such items in something like the way in which you receive information from another, you do not issue them in anything like the way in which he does. In fact, if issuing is an action, you do not issue them at all. For your will cannot attach itself to any part of the project as it could in the previous case, where what you did was to refrain from seeking further evidence. The use of metaphors, such as 'spelling out',[4] cannot obliterate this crucial difference. Such deliverances are immediate, and though wishes may influence them directly before they are issued, no such direct influence can be consciously planned.

Perhaps you might plan a course of self-discipline designed to bend your memories in a desired direction, but it is difficult to see what your procedure would be. Getting drunk in order to forget something would involve the wrong kind of causation, because making another person drunk with that end in view does not count as deception. Your treatment of yourself would have to be some kind of intellectual exercise, preferably one which might look as if it could improve your memory. In any case, the causal influence of the exercise would be too indirect for it to be anything like lying, and it would be more like causing another person to lie to a third person.

If the type of self-deception now under scrutiny does not have to be assimilated to straightforward lying to another person, (3) does not look so difficult. Self-deception might be a lengthy process somewhat like the process of conditioning another person by a prolonged campaign of subtle deceit. The difference would be that in one's own case the truth-seeking faculty itself has had to be held in check. But though this faculty is usually conceded complete sovereignty, it can sometimes be rational to curb it when the object of inquiry is oneself or a person closely

4. See Fingarette, *Self-deception*, passim.

associated with oneself, because in such cases the belief can alter its object (cf. the existentialist paradoxes about sincerity). The real difficulty is the other kind of irrationality, incoherence.

In *A* Sartre goes too far when he argues that we cannot appeal to lapse of time in order to remove the incoherence. True, we cannot if the act is a motivated lie no sooner planned than told. But the type of self-deception which is now being examined is never lying to oneself and it usually takes time. For the belief that *p* must not only be manufactured but also maintained, and so the plan will be in existence for some time. It is therefore worth asking whether this makes it possible for it to avoid incoherence through some change in its elements, or in their relation to one another.

In the discussion of wishful thinking it was pointed out that two facts had to be screened: the fact that the contribution made by the wish was needed, and the fact that therefore there was some uncharacteristic distortion in your mental processes. They also have to be screened in this type of self-deception, because here too the sovereignty of the truth-seeking faculty cannot be manifestly infringed. But *B* draws attention to an unwelcome consequence of supposing that in this kind of case the first fact has to be screened. For this implies that your rational tendency to believe *not-p* has to be screened. But if this is progressively screened, the motive behind the execution of the project will gradually lose its force as the project approaches completion.

This is evidently a conclusive argument against interpreting planned self-deception as anything like straightforward lying to another person. For part of the liar's motive for saying *p* has to be that all the time he believes *not-p*. But a more interesting question is whether the argument achieves anything more after the analogy with lying has been dropped.

The argument tries to exploit the fact that in this kind of planned self-deception you start with strong evidence for *not-p*, and when you argue for *not-p* in another person's case you show that you appreciate its strength: for example, *p* is the ascription of a desirable character trait, and the evidence for *not-p* in your own case is your behaviour and the reactions of other people to it. You might even start by believing *not-p*. In some cases it would be an exaggeration to say this, but at least there is a big difference between this kind of case and the case described earlier, in which you only suspected that possibly *not-p*, and so refused to collect any more evidence.

Now the fact that you have a rational tendency to believe *not-p* is only part of your reason for beginning to do whatever you do to persuade yourself that *p*. The other part is your wish to believe *p*. You are rather like a patient who is aware of his illness and wishes to get well, and begins to take the appropriate medicine. So the first point to be made against the argument from the vanishing motive is that this patient might decrease his dosage as his health improved, and similarly you might reduce your intellectual exercises, as your belief that *p* increased in strength.

But this is only a superficial point, because it takes no account of the fact that underneath your increasing belief that *p* there will still be your undiminished rational tendency to believe *not-p*. Naturally, this must be screened from you. But, contrary to Sartre's assumption, the fact that it is screened from you will not necessarily deprive it of its motivating force. Your wish to believe *p* emerges as the plan to deceive yourself that *p* only because you have a rational tendency to believe *not-p*. The fact that you have this tendency may continue to produce its effect even when it has been screened from you.

However, the argument from the vanishing motive does achieve something more than the destruction of the analogy between planned self-deception and straightforward lying. It shows that any plan that there is in this kind of case cannot be fully reviewed when it approaches completion. In the later stages either my original motive must be screened, or it will come through in a version that does not include my rational tendency to believe *not-p*. So if there is a plan here, it cannot contain all the elements of an ordinary plan at every stage in its existence. But if there is no element which it cannot contain at some time, then, contrary to what Sartre implies, its duration is important. For the incoherence indicated by (3) can be removed without eliminating any single element for the whole time. No doubt when things have gone a long way you cannot review what you are doing in words such as these: 'I am dwelling on certain aspects of my behaviour and relations with other people because I have a rational tendency to believe *not-p*, which I wish to inhibit.' At some point in your progress it must become impossible for you to see through what you are doing to your motive for doing it. When this happens, you still have to be able to describe what you are doing in a way that does not mention your motive. For if you could not describe your action in any way at all, it would not be an action under your conscious control. But at the beginning you can include your motive in the formulation of your plan: 'I shall dwell on certain aspects . . . etc.'

Here there is another important difference between the self-deceiver and the patient taking the medicine. It is unlikely that the patient would continue taking his medicine if he forgot why he had started taking it. But it is not at all unlikely that the self-deceiver would continue his intellectual exercises when his awareness of his motive for starting them began to be blurred. For in this case all the action is in the mind, and so it is easier for the motive to exert its force stealthily, and perhaps without even being questioned by the agent.

Whether it is at all common for people to embark on self-deception in this candid way is another question. My point is only that it can be done. I want to discover the minimal adjustments that are needed to remove incoherence from this kind of plan, and, if the self-deceiver's full motivation is gradually screened from him as he proceeds, that is enough to remove the incoherence indicated by (3).

However, this answer to (3) fails to deal with a point which came up in the earlier discussion of wishful thinking. Suppose that you start by formulating your plan to deceive yourself that *p*. Then, as has just been conceded, if this plan is going to succeed, there must come a stage in its execution at which you cannot review it in a way that brings in your motive. Moreover, at the beginning you will know that such a stage is necessary, and so you will have to include it in your original plan as an extra task. But in the execution of this task too, there must come a stage at which a review of the plan that brings in your motive is impossible. So the attempt to complete the formulation of your initial plan will lead to an infinite regress. This regress cannot be stopped in the way that the similar regress was stopped in the case of wishful thinking. For in this example you are in the position of a gang-leader who is planning an assassination but cannot trust the assassin not to talk; and if he arranges the assassination of the assassin, cannot trust that assassin not to talk . . . etc. It is evident that such a plan would necessarily remain incompletely formulated, and would therefore rely at some point on luck. So too, if someone really did start a course of self-deception, his initial plan could never be completely formulated before he began.

But beneath the similarity between these two plans there are important differences. The gang-leader relies on luck, but if at any stage he discovers that he is likely to be unlucky, he can resort to a further assassination. So at the beginning he plans to do whatever he discovers to be needed, hoping that there will come a time when he is lucky and need do no more. But if the self-deceiver plans to do whatever is needed, he has no usable method of discovering at any stage whether further action is needed. For if he investigates his progress with this question in mind, it will follow that further action will be needed. On the other hand, he has an advantage over the gang-leader: what he relies on is not luck, but the discreet operation of his own wish to believe *p*. So though it is true that in the hierarchy of levels there will be one at which he does what happens, it is reasonable for him to expect it to happen.

The main conclusion that I would like to draw from the examination of this type of planned self-deception is that it is possible for it to approximate very closely to one type of ordinary deception. It cannot be at all like straightforward lying to another person, but what it can be like is a carefully planned campaign of deceit, during which you persistently put gentle pressure on him, slightly distorting the evidence or presenting it in a false light. But even this analogy is imperfect, because, when you deliberately set out to deceive yourself in this way, you cannot see every rung of the ladder before you climb it, and at some point you must lose your clear picture of your starting point and of the reason why you have to use this particular ladder to reach your destination. These are important imperfections in an analogy which, nevertheless, remains large.

However, the case, as described, is extreme. In real life it nearly always happens that much more is screened than needs to be. It is rare for anyone who believes *not-p* deliberately to set out to deceive himself that *p* and to plan the strategy of his campaign in advance. What usually happens is that his project seems to improvise itself as it proceeds. When there is a conscious method, it is more often the negative procedure described in the previous case, in which you deceived yourself about the other person's honesty. It is far easier to avoid looking at what is there than it is to discern what is not there. If this is done for long enough the buoyancy of the wish may be relied on to support the belief that *p*. So the commonest cases of what we regard as purposive self-deception are mixed cases. Their most conspicuous feature is systematic wishful thinking, but this is punctuated by episodes of deliberate action, which is usually only averting one's gaze, but which is sometimes something more positive.

This brings me to the final, and perhaps the most difficult question that I want to raise. In my comments on the last case of self-deception I did not deal with the whole of (3), or with (4). The argument of the final part of (3) was that, if the self-deceiver's rational tendency to believe *not-p* is screened from him, he will not be able to plan the strategy of his campaign against it. The argument of (4) was that, if our response to this is to say that the whole plan, together with everything mental that it requires for its existence, is screened, we shall merely be shifting the difficulty to a different point where it will remain unsolved. Sartre puts the two points very clearly in his polemic against Freudian theory: '. . . the resistance of the patient implies on the level of the censor an awareness of the thing repressed as such, a comprehension of the end toward which the questions of the psychoanalyst are leading, and an act of synthetic connection by which it (the censor) compares the *truth* of the repressed complex to the psychoanalytic hypothesis which aims at it.'[5] From here it seems a short and easy step to the conclusion that all the difficulties described by (3) must now be located in the deliberations of the censor.

These problems are a threat to the thesis that I have been developing. If it is true that any piece of self-deception must contain some mere wishful thinking, and that most pieces will contain a lot, then the case for calling these pieces of self-deception 'purposive' will rest very heavily on the fact that the

5. ibid., p. 53.

wishful thinking is systematic. But if it is systematic, then it may look as if behind the screen there must be another agency which synthesises the plan and guides its implementation. If this is so, nothing has been gained.

It would take another paper to answer this objection adequately. I shall merely make three brief points in defence of my treatment of the paradoxes of self-deception.

(1) We ought to distinguish between an ordinary shallow case of self-deception, in which the rational tendency to believe *not-p* is pre-conscious (easily recoverable), and a deep case, in which it is unconscious (too strongly repressed to be recovered easily). In the first kind of case the structure of the so-called 'plan' will usually be simple and the wish to believe *p* can do its work without any detailed knowledge of the underlying tendency to believe *not-p*. But the second kind of case is very different, and it may well seem that the patient could not parry the psychoanalyst so effectively unless he had behind the screen much detailed insight into his own case.

(2) However, Sartre's presentation of the Freudian theory about the deep kind of case is excessively intellectualised. Here what has been repressed will not be a single belief but a whole complex of beliefs and feelings. Moreover, the forces stored in this complex will have had a long time to produce other beliefs and feelings of which the patient will be aware. For example, it will produce an elaborate reaction-formation if he is an obsessional neurotic. It would be absurd to describe such a man as simply deceiving himself that *p*, even if *p* were a very complex proposition about himself. His reaction-formation could not be represented as a purely intellectual structure because it would also include feelings, and his resistance to the psychoanalyst would be a natural manifestation of this part of his character. Sartre is quite mistaken when he presents this resistance as a piece of clever acting based on inside information.

(3) Behind this controvery there is a profound question which is hard to formulate correctly. Suppose that we start by considering a shallow case of self-deception. We notice that the process by which the belief that *p* is manufactured and maintained is largely wishful thinking. Then we ask ourselves whether the systematic character of this wishful thinking justifies us in treating the self-deception as purposive. But what does

this question mean? If the process is at all complex, it may mean: 'What degree of complexity would require unconscious foresight, calculation, feed-back and control?' But how are we supposed to answer this question? We have no reliable way of comparing this kind of process, where all the action is in the mind, with a skill learned and exercised in the external world. But our difficulty is not merely that we lack a method of answering the question. Its meaning is in doubt. So we try to fill in the disputed part of its meaning by taking all the elements of ordinary agency and imagining that they are screened from the person himself but not from one another. But even if this has a clear meaning, why must it be true? Why must the structure of whatever is behind the screen reproduce the structure of ordinary agency? Why should it not produce its effects without satisfying the requirements of a coherent plan? The original state of the person might simply cause what follows without that irrelevant constraint. Naturally, no creature's mind could contain a mechanism which eliminated too many of its well-founded factual beliefs. But such a mechanism has a certain survival value for social creatures when its operation is confined to beliefs about themselves and about each other.

5 Sketch for a Causal Theory of Wanting and Doing

There are three problems about wanting and doing which are so closely connected that a solution to the first would have to include a solution to the second, which in turn would have to include a solution to the third. The first problem is about the connection between wanting to do something and doing it. Is it a causal connection? If so, it might be thought that it must be possible to describe the cause without mentioning the effect and the effect without mentioning the cause. But can they really be described in isolation from one another? The second problem is concerned with the agent's reason for his action. When he states it, does his statement entail any general proposition covering the particular case? It ought to, if it is a causal statement, but in fact it is difficult to find any general proposition to which he would take himself to be committed. The third problem is that the agent nearly always knows immediately what he wants to do, or why he did what he did, and it is not easy to see how this fact can be reconciled with the fact that what he knows is not confined to the present moment, or with the theory that its spread is causal.

These difficulties appear to come from trying to fit the agent's knowledge into a causal framework. So perhaps this is a misguided enterprise. Everything is what it is and not another thing. The connection between desire and action is not the same kind of connection as that between impact and motion. Nor is the agent's foreknowledge of his own actions of the same kind as his foreknowledge of the weather when he looks at the barometer. Nor is his retrospective knowledge of his reason for an action of the same kind as his knowledge of the cause of a fire. So would it not be better to describe all these things as they are, without assimilating them to other things or theorising about them?

But this is too simple a diagnosis. For one of the problems is not peculiar to the causal theory, but is inherent in the facts on any reading of them. Immediate knowledge of something that is not confined to the present moment is intrinsically difficult to understand. It is true that the other problems do arise from the causal theory. But any attempt to understand the facts must lead to some theory, and at certain crucial points there does not seem to be any alternative to the causal theory. If the connection between desire and action is not some kind of causal connection, what kind of connection can it be? Perhaps the adoption of a causal framework is not a mistaken choice, not because it is the correct choice, but because it is inevitable, and the argument should really be about the way in which the facts should be fitted into this framework. I shall discuss the three problems in this spirit. Where critics of the causal framework argue that there is a misfit, I shall try to show that there is a fit, but a complex one, and that the difficulties are all in the dissection of its complexity.

I shall not attempt to deal with all the difficulties, but only with the three that have been mentioned. So what is offered is only a sketch for a causal theory. A complete theory would have to include a causal analysis of the connection between wanting and doing. This sketch only aims to establish that, in spite of the three difficulties, the connection must exhibit a certain causal pattern. But the description of the causal pattern that I shall give will not be complete. So it will apply not only to the kind of connection between wanting and doing that is typical of intentional action, but also to other kinds of connection between them. No attempt will be made to exclude the other kinds by completing the analysis. Nobody has yet solved that problem, which has a counterpart in the causal theory of perception. But there seems to be no reason to regard it as insoluble.

Part I

Does a human agent's desire to perform a particular action cause him to perform it? If the same question were asked about a physical need in a simpler organism and the movement that leads to its satisfaction, the answer would be affirmative. But human agency is more complex, and so, if the connection is causal in this case, it will be a more complex example of causation. The main source of the extra complexity is the fact that the process does not start from a need but from a desire to perform a particular action. For such desires are nearly always conscious, or potentially conscious, and therefore subject to the influence of deliberation. The agent knows what he wants to do and is in a position to review the project and possibly revise it. It is often argued that complications of this kind cannot be described in causal terms.

On the other hand, revision is seldom endless, and, when it has terminated, the agent's final desire does seem to cause his action. For there does not seem to be any other kind of connection which would give him his knowledge that he will perform it. This knowledge is most impressive when it is based on a decision, because in such cases the finality of the desire is the result either of the assumption that it is unquestionable, or of deliberation, and so his certainty is greater. But how can he be so certain of his future action unless his present state in some way causes it? His certainty evidently does not lack a present basis, like a premonition. It might be suggested that his decision is non-causally connected with his future action. But even if it were clear what a 'non-causal connection' is, this picture omits the more important connecting lines. His decision and his action are both produced by his desire, and, without these two connections, the connection between his decision and his action would be very weak. True, you can do something merely because your diary records your decision to do it. But such a case would be exceptional, and normally the line that runs from decision to action starts from an antecedent desire which endures. So the crucial question is, how the agent knows that its degree is still sufficient and that it will continue to be so. The answer cannot be that his knowledge is based on a second decision to make his action fit his first decision, because that would lead to a regress. The observation that it is characteristic of human agents to know immediately what they will do is no explanation. Thus we appear to be driven to the conclusion that there must be a causal connection between desire and action, because there seems to be no other theory that fits the phenomena.

The argument for this conclusion is conceptual: the only concept that makes the connection intelligible is the concept of cause. The strongest objection to it is also conceptual: the resulting theory is incoherent. This is the line taken by those who argue that, if the desire to perform a particular action did cause it, it ought to be possible to describe the cause in isolation from the effect, and the effect in isolation from the cause, but that, since no such descriptions are available, the connection cannot be causal.

The plausibility of this objection depends on the precise meaning of the requirement on which it is based. What sort of isolation is being demanded? Suppose that the alleged cause is described as 'the desire to do A', where 'A' signifies the particular action. Then A is the alleged effect and it is mentioned in the description of its alleged cause, and this is one way of failing to achieve isolation. But though A is treated as the effect in the theory under attack, it is not specified as such in the description of the desire that is said to be its cause. It is only specified as the object of that desire. This raises the question whether this particular way of failing to achieve isolation in a description prevents us from regarding what is described as the cause of the actual occurrence of its object. The answer seems to be negative. For it is easy to find examples of psychological attitudes which are described in a way that mentions their objects, and yet which are said to cause those very objects to exist. For instance, it is said that fear of stammering causes some people to stammer, and in some fairy stories a wish for an object, if it is accompanied by a certain ritual, will bring about that object. In these examples the thing that is said to be the effect is mentioned in the description of the psychological attitude that is said to be the cause, but it is only specified as the object of the psychological attitude. So long as the specification is done in this way, there is nothing wrong with the suggestion that the psychological attitude causes the thing so specified.

If we consider the rationale of the objector's requirement of isolation we can see that he demands too little in one way, but too much in another. He is claiming that such psychological attitudes can be regarded as the causes of their objects' actual occurrence only when they can be described in a way that does not mention their objects. But there are two different things that might be meant by his claim. It might mean merely that, when we want to refer to the psychological attitudes, we can avail ourselves of many definite descriptions which do not contain any kind of mention of their objects, and that, if this were not so, we could not regard them as the causes of the actual occurrence of their objects. For example, we could describe the fear as the dominant feeling of the speaker as he mounted the rostrum. But if this is what is meant by the objector's claim, it makes too small a demand. Of course, any psychological attitude will satisfy many definite descriptions of this kind, and some of them will be known to us. But a psychological attitude that is the cause of the actual occurrence of its object, must satisfy a stronger requirement. It must be describable in a way that assigns it to a class each of whose members is followed by a member of a single class to which the effect belongs. This interpretation makes the claim more interesting, because it gives it a rationale. The idea would be that it is self-contradictory to suggest that a cause might not belong to any such class, and that, if anyone could not assign it to such a class, he could not recognise it or predict its effect in other cases.

If the claim were left in this form, it would be acceptable. But the objector adds the stipulation that this generalisable description of the psychological attitude must contain no kind of mention of its object. But this is to demand too much. For 'X's fear of stammering' might be the only generalisable description that applied to his psychological attitude, and, more obviously, it might be the only generalisable description known to a psychologist who used the attitude as a basis for predicting X's bouts of stammering. So both reasons for adding this stipulation to the claim are invalid.

If we modify the additional stipulation, we get a more plausible formulation of the requirement of isolation. Instead of requiring that a cause be describable in a generalisable way that does not contain any kind of mention of its effect, we require only that a cause be describable in a generalisable way that does not imply that it causes its effect. This requirement is more plausible because it allows the generalisable description of the cause to mention its effect provided that it does not specify it as its effect. The two counter-examples to the extreme version of the requirement meet this version of it, because in their generalisable descriptions of the psychological attitudes they specify their effects only as their objects, and so satisfy the less extreme condition.

There are also more positive reasons for adopting this moderate requirement of causal isolation. If it is self-contradictory to suggest that a cause might not belong to any class each of whose members is followed by a member of a single class to which the effect belongs, then it would be vacuous to try to avoid this self-contradiction by pointing out that a cause is always assignable to the class of things that cause its effect. Even if there only has to be a general, and not a universal, connection between some generalisable description of the cause and some generalisable description of its effect, this kind of response is vacuous. In fact, it is what is meant by calling a cause 'occult'. If this charge meant only that the general description of the cause happened to be unknown to the speaker, or perhaps to everyone at the time of speaking, that would be a much less serious matter. For presumably, the cause would satisfy some non-vacuous generalisable description, and the only trouble would be that the speaker, and possibly his contemporaries, would not know what that description was. But there would still be definite descriptions that the cause was known to satisfy. Otherwise people would be unable even to identify it, and a cause that was occult in that sense would merely be an unknown cause.

An example will demonstrate the plausibility of the moderate version of the requirement of causal isolation. We grant the intelligibility of a coroner's verdict that a man died of a fatal dose of barbiturate, because such a dose is specifiable in a way that does not imply that it causes death in human beings – perhaps as twenty grains. Of course, the person who found the dead man could say that he died because he took all the pills in the bottle beside his bed, and neither he nor anyone else need know what the fatal dose is. But if we did not believe that some independently specifiable dose is fatal, we would at first treat the coroner's verdict as false, and, if it turned out that he shared our disbelief, we would treat his view of the case as self-contradictory and, therefore, unintelligible. If the cause of the death merely happened to be occult to the first witness on the scene, in the sense that he did not know the independent specification of the fatal dose, he would be unable to recognise it or predict its effect in other cases. As a practical disadvantage this would be serious, but it would not introduce any incoherence into the witness's view of the case.

This account of the operation of the moderate requirement can be checked on the two counter-examples to the extreme requirement. 'X's fear of stammering' is a description which does not even contain the covert implication that it causes stammering. Even if we perversely included this implication in the meaning of the description after we had discerned that in fact it did cause X to stammer, we could still revert to the original meaning of the description in response to the moderate requirement. Nor is there any doubt that the description, meant in the original, straightforward way, provides the psychologist with an adequate basis for his prediction. It is obvious that the wish accompanied by a magic ritual meets the moderate requirement in the same easy way.

It might be thought that the second part of the rationale of the moderate requirement is less important than the first part. For so long as there is an independent generalisable description of the cause, it is not theoretically important whether anyone has yet discovered it. In fact, the point of scientific realism is that the first identifications of things are often superficial, and their more important, and perhaps essential, properties are discovered later. But the application of this idea seems to be limited in some parts of the philosophy of mind. Certainly, the causal theory of desire and action relies not only on the existence, but also on the availability to the agent of a generalisable description of his desire to do A which meets the moderate requirement. Of course, his foreknowledge of his action is immediate, but, according to the theory, this foreknowledge would be unintelligible if he could not predict his action inductively from his desire identified under an independent, generalisable description.

However, this part of the causal theory is controversial, and it will be defended later. So it is worth observing now that there is a general reason for assuming that the properties mentioned in some ordinary identifications of mental entities cannot be regarded as superficial. The reason is that some of these properties are the basis of a pre-scientific theory of human nature which works well enough to have become the framework of our lives. This is conspicuously true of the psychological properties through which desires are identified. These properties allow us to systematise all the manifestations of an agent's desires, including his actions, and in many cases to connect them with his needs. If the system is rough and untidy, some of the anomalies can be removed by hypothesising unconscious desires.

Perhaps an even neater explanation of his actions might be achieved by a neurological theory which identified their causes in ways that are not yet available. But if the points at which it proved impossible to map the neurological theory onto the psychological theory became more and more numerous, we would be increasingly reluctant to identify the neural causes with desires and to maintain that we were discovering the true nature of desires. This reluctance would not merely be an expression of a conservative preference for the pre-scientific criteria of desires, perhaps with unconscious desires grudgingly admitted to the scheme. For there is a stronger reason for treating the agent's identification of his desires as the basic identification of them, which captures their essence and which, therefore, cannot be given up. His desires control his actions from moment to moment, and if they were not accessible to him, this control would be successful only in stereotyped sequences of actions, and then only when there was no need for cooperation with other people. But they are accessible to him only through their psychological descriptions. When they are identified under these descriptions, he can plan his actions, others can count on them, and all can understand them. Thus the pre-scientific criteria of desires are more entrenched than the pre-scientific criteria of gold.

Is there really a generalisable description of the agent's desire to do A which is available to him and which meets the moderate requirement of causal isolation? This is a complex question, and it might be better to begin with the question about the alleged effect. For that question is simpler, and the contrast may throw some light on the problems besetting the alleged cause.

If the action A is the effect of the agent's desire to perform it, it will also be describable in other ways. The question is this:

In what other way must it be describable, if it is going to be possible to regard it as the effect of the agent's desire? First, there obviously must be a description of it that meets the minimal version of the requirement of causal isolation. For an effect must have other properties in addition to being the effect of its cause. But this requirement is easily met from the wealth of available physical descriptions of A. It is a bodily movement of a certain kind made by this agent at a particular time and place. But does there have to be a physical description of A which not only meets the minimal version of the requirement, but is also generalisable and available to the agent? In order to answer this question, we need to look at the general propositions, which, according to the causal theory, underwrite the connection between desire and action.

If this connection is causal, a desire of one kind (K_1) will always be followed by an action of the appropriate kind (K_2). Now 'K_1', according to the preceding argument, must be a description which is available to the agent and which meets the moderate requirement of causal isolation, and the task of finding a description to fill that bill has not yet been attempted. Can a similar argument be used to prove that 'K_2' must be available to the agent? First, we must determine what description 'K_2' will be. Fortunately, this task is not so difficult as it is in the case of 'K_1'. Since 'K_2' appears in the general proposition which underwrites the causal connection, it must meet the moderate requirement of causal isolation. So it will be a physical description of the kind of bodily movements and their consequences that would count as A-type actions if they were caused by the desire to perform an A-type action. Naturally, there will often be considerable flexibility in 'K_2', because the bodily movements and consequences that would count as A-type actions, given the causal condition, will vary from situation to situation. So it will not always be necessary to formulate 'K_2' completely. But it must always be possible to formulate the part of it that is relevant to the agent's situation.

But must the agent himself be able to formulate this part of it? Apparently not. For when he plans his action and executes the plan, he will usually think of its stages not under descriptions like 'K_2', which meet the moderate requirement of causal isolation, but under action-descriptions, which imply that they will be brought about by his desires. In fact, in many cases he would be unable to produce a description like 'K_2', or at least unable to produce one without a much more thorough analysis of his action than is normally needed. So the argument used to prove that 'K_1' must be available to the agent does not prove that 'K_2', or the relevant part of K_2, must also be available to him. However, it would be unintelligible to suggest that the action was the effect of his desire, if the action could not be described in a way that met the moderate requirement of causal isolation. So whatever action-descriptions are used by the agent or by anyone else, they must be underpinned by descriptions like 'K_2'.

A further development of the requirement of causal isolation might be proposed at this point. Since a given bodily movement can be caused in two different ways – either by the desire to make it, or by something quite different, such as a reflex arc – it might be thought that there must always be a difference in the effect corresponding to this difference in the cause, and that this difference in the effect must be describable in a causally isolated way. But there does not seem to be any reason to suppose that there must be such a difference in the effect. True, there may be, and in fact there often will be, such a difference, and, when there is, it must be describable in a causally isolated way. But there need be no such difference, because, in general, it is possible for two or more independent prior sufficient conditions to produce the same effect. However, when the effect is a bodily movement, which may or may not be an action (depending on its causation), there nearly always will be some difference in the effect in the two cases, and some sequences of bodily movements are so complicated that they can only be the effects of desires. But the existence of a difference in the effect is only contingent, and, when it does exist, neither the agent nor anyone else need be aware of it. The causal theory certainly does not imply that it is always possible to infer the cause from the effect.

So there are three distinct contrasts between the descriptions of the cause and the descriptions of the effect in the causal theory of desire and action. In the general proposition which underwrites their connection the description 'K_1' applies to the cause and the description 'K_2' applies to the effect. The first difference is that the same cause cannot produce different effects, but the same effect can be produced by different causes. Consequently, there cannot be any difference between the effects of desires which satisfy 'K_1' in exactly similar circumstances, but there can be a difference between the causes of bodily movements which satisfy 'K_2' in exactly similar circumstances. For the cause might be the desire to produce the bodily movement, or it might be a reflex arc. Second, if the K_2 bodily movements do not differ in these two cases, nobody will be able to infer the cause from the effect; whereas anyone who is aware of the K_1 desire will be able to infer its effect. Third, in fact the agent generally is aware of his own desires and so can make inferences from them to their effects, whereas anyone can observe their effects. Therefore, though 'K_1' and 'K_2' are both indispensable, and, though both satisfy the moderate requirement of causal isolation, 'K_1' must, but 'K_2' need not be, available to the agent.

These differences make it more difficult to see what sort of description 'K_1' will be than it is to see what sort of description 'K_2' will be. According to the causal theory, 'K_1' is a description of the agent's desire which not only meets the moderate requirement of causal isolation but is also available to the agent himself. It is the second of these stipulations that makes it difficult to find a suitable candidate. The moderate requirement of causal isolation without this extra stipulation could be met by invoking neurological facts which have yet to be discovered. For presumably there is some causally isolated neurological description of the agent's desire, although nobody knows it yet. If this is so, it is enough to make the causal theory intelligible. But it does not meet the further requirement that 'K_1' be available to the agent. It seems that the only way to meet this requirement would be to extract 'K_1' from the agent's psychological scene. But the trouble is that this is a much more restricted source of material than the physical setting of his bodily movements. There are in fact two ways in which it is restricted. First, there is so little that is relevant going on in his mind. Second, what there is seems to absorb its so-called effects as criteria of its own existence so that it seems to be impossible to meet the moderate requirement of causal isolation. This difficulty has often been regarded as insuperable by critics of the version of the causal theory that is being defended here. It would decrease, and perhaps even vanish if the theory did not include the extra requirement that 'K_1' be accessible to the agent.

Can the extra requirement be kept and the resulting difficulty overcome? There are three things here whose relations with one another are in question.

(1) The agent's sincere statement that all things considered he wants to do A.
(2) His desire to do A, all things considered.
(3) His doing A.

There are difficulties about the criteria of (1), but nearly always the agent himself will know whether his statement is sincere. But what is the relation between (1) and (2)? According to a theory which I shall call 'T_1', the sincerity of the agent's statement entails its truth, and so the existence of (1) entails the existence of (2). But according to another theory, which I shall call 'T_2', the existence of (2) in its turn entails that, given certain conditions, (3) will follow.

It is evident that, if the conditions mentioned in T_2 are specified and turn out to have independent criteria, T_1 and T_2 cannot be combined as they stand. For taken together they would imply that it is conceptually impossible that, given the conditions, (1) should exist without being followed by (3). But this would be absurd. The furthest that we could go in that direction would be to say that in fact this is a possibility that is never realised. For though it may be a fundamental feature of human nature that, given the conditions, (1) is always followed by (3), and though our conceptual scheme may rest on this feature, it can hardly guarantee it.

But is it realistic to move so far in that direction? In order to answer this question, we need a specification of the conditions which should be mentioned by T_2. These are of three kinds. First, if (1) occurs appreciably before the moment for action, it is obviously necessary to stipulate that the agent's desire to do A, all things considered, must not have diminished in the interim, either because he has definitely changed his mind, or in some less palpable way. The second kind of condition is concerned with the possibility of the action: there must be no insuperable obstacles, either physical or psychological, to his performance of it. The third kind of condition covers the agent's factual information: he must be aware that he is able to perform the action and, when the opportunity comes, that this is it. Now the details of these conditions are much more complex than this very schematic account of the behavioural test of (2) suggests. But a general point of some importance does emerge from it. There are independent criteria for the fulfilment of each of the three kinds of condition, and, though it is sometimes difficult to establish that the first two are fulfilled, there are many cases in which the fulfilment of all three can be established beyond reasonable doubt, independently of (3). The question then is, whether it is realistic to maintain that in all such cases (1) is, as a matter of contingent fact, always followed by (3).

It is obvious that this is what happens in the great majority of such cases. But it is equally obvious that it does not always happen. The easiest way to prove that it does not always happen is to produce examples in which the agent fails the behavioural test and so is judged to have exaggerated the degree of his desire to do A, perhaps under the influence of a wish to conform to some image of himself, but not necessarily insincerely. But it is worth asking how people are supposed to know that this is the correct interpretation of the examples. For all that they are given in a case of this kind is the fact that (1) is not followed by (3) in spite of the fulfilment of the three conditions. So why could they not conclude that the connection between (2) and (3) had broken down, instead of the connection between (1) and (2)? If T_1 is doubly mistaken, because it denies the conceptual possibility of something which is not only conceptually possible but also actually happens, perhaps T_2 is doubly mistaken.

This suggestion may appear to be the turn of the screw which loosens the criteria of (2) to the point of detachment. But a review of the process of relaxation might indicate that this is not really so. The two theories with which we started, T_1 and T_2, were so rigid that their combination led to an absurdity. So anyone who held both would have to modify at least one of them by substituting a contingent connection for a conceptual connection. For it is, at best, a contingent truth that (1) is always followed by (3) given the fulfilment of the three conditions.

But in fact this is not even contingently true without exception, and the exceptions force a more radical modification on at least one of the two theories: one of the two connections cannot be a universal contingent connection, but only a general one. But is it not quite arbitrary to refrain from modifying the other theory too in this more radical way?

The reply might be that (2) must be conceptually anchored either to (1) or to (3). Otherwise, it would slide along the line that marks the contingent connection between (1) and (3) and the agent's report of it would not have a determinate sense. In fact, it might be argued, it is evident that it is the connection between (2) and (3) which is conceptual, rather than the connection between (1) and (2). For if an agent has all the relevant factual information, the thrust of his desire against the facts is such that the only conceivable cause of inaction is impossibility. This is why, when (1) occurs without (3), and (3) is not impossible, and the agent has the requisite information, people infer that he must have mistakenly reported the existence of (2).

But this reply is too simple. First, a distinction should be drawn between cases of (2) with the information, but without (3), which we can explain by establishing the impossibility of the action by independent criteria, and cases of (2) with the information, but without (3), which we can explain only by saying that the action must have been impossible in some way that we cannot yet establish independently. Now the second kind of case does not yield a usable conceptually necessary condition of (2). The hypothesis that the action must have been in some way impossible is open-ended, and what it offers is not a criterion but only a promissory note which may one day be exchanged for a criterion. But if the objector falls back on the first kind of case of (2) with the information, but without (3), he cannot claim that it is conceptually necessary that (3) be impossible by independent criteria. For this is contingently false. So if we confine ourselves to things that we can now use as criteria, it is evident that we treat the connection between (2) and (3), given the conditions, as a general connection rather than a universal one, like the connection between (1) and (2). On the other hand, the permanent loophole, conjectured impossibility, does allow us to explain cases of (1) with the information, but without (3), without imputing a mistake to the agent, and our choice between the two alternatives, mistake or impossibility, if we feel able to make it, is governed by our knowledge of the particular case.

There does not seem to be any general objection to concepts with criteria like those that are here suggested for the concept of (2). Newton's concept of force is free to slide along the line marking the connection between the other variables in his laws, and yet its meaning is sufficiently determinate. It is true that the psychological concept has features which are not shared by the physical concept. For the psychological 'law' connecting (1) with (3), given the conditions, is not valid without exception, when possibility is judged by independent criteria. Also, the psychological concept has been built into a pre-scientific theory which has become the framework of our lives, and so new discoveries are less likely to lead to refinements of the old concept than they are in physical cases. But this reversal of the normal order of importance is intelligible, and the exceptions to the psychological 'law' are not sufficiently numerous to render the concept unusable, although it is sometimes much more difficult to use than physical dispositional concepts.

If this account of the criteria of (2) is correct, we can identify a description 'K_1' which applies to (2), is available to the agent, appears in a causal generalisation connecting (2) with (3), given the conditions, and yet meets the moderate requirement of causal isolation. 'K_1' is 'the psychological state of the agent which is nearly always the state that produces (1)'. There are two reasons for inserting the phrase 'nearly always' in this description. (1) may be mistaken, or (2) may exist without his being aware of it. The preceding argument has exploited the possibility of the first kind of mistake, but the second kind is important too. The fact that K_1 produces (1) is not intended to yield an analysis of the meaning of (1). That would require, at the very least, a more specific characterisation of the connection between K_1 and (1).

It is clear that the existence of 'K_1' makes it possible to maintain that (2) causes (3), given the conditions, and that its availability to the agent enables him to predict (3) from (2) inductively, given the conditions. So the theory, that the relation between (2) and (3) is causal, is reconciled not only with the fact that (3) is (2)'s object, but also with the fact that (3) is one of (2)'s criterial points of attachment to the world.

At first sight it might seem that there is only a marginal difference between the description 'K_1' of (2) and the description of it that mentions (3) as its effect. For the second description will be satisfied in almost every case in which the first is satisfied. In fact, if this were not so, the concept of (2) could not be maintained in use. Perhaps then 'K_1' meets the requirement of causal isolation so marginally that it cannot be invoked in defence of the causal account of the connection between (2) and (3).

But this criticism overlooks the fact that 'K_1' attaches (2) criterially to (1). It is true, and essential to the concept of (2) that, when (2) is judged by this criterion, it almost always produces (3), given the conditions. But that does not show that there is only a marginal difference between 'K_1' and the description of (2) that mentions (3) as its effect. On the contrary, it is a remarkable fact that (1) provides (2) with a second criterial point of attachment to the world which very seldom conflicts with the first one.

At this point the objector might propound a dilemma. Either we must adopt T_1, which makes the criterial connection between (1) and (2) so rigid that it is conceptually impossible for (1) to occur without (2), or we must relax T_1 and allow that this possibility is occasionally realised. But on the first alternative mistakes are ruled out, which is unrealistic, and on the second alternative the cause of (3) is not being specified as '(2)', but as 'something which the agent, perhaps mistakenly, takes to be (2)', which is not what the theory requires.

But the second horn of this dilemma is too fragile to be effective. It is true that, according to the theory, the criterial connection between (1) and (2) does not hold without exception. But neither does the criterial connection between (2) and (3), given the conditions and given that impossibility is independently established. So it is begging the question to say that, when the theory uses the criterial connection with (1), it does not specify the cause of (3) as '(2)'. For, according to the theory, this is one of the two best possible ways of specifying the cause of (3) as '(2)'. The only effective way to criticise this part of the theory would be to demonstrate that this account of the criteria of (2) leaves its meaning insufficiently determinate. But that does not seem to be demonstrable.

Another objection, of a quite different kind, would be that all these manoeuvres have produced a very meagre result. Of course, the agent can reflect on (1) and can argue inductively from his spontaneous inclination to make (1) to (2), in much the same way that a clairvoyant can argue inductively from his spontaneous inclination to make a sincere premonitory claim to the future event. But what is the importance of this possibility? Surely what actually happens is more important, and what actually happens is that the agent knows immediately what he will do, just as the clairvoyant knows immediately what will happen.

But this does not show that the possibility that the agent might use the inductive argument is unimportant. On the contrary, the concept of '(2)' rests on the fact that (2) is nearly always followed by (3), given the conditions. The reason why he seldom actually uses the inductive argument is only that he takes this fact for granted. This is one difference between his foreknowledge and that of most clairvoyants. Another difference emerges when we ask for an explanation of the agent's foreknowledge, rather than a mere description of it. The clairvoyant's premonition comes unheralded and its causation is unexplained, but the agent's conviction that he will perform the action does not come unheralded and its causation is evident. Both it and (3) are caused by (2), and, if this were not so, his foreknowledge would be as inexplicable as that of the clairvoyant. So though it is true, and important, that the agent can reflect on his spontaneous inclination to make (1) and can argue inductively from it to (2), this is far from the whole truth. He can also ask himself how much he wants to perform the action, and, if his desire seems to him to amount to (2), he will be convinced that he will perform it. This inquiry is often accompanied by rehearsal in imagination and inner reactions, and these processes and results are the forerunners which explain his eventual conviction in a very simple way: they are all effects of (2).

It is clear that this account of the agent's mental processes raises the original problem in a more precise form. Just as it was necessary to find a description of the nature of (2) which was causally isolated from (3), so too it is now necessary to find a specification of the degree of (2) which is causally isolated from (3). This is merely a more precise formulation of the problem that has already been solved. In fact, it is the formulation that locates the crux of the problem. For when the agent asks himself whether he really wants to do A, he does not have to discover whether his desire really is the desire to do A. That is how it is specified in his question, and what he has to discover is its degree. But its degree is not independently measurable, like a physical force. So it needs a causally isolated specification, and the only available candidate seems to be 'the degree which nearly always convinces the agent that it does amount to (2)'.

This reply to the objection to the causal theory consists of three parts, and it is important to see how they fit together. For though the details of the answer are complex, its guiding principle is extremely simple. This, of course, is the fault not of the answer, but of the objection.

The objector claims that it is necessary to the causal theory, but, in fact, impossible, to find a generalisable, causally isolated description of (2) available to the agent. The first part of the reply is to generalise the problem to other cases of immediate knowledge separated from its object by an interval of time. Memory is one such case, but premonition is a better one because, if its exists, it reaches into the future. In all such cases the interval creates a problem, because it must be crossed by some kind of causal linkage, even if none is evident. Now memories and premonitions are effects, but they are effects of a special kind – they are impressions of their causes. This makes it difficult to find generalisable descriptions of them which do not entail the appropriate causal linkage. It is not enough to describe them as matching their causes. For they could do this without the person's believing that they did it. So the only available candidates are descriptions that mention his conviction that the particular event occurred, or will occur, or the sincere claims that express these convictions.

Few philosophers are disturbed by the fact that in cases of these two kinds the only available description is reflexive in the following special way: although it does not mention the object (the event) as the cause it does mention the object as the claimed cause (where the claim itself is an effect). The second part of the reply to the objection is to explain why they are right not to be worried by this special kind of reflexivity in the description. Now it is understandable that in this kind of case of immediate knowledge no other specific description of the effect is available. The reason is that in such cases one cannot analyse the state to which one is reacting, as one can when one is reacting immediately to some external physical object, and so one is reduced to describing the state as the kind of state that produces the reaction. This looks incoherent, because the reaction is a claim about the cause of the state. But it is easy to see that it is not really incoherent.

Imagine a world in which premonitory claims were never reactions to purely intentional impressions that the events would occur, but always reactions to a psychological state which could be partly described in an independent way – e.g. the thought of the event was coloured by inappropriate feelings. Clearly there is no incoherence in the view that in such a world premonitory claims would be reactions to natural signs of coming events. Now if in our world premonitory claims are reactions to a psychological state which can never be partly described in an independent way, but only purely intentionally, why does that make it incoherent to analyse the causal linkage in the same way? True, the psychological state cannot be classified as an ordinary natural sign, because any description that specifies it will mention our interpretation of it. But that does not show that it cannot be the effect of the future event.

We cannot use exactly the same argument about memory-claims, because it would not be possible for all memory-claims to have been reactions to a psychological state which could be partly described in an independent way. For in such cases an inductive argument would have to be used, and, therefore, remembered, and this carries the threat of an infinite regress. But some memory claims could have had such a basis, and from this point the argument proceeds as it does for premonitory claims.

Why, then, are so many philosophers disturbed by the logically similar constraint on cases where it is the cause that is psychological rather than the effect? The answer to this question is the third part of the reply to the objection. Now the explanation may be that the pattern of connections is different in the case of wanting and doing. For the agent's foreknowledge of his own action is an effect of a cause of its own object. But this is hardly a justification of their attitude. For it is no more difficult to find a causally isolated generalisable description of (2), the common cause of the foreknowledge and of the action, than it is to find such descriptions of the effects in cases of memory and premonition.

It may be that another difficulty is felt at this point. The causal theory identifies desires, memories and premonitions by psychological properties that are dispositional, and it may be felt that causes must be identifiable in some other way. This raises a general question about latent mental states and their neurological basis, and it is beyond the scope of this paper to try to answer it. But it is worth observing that the same problem arises for memory.

But, though these problems and their solutions are symmetrical, there is also a difference, and it is with this difference that the third part of the answer to the objection is concerned. The difference is that this kind of 'practical knowledge' is not the cause of its object, as 'theoretical knowledge' is the effect of its object. The suggestion that there is symmetry at this point too is not only false but incoherent. 'Practical knowledge' is the effect of the cause of its object, and we understand the causation because the common cause produces other inner effects. This view of 'practical knowledge' is really forced on us. For though it is possible to construe premonition as retro-causation, at least in the sense that some do construe it in this way, it is obvious that we cannot treat 'practical knowledge' as the effect of the future action. For, even if our desires were as inscrutable as some physical needs are, it would change the concept of a desire to regard 'practical knowledge' that accompanies it as the present effect of its future fulfilment. It is a little less obvious, but no less true, that we cannot regard 'practical knowledge' as the cause of the future fulfilment of the desire on which it is based. So even if we reject the hypothesis that the premonitions of the boy in D. H. Lawrence's *The Rocking-Horse Winner* were the effects of the horse's physique, just like its later victory, we are forced to accept some such hypothesis in the case of wanting and doing.

Part II

So far nothing has been said about the possibility that the agent might want to do A for further reasons. The only description of his desire that has been exploited is 'His desire to do A all things considered'. But he may consider more things than doing A merely because he wants to do it, and his reflections on the project may be more than experimental rehearsals in imagination. Deliberation often introduces one or more extra descriptions of the project, each relating it to some further goal of the agent's. I shall call these descriptions 'diagnostic', because they give the agent's reasons for his action and provide the kind of explanation that is often called 'rational'. Of course, it may happen that the agent had no further goal, but did A merely because he wanted to do it. In such a case the description 'A' will itself be diagnostic, and anyone who offered it as such ought to indicate that he was excluding other diagnostic descriptions. For the comment, 'He did A because he wanted to do it', need not convey any more than that it was an action rather than a mere bodily movement, and that under the description 'A' it was done intentionally and perhaps voluntarily. If more is meant, it should be indicated by the insertion of the word 'merely' before the word 'because', or in some such way, and then it will be clear that the description 'A' combines two functions, identifying a particular intentional action and explaining it rationally. However, it is more common for each of these two functions to be assigned to a different description, as in 'I did A because I wanted to achieve B (because I believed it to be achieving B which is what I wanted)'.

There are many problems about the distinction between diagnostic and non-diagnostic descriptions of actions. If 'A' is a description under which an action was done intentionally, what is the precise line between diagnostic 'A' and non-diagnostic 'A'? How far does practical reasoning have to be taken back before it reaches something which counts as a goal, and how closely does a diagnostic description have to relate the action to the goal? But I want to concentrate on the question of entailed general propositions, and so I shall evade these questions by selecting descriptions which would be diagnostic on any view. For example, someone votes for the Labour candidate, or chooses the most intelligent applicant for a job. In each of these cases the description is diagnostic because it relates the more immediate action to a further goal of the agent's. He votes for Smith because he wants a Labour M.P., and he chooses Jones because he wants the most intelligent man on the job. My question is this: Do these rational explanations of actions entail any general propositions concerning the particular case?

Before this question can be discussed, some preliminary analysis is needed. The agent says, 'I did A because I wanted to achieve B'. But how is this desire related to his desire to do A all things considered? Now if he had said '. . . because I wanted to achieve B and C', he would have meant that these two desires were components of his desire to do A all things considered. So when he says '. . . because I wanted to achieve B', he is specifying its only component. In the limiting case, in which he does A merely because he wants to do it, the desire to do A all things considered has only the desire to do A as component, and so is atomic. It is also necessary to extend the concept of 'a component desire' to cover the more complex kind of case in which the agent says, 'I did A because I wanted to achieve B, and in spite of the fact that I did not want to achieve D'. This means that the second component reduced the degree of his total desire to do A. For when a component is an aversion, it is a minus quantity instead of a plus quantity. In both cases what relates a component to the agent's total desire will always be his factual information.

Although this preliminary analysis is only approximate, it does put us in a position to distinguish between various types of rational explanations of actions. For example, if an agent says, 'I did A only in order to achieve B', he will mean that his desire to achieve B was the only component of his total desire to do A, and so, given that he actually did A, that it was sufficient to raise it to the requisite degree. This does not imply that it was sufficient to produce the action without any further help. For his performance of the action also depended on the fulfilment of two of the conditions specified in Part I – *viz.*, on the possibility of the action and on his possession of the relevant factual information. But his statement does imply that his desire to achieve B was not reinforced by any other desire, and so that it was sufficient in itself to fill the bill under the heading 'component desires'. If he had said, 'I would not have done A unless I had wanted to achieve B', he would have meant that this component was necessary in order to fill the bill. So these two types of rational explanation have precise meanings. But they are less common than the statement, 'I did A because I wanted to achieve B', which is conveniently vague and may mean no more than that this is the component which in the context is most worthy of mention. But even claims of this kind must fit some schema constructed out of the concepts of sufficiency and necessity. For example, the vague statement often means that the desire to achieve B was the most important insufficient but necessary component of a set which was unnecessary but sufficient to fill the bill under the heading 'component desires' (i.e. a special case of J. L. Mackie's I.N.U.S. condition).[1]

This account of the meaning of rational explanations of actions suggests that they entail general propositions that are familiar and available for everyday use. For if a component desire is sufficient to fill the bill on one occasion, it should be sufficient to fill it on another, similar occasion, and it should be possible to specify what counts as a similar occasion, and so to test the agent's explanation of his original action by seeing what he does next time. It should also be possible to test the alleged necessity of a component desire in a symmetrical way. I shall call the theory that these possibilities are realised 'T_3'. T_3 has two main rivals. One is the theory that no general propositions are entailed by the sufficiency or by the necessity of component desires (T_4). The other is the theory that they do entail that there are general propositions covering the particular case, but that nobody yet knows what those general propositions are (T_5).

It is arguable – and I shall argue later – that T_4 is neither a causal theory nor an intelligible theory. T_5 is a causal theory, but it is subject to a limitation that was mentioned in Part I. Unlike T_3, it does not require that the agent's desires should be fitted into an explanatory theory which identifies them through their objects. But the pre-scientific theory, which we use in

1. 'Causes and conditions', *American Philosophical Quarterly* 2, 1965.

everyday life when we want to esplain the actions of a particular agent, does identify them in this way. Therefore T_5 might lead to a theory that was quite different from our pre-scientific theory. It might even lead to a theory that lacked any connection with our pre-scientific theory, because it identified the causes of actions under descriptions which were not even approximately coextensive with the descriptions of desires through their objects. Of course, such a theory might well be more precise and complete, but, if these advantages are secured by identifying the causes of actions under descriptions that are not even approximately coextensive with the descriptions of desires through their objects, the essence of rational explanation will have been lost. For it is essential to rational explanation that the causes of actions should be the agent's desires, identified as he identifies them when he deliberates, and that they should be systematised under his intentional descriptions of them. Naturally, there will be occasional divergences – for example, the theorist may disagree with the agent's account of his motivation on a particular occasion, and in certain cases he may claim that an unconscious desire was at work. But the basic method of identifying the causes of his actions will always be his method, and, if a second method is added to his method, its descriptions must be approximately coextensive with his descriptions. Otherwise rational explanation will not be improved but abandoned.

If rational explanations of actions cannot give up the agent's method of identifying desires, and must construct general propositions out of the familiar pre-scientific material, how much systematisation can they achieve? The best argument for T_3 would be to demonstrate that they do achieve a fair amount of systematisation of the kind that it specifies.

Consider the agent's statement, 'I did A only in order to achieve B'. This implies that the desire to achieve B was sufficient to fill the bill under the heading 'component desires'. But how can the implication be tested? The entailed contrapositive, 'If I had not done A, I would not have wanted to achieve B', is counterfactual, and, therefore, not directly testable. So if we want to test this implication of sufficiency, we have to look further afield and find out what this agent does in other similar situations. But what counts as a similar situation for this purpose?

First, and most important, the component desires, which, according to the agent, were engaged on the original occasion, must not have decreased in number or in degree in the interim. If they have decreased in either of these two ways, the situation will be relevantly dissimilar and the test will not show what it is intended to show. In the example given the agent claimed that there was only one component desire, the desire to do B. So at the time of the test he must still want to achieve B as much as he did on the original occasion. The reason why this must be so is not that the truth of a rational explanation of an action requires the constancy of the desires on which it is based. This was Professor Ryle's theory in *The Concept of Mind* (Ch. 4), and it is vulnerable to the objection that it is possible to act from a desire that is fitful and uncharacteristic. But T_3 does not make the constancy of the desires adduced in a rational explanation a necessary condition of its truth. It only requires that they should not have decreased in number or in degree on the later occasion when it is being tested for truth. The idea is that a negative result on this occasion will falsify the original explanation only if this condition is fulfilled.

But this is not the only condition that has to be fulfilled if the test is to show what it is intended to show. For it is not enough that the original component desires should still exist in the same degree at the time of the test. It is also necessary that the situation should possess whatever features are needed to engage them. This condition must be supplemented with one of the conditions that was specified in Part I: the agent must know that the situation at the time of the test possesses these features. More generally, he must have all the relevant factual information. For if he does not have it, his failure to perform another A-type action would not falsify the original rational explanation, because it would not show that the component desires adduced in it were not sufficient to fill the bill. For the same reason, another condition specified in Part I must be fulfilled: the action must be possible.

It might appear that we now have a complete list of the conditions that have to be fulfilled on the occasion of the test, and that, given their fulfilment, non-performance of an A-type action would falsify the rational explanation of the original action. But that would be an illusion produced by concentrating on the plus quantities and neglecting the minus quantities. For suppose that between the time of the original action and the time of the test the agent developed a new aversion, which happened to be engaged by some feature of the testing situation. Then non-performance would not count as falsification because it would be attributable to an aversion which did not exist on the original occasion. If the aversion had existed and had been engaged on the original occasion, and if the agent had done A in spite of it, and because of his desire to achieve B, then we might legitimately expect the same outcome on the testing occasion. But if the agent developed the aversion in the interim, we cannot construe the matter in this way, and so cannot count non-performance as falsification. So we must add the further condition that the testing situation must not possess any feature which engages an aversion developed by the agent in the interim.

Does this complete the list of conditions that have to be fulfilled on the occasion of the test? This is not an easy question to answer, because there is another condition concerned with aversions, which may sometimes have to be fulfilled. Suppose that the testing situation possesses a feature that engages an aversion which did exist at the time of the original action, but which was not then engaged. Would non-performance in such a case falsify the agent's rational explanation of his original action? For example, the agent is selecting people for a certain kind of job and he is using a short list of requirements. He accepts a particular candidate and he says that he accepted him only because he met the requirements. Then on a later occasion he rejects another candidate who meets the same requirements, and he says that he rejected him because he had a defect which the first candidate did not have. Does this falsify his rational explanation of his selection of the first candidate?

This question is difficult, and it will be discussed in detail later. The case for saying that the result described would count as falsification rests on the fact that the agent's rational explanation of his selection of the first candidate was offered as a complete explanation. His statement was supposed to mention all the component desires that were then operative. So ought it not to have included the desire to choose only applicants without that particular defect? If he relied on a handbook which actually mentioned absence of the defect as one of the requirements, this question would have to be answered in the affirmative. But suppose that its absence was something so obviously and so generally desirable that it was taken for granted. Then it would not be so clear that his rational explanation of his selection of the first candidate had been incomplete. The issue depends partly on the concept of completeness that is being used.

This problem will be discussed later. Meanwhile, to make T_3 watertight, I shall impose the further condition that the testing situation must not possess features that engage aversions which existed at the time of the original action but which were not engaged by any features of the situation at that time.

The addition of this last condition gives us a strict – in certain cases perhaps an excessively strict – list of the requirements that must be met by any testing situation. When they are met, non-performance really will falsify the rational explanation of the earlier action. For it will show that the agent's tally of the component desires operative on the earlier occasion was incomplete, and this will be confirmed if we can find a further desire which we can add to his list as a likely auxiliary. If this account of the pattern of falsifiability of rational explanations of actions is correct, it can easily be extended to the much simpler cases in which the agent merely claims that a particular component desire was necessary. Thus rational explanations of actions entail general propositions constructed out of the familiar pre-scientific material, and this was what T_3 claimed.

There are various objections to this version of T_3, some of which are serious. But there is one objection to which it is possible to give a quick answer based on the arguments of Part I. Suppose that someone objects that, when rational explanations of actions are analysed in this way, the alleged cause does not meet the moderate requirement of causal isolation. If he means that it can be described only as the desire to do A, then his objection will get a foothold only when the agent does A merely because he wants to do it. But in such cases the arguments of Part I show that the moderate requirement of causal isolation can be met. However, the more interesting cases are those in which the agent explains his action by adducing one one or more different component desires – for example, he says that he did A only because he wanted to achieve B. If the objector means that, when the desire is described diagnostically in this way, the action must be given the matching description 'achieving B', this is never true. For in such cases the action can always be described in the non-diagnostic way – in this example, as 'doing A'. Moreover, even if it were true, it would merely present a special case of the general problem which has already been solved in Part I.

It is worth adding that the main point of a rational explanation is to give the components of the desire to perform the action all things considered, and this part of what it says will always be contingent in a straightforward way that does not even raise the problem of causally isolated descriptions. In the example used the desire to do A was said to have only one component, *viz.*, the desire to achieve B, and this statement is clearly contingent. For the desire to do A might have had several components, and some of them might have been aversions, and, if this was not so, it is a contingent fact that it was not so. Even if the agent did A merely because he wanted to, so that his desire to do A all things considered was atomic, that would still be a contingent fact. This part of the content of a rational explanation of an action is contingent in a way that does not even raise the problem discussed in Part I.

A more serious objection to T_3 is that it describes a pattern of falsification which can seldom be used in order to test rational explanations of actions. This point would not be very damaging in itself, because it could be countered with the observation that, when we notice what the agent does in other similar situations, we can often cast doubt on his rational explanation of an action, even if we cannot actually falsify it. It is notoriously difficult to achieve certainty about a person's motives, especially if the aim is to get a complete account of them. However, the objection can be made more damaging, if it is reinforced with an appeal to the agent's own immediate impression of his motivation. For it might be argued that this is the main source of rational explanations, and that T_3 is quite wrong to attach so much importance to entailed general propositions which are too loosely formulated and too open-ended to be used. Here it might be suggested that T_3 is unduly influenced by the analogy between rational explanations of actions and ordinary causal explanations of purely physical events. A supporter of T_4 would go even further and deny that rational explanations of actions entail any general propositions, usable or unusable.

The remainder of this paper will be an attempt to answer this objection. The following strategy will be adopted. First I shall argue against the extreme position occupied by T_4. The argument will be that, though it is correct to attach great weight to the agent's impression of his own motivation, it is not correct to make what he says on the basis of his impression logically independent of anything that he does on other occasions. For that would make what he says unintelligible. The argument against the rest of the objection will be less uncompromising, because it is true that the entailed general propositions can be used less often than T_3 suggests. So the defence of T_3 must include an explanation of this fact. I shall try to explain it by pointing to certain differences between rational explanations of actions and ordinary causal explanations of purely physical events. The idea will be that, though rational explanations of actions do entail the general propositions specified by T_3, the differences prevent us from using them as much as we might have expected to be able to use them. So though the theoretical importance of the entailed general propositions is very great – without them, rational explanations of actions would be unintelligible – it is not matched by their practical importance.

The argument against T_4 is simply that it flouts the maxim, 'Same cause, same effect', and so removes an essential part of the meaning of rational explanations of actions. It is essential to the meaning of the statement 'I did A because I wanted to achieve B' that it should imply more than is implied by the statement, 'I wanted to achieve B and I did A'. The extra implication is that the desire to achieve B was enough in those circumstances to lead the agent to do A, and this is incompatible with the assertion that, if he wanted to achieve B as much on another similar occasion, the outcome could be different. This holds for rational explanations of actions as impregnably as it holds for ordinary causal explanations of purely physical events.

Since any supporter of T_4 would reject this argument as a piece of dogmatism, it is worth inquiring what positive account he would offer of the connection between component desires and action. What is offered is nearly always a theory about the way in which the agent apprehends the connection, rather than a theory about its nature. For instance, it is said that he apprehends it immediately. This is also said about certain cases of purely physical causation. For example, a child who watches sulphuric acid burn paper for the first time would be described as apprehending this causal process immediately. It is admitted that there are differences between the two cases, but the differences strengthen the argument for T_4. For the agent's experience of the force of his own motives within himself is more direct and immediate than any observation of external physical causation, and he knows the descriptions of his motives which explain their effects. His experience is, therefore, sufficient in itself and self-contained, and the statement that he bases on it is not tied by any general proposition to other occasions in his life. In any case, it will be objected that the general propositions specified in T_3 are too loose and open-ended to yield a real test.

But this argument confuses a theory about the way in which a connection is apprehended with a theory about its nature. Hume sometimes makes this confusion and puts his theory about the nature of causal connection in needless jeopardy by tying it to a theory about the ways in which we can tell the difference between a case in which X is the cause of Y and a case in which X is merely followed by Y. In fact, we can sometimes tell that X is the cause of Y even if we have never observed a similar conjunction before. But that is no reason for rejecting his account of the nature of causal connection. As a matter of fact, the child's awareness of the cause of the paper's combustion is not such an extreme case of immediacy. For he can argue that there are no other suitable causal candidates around, and we can see how he learned to use that argument. But suppose that he had no such argument in reserve, and, in general, that human beings had an innate ability to detect causes, and that they were often completely unable to represent the process of detection as a compressed argument. Even that would not undermine Hume's theory about the nature of causal connection. Therefore, even if the agent's awareness of his own motivation is a more extreme example of immediacy than the child's awareness of the cause of the paper's combustion, that still would not undermine T_3.

If it could be shown that the agent's sincere account of his motivation was immune from error, that could be used as the basis for an argument against T_3. For T_3 would then credit human agents with infallible self-knowledge extending far beyond the confines of the present moment, and this would be very implausible. Even when claims to self-knowledge are confined to the present moment, infallibility would be quite an achievement. But when the claims extend outside the present moment, it would be miraculous. Therefore, T_3 must be abandoned.

This is a valid argument from a false premise, unlike the argument from immediacy, which is an invalid argument from a true premise. For if the agent is required to give a complete account of his motivation, it is easy to find examples in which he omits an important element by mistake. It is also possible for him to make the mistake of including an element which made no contribution at all to his motivation.

The immediacy of the agent's awareness of his motivation is no obstacle to T_3. Immediacy does not entail immunity from error. However, if it could be shown independently that agents' sincere accounts of their motivation were immune from error, that would create a difficulty for T_3. But this cannot be shown. Therefore the epistemology of rational explanations of actions yields no valid objections to T_3's account of the connection between component desires and actions.

However, it is a more complex matter to defend T_3 against the objection that the entailed general propositions to which it attaches such great theoretical importance have very little practical importance and can seldom be used as an effective test. This too is an epistemological objection, and there seem to be two ways of answering it. One is to show that it is possible to rely on the entailed general propositions for an effective test in certain cases. The other is to explain what makes this impossible in other cases. Since the cases in which it is impossible are more common in this area than in the area of purely physical causation, the explanation will largely take the form of a list of differences between motivation and purely physical causation.

First, it is necessary to point out that the objection is exaggerated. The entailed general propositions are not theoretical appendages which can never be used. In fact, it is only too easy to think of everyday examples which would illustrate their use. If someone happened to be influenced by racial prejudice in his selection of applicants for a certain kind of job, he might well want to conceal this fact. So his statement of his reasons for accepting a particular candidate would not mention race, but only the qualifications needed for the job. But on a later occasion he might reject a second applicant who had all the qualifications given as reasons for accepting the first one. There would be various possible explanations of this inconsistency. First, it would be necessary to exclude the hypothesis that the selector's factual information was inadequate, and the hypothesis that either or both of his decisions were made because the alternatives were impossible. The exclusion of explanations of those two kinds would focus the inquiry onto his component desires on the two occasions. It would appear probable that the second applicant had some characteristic which was counted against him and which the first applicant did not have. If this was so, the selector's statement of his reasons for accepting the first applicant ought to have included the absence of that characteristic. So, since it was offered as a complete statement, it would be false. This explanation of his inconsistency would be acceptable, even if it could not be confirmed by the identification of the component desire which was concealed by the selector – in this example, the desire to accept only those applicants who belonged to the favoured race. If it could be confirmed in this way, it would be established beyond reasonable doubt.

There are several features of this example that ought to be emphasised. First, the evidence against the selector's statement of his reason for accepting the first applicant might all be drawn from his behaviour on other occasions. There is no need for an admission. Second, the case against him might be conclusive in spite of the fact that sometimes it is not easy to tell what counts as a complete list of component desires. This is because he would be using a number of quite definite principles of selection, unlike a person choosing where to spend a holiday. So when he said that he selected the first candidate only because . . ., his list of component desires ought to have included every desire which corresponded to one of his principles of selection and which was operative on that occasion. The items on his list ought to have added up to a total which was sufficient to fill the bill under the heading 'component desires'. Therefore, it ought to have included the desire to select only applicants belonging to the favoured race. No doubt, it is sometimes difficult to use the concept of 'a complete list of operative component desires'. But there is a difference between the case against the selector and the case against a person who was suspected of concealing one of his reasons for choosing a place to spend a holiday. The list even of one person's grounds for the latter choice is very open-ended, and this would weaken the case against him, whereas the list used by the selector of personnel would be much less open-ended, and, perhaps, definitely closed, so that the case against him could be made much stronger.

The complications introduced by the concept of 'a complete list of operative component desires' do not arise when the agent only says that a certain component desire was necessary on a particular occasion. This claim can be falsified in a much simpler way. All that is required is a second occasion which engages only the component desires engaged on the first occasion, with the exception of the one that the agent claimed to be necessary. If he nevertheless performs an action similar to his first action, it will be very probable that his original claim was false. This conclusion would be confirmed if the allegedly necessary component desire was respectable, or face-saving, or some such thing.

There is a third feature of these examples which needs comment. They are all cases of falsehood attributable to straightforward insincerity, rather than to self-deception or downright mistake. This is not because cases of the two latter types do not occur. They do occur, but the thesis, that the entailed general propositions yield a usable test, does not depend on their occurrence. Even if all falsehood in this area were attributable to insincerity, the thesis could be successfully defended against the objection that the test is unusable.

These examples show that the objection is exaggerated. The entailed general propositions sometimes yield a decisive argument against an agent's rational explanation of his action.

Even when the argument is not decisive, it is often sufficient to convince us that his statement was false. No doubt, there are also many cases in which this conclusion is no more than probable. But our task is to construct the most probable rational explanation of a sequence of actions performed by this particular agent, and, if we often have to rest content with the most probable hypothesis, that is a predicament to which we are accustomed.

However, there is a valid point beneath the objector's exaggeration. For there are many rational explanations of actions which are beyond the reach of this kind of test, and many against which it can produce only very weak evidence. Even in the favourable examples that have been described there are two important sources of uncertainty which are not parallelled in the investigation of purely physical causation. First, impossibility is the limiting case of difficulty, and, when performance is difficult, we may have to take account of the fact that the agent knows this and thinks that the project is not worth it, whereas in purely physical processes future obstacles do not impair, but only impede, the operation of present causes. Second, when the agent enters the test situation, how is it known that his desires have not altered in a way that would invalidate the test? For instance, the selector might simply have changed his principles of selection some time between his acceptance of the first candidate and his rejection of the second. There are further sources of uncertainty in less favourable examples, in which the agent does not formulate a regular policy for dealing with a recurrent type of situation. In many cases of this kind it is not even clear what would be meant by 'a complete list of the agent's operative component desires', and in many others it would be impossible to construct a consistent theory about the permanent weights that he attaches to their objects. A similar difficulty may occur in some cases of purely physical causation, but if it does occur, it is not necessarily insuperable. For new ways of identifying and measuring physical factors may always be discovered, but we are seldom in a position to do this for psychological factors, and sometimes it cannot be done without changing the character of the original theory.

These are valid points, and the defence of T_3 can proceed only by admitting them, and by trying to explain them without abandoning the thesis that rational explanations of actions do entail general propositions constructed out of the familiar, pre-scientific material. What has to be accounted for is not the fact that such explanations do not fit actions into a recognisable deterministic framework. Even the neatest explanations of purely physical events do not quite do that. What has to be accounted for is the fact that rational explanations of actions rest on the agent's impression of his own motivation so much more heavily than explanations of purely physical events ever rest on the observer's immediate awareness of causation. No doubt, in order to account for this fact, it will be necessary to show why the entailed general propositions are looser and more open-ended in the case of motivation. But the standard arguments against psychological determinism will be irrelevant. For instance, even if an agent could always falsify any prediction of his own future action after he had heard it, that would contribute almost nothing to the solution of the present problem, because in real life agents are seldom influenced by counter-predictiveness. What is needed here is a description of the many striking differences between ordinary causal explanations of purely physical events and ordinary rational explanations of actions. This will be a description of the differences between the two types of explanation as we know them and use them, and not after conjectural improvements. It must be based on the familiar material of rational explanations of actions, and it may not draw on neurological data or speculations. For here the surface is the thing.

The first, and perhaps the most conspicuous, difference between the two types of explanation is that there is a peculiar difficulty about establishing that the agent enters the test situation with all his relevant component desires unaltered, or at least not altered in ways that would invalidate the test. In the example used, how do we know that the selector has not developed a new aversion between his acceptance of the first applicant and his rejection of the second? Why should he not say that he really did give a complete list of his component desires on the first occasion, and so his present aversion must be new? Or, to take a different form of the same difficulty, suppose that, instead of claiming that he has a new aversion, he offers the different explanation, that one of his original component desires has decreased. How can we tell whether this is true or false? Now there are also purely physical cases in which it is difficult to establish which causal factors are present, and in what degree on the occasion of a crucial experiment. But there is no general source of uncertainty in that area, whereas we seem to be generally uncertain about the repetition of an agent's component desires. It might even seem that a negative instance could always be explained by the hypothesis that his desires have changed in a way that would invalidate the test, even if we would often be reluctant to accept that explanation.

There certainly is a difference here, but the last suggestion exaggerates it. It is true that, when we wonder whether one of the agent's relevant component desires has decreased in the interim, there often does not seem to be any way of getting an absolutely certain answer. If we ask him whether this did happen, he will probably say that, judging by his attitude to the project on the second occasion, it must have happened. But this will not help us. We want an estimate that is independent of his attitude on the second occasion, and we shall not get this from him at the time. However, we can put our question to him before he enters the testing situation, and his answer will then be independent of the result of the test, and so may serve as part of the basis of the case against his statement of his reason on the first occasion. We also have other resources. We can accumulate evidence for the degree of his component desire by examining his behaviour over a longer period both before and after the occasion of the test. This sort of evidence can be very impressive. If his later history agrees with his earlier history, leaving an alleged decrease in the component desire isolated on the occasion of the test, we might feel practically certain that it had not decreased, and on this basis we might find the case against his original statement of his reason convincing. But actual discovery of the extra motive on the first occasion would always add to our confidence in the verdict.

However, all this evidence is indirect in two distinct ways, and, therefore less good than the best evidence for the presence of purely physical causal factors on the occasion of a crucial experiment. First, the degree of the component desire is always judged by its effects, because it is a dispositional entity with no non-dispositional basis that is yet known to us. In this it is unlike physical causal factors, which either are non-dispositional, or else have non-dispositional bases, available for use as criteria of their presence. Second, the evidence must be collected at times other than the time of the test, because the only way to collect it at the time of the test would be to ask the agent, and his answer would not be independent of the development of the result of the test. There is no exact analogue to this limitation in cases of purely physical causation.

This difference between motives and physical causes provides part of the explanation of the fact that we rely more heavily on the agent's impression of his own motivation than on the observer's immediate awareness of physical causation. The weakness of the test of an agent's statement of his reason for his action is that it is difficult to know how a negative result should be interpreted, and this leaves it open to us to put more weight on his impression. However, this does not explain why we take this option and actually do put more weight on his impression. For we might have been content to admit that we very often do not know the motivation of our own and other people's actions.

The same is true of other differences which make tests of motivation less reliable than tests of physical causation. For instance, any attempt to reduce all motives to one is bound to be speculative, and even theories which attempt to derive all actions from a few basic motives do not achieve a precise fit with the facts, whereas the concept of physical force is empirical and exact. One reason for this difference is that descriptions of motives overlap one another producing a pattern which can be construed in various ways. Another is that, even when a particular motive can legitimately be isolated, it cannot be measured independently, as a particular physical force can. So the surest test of an agent's account of his motivation will be one that does not depend on comparative estimates of degree, but only on the constancy of a particular set of motives, whatever their relative degrees. But a theory about a particular agent's motivation that is constructed in this way cannot be very powerful because, if it is extended beyond a sequence of actions of a specific type, its probability will necessarily decrease. However, these differences too only explain why it is open to us to put more weight on the agent's impression of his own motivation. They do not explain why we actually do put more weight on it.

The explanation of this fact is to be found in the experience of motivation. No doubt, this is a crude description of the phenomenon, because it suggests too close an analogy with the experience of physical causation. If the agent feels his action issuing from his desire, he feels this happening within himself, and so his report of the event is more closely connected with the event itself than it is in the other case. But this does not prevent us from distinguishing between the event and his awareness of it. Nor, of course, does the fact that very often he will not pause to reflect, prevent us from distinguishing an automatic response from a considered report. Perhaps the word 'experience' is often too heavy to be appropriate. But the same might be said of the phrase 'the experience of physical causation'. If it is objected, from a different angle, that the causation of the action is an ineliminable part of its description, the answer to this has already been given: the action can be redescribed as a bodily movement, or the desire to do A can be redescribed by its components. There seem to be no valid objections to the thesis that the agent feels his action issuing from his desire, and the simple fact that this happens within him provides part of the explanation of our reliance on his own impression of his motivation. We do not merely rely on it *faute de mieux*, but for a positive reason.

But the positive reason is much stronger than this. For when an agent feels his action issuing from his desire, he nearly always identifies his desire in a way that explains its connection with his action. It is true that this is not always so, because a desire may be masked, and its identity may be hidden from the agent himself. But in most cases of motivation the desires that are operative are identified by the agent in an explanatory way, either as 'the desire to do A', or as 'the desire to achieve B', where B is some further goal which he believes to be attainable by doing A. So desires are seldom inscrutable causes, unlike causes in the physical world, which are often inscrutable, because the observer can identify them only in a way that does not explain their connections with their effects. This increases the credibility of the agent's impression of his own motivation. For we do not have to rely on the weak argument, that it is very likely to be correct because it is an impression of internal causation. We can add that in the system of desires and actions superficial descriptions are explanatory descriptions. Here the surface is the thing, and the order of importance corresponds to the order of discovery, whereas the reverse is true in the physical sciences.

There is also something else which increases the credibility of the agent's impression of his own motivation. Often his desires operate only because he is aware of their existence and their tendency. For it can be a complex and difficult task to bring his desires to bear on a particular predicament, and so he has to deliberate, and his deliberation, not being merely hypothetical, requires his awareness of the existence and tendency of the relevant desires. In such cases the agent does not play the role of a spectator who notices things that would have happened anyway, even if he had not noticed them. He is aware of the existence of a desire, and of its tendency to operate in a certain way, and this very awareness helps it to operate, and may even be a necessary condition of its effective operation. Evidently, it is not always necessary, because some of his desires would operate even if he were unaware of their tendency or even of their existence, and some would operate only if he were unaware of their existence, or, at least, of their tendency. So the importance of consciousness in the system of desires and actions must not be exaggerated. The truth is only that in many cases it is a necessary condition of the operativeness of a desire.

But this is an important truth, because, when an impression is a necessary constituent of the total process part of which is its object, its credibility may be increased. For in such cases the desire would not operate without the agent's impression of its tendency, and this impression would be less likely to contribute to the outcome if it were not reinforcing a tendency which already existed, and, therefore, if it were not correct. Naturally, this is not the only function of consciousness, which also tells the agent what he would have done anyway. Now this information, like the information derived from the more complex kind of case, in which consciousness plays an active role, is the basis of the agent's image of his own agency. But though this gives a special importance to his impression of his own motivation, it does not increase its credibility. The only factor which may increase its credibility is the active role of consciousness. For when consciousness operates in this way it will usually be reinforcing a pre-existing tendency.

My aim is to show that these considerations, or at least those of them that are valid, show why we attach more weight to the agent's impression of his own motivation than to an observer's immediate awareness of purely physical causation, without detaching its general implications. The first, and most important point that needs to be made is that there is a limit to the information that can be extracted with any certainty from the agent's impression. Even if it were legitimate to assume that the description of his action would always match some desire from which it issued, it would not follow either that he could give a complete list of the components of that desire or that he could be sure that a particular component was necessary. For example, even if he could rely on his impression for the information that he did A intentionally under the description 'A', he could not rely on it either for the information that his only motive was to achieve B or for the information that that motive was necessary. These two explanations of his action go beyond his impression, and they would be defeated if the entailed general propositions could be rigorously tested and falsified. Naturally, his impression supports the two explanations, and the preceding discussion shows that the support provided by it is stronger than the support provided by an observer's immediate awareness of causation in the other kind of case. But this does not free either of the two explanations from their dependence on the truth of the appropriate general propositions. It is one thing for an explanation to receive unusually strong support that is independent of such tests, but quite another thing for its truth to achieve independence of their results.

In any case, it is not always safe to assume that the agent's description of his action will always match some desire from which it issued. This depends on how much is implied by the claim that, if he did A intentionally under the description 'A', then the action issued from the desire to do A. If 'A' is a description of the action under some immediate aspect, such as 'walking out of the room', it may be that no more is implied than that the action was performed under the guidance provided by that description of it. If so, the agent's impression, that he moved his legs in the appropriate way because he wanted to walk out of the room, would be very unlikely to be faulted by any subsequent test. It is, of course, conceivable that, as a result of neural surgery, this desire might produce entirely different movements on different occasions, so that it was mere luck that his impression was correct on this particular occasion. But that is a marginal possibility of no practical importance.

However, the agent's claim might imply more than this. For if his description of his action were more remote – e.g. he said 'I was going to the kitchen', or 'I wanted to gain time to think about the suggestion', or 'I wanted to get away before the others arrived' – he would be giving his motive for walking out of the room. But in that case his impression might be mistaken. For these might be spurious motives masking his true motive even from him. It is interesting to observe that, when a description gives a further motive, as these descriptions do, we cannot defend the agent's claim by cutting it back to the minimal implication, that at least he must have performed the action under the guidance of that description, because he felt it guiding him. For this would omit any claim about his motivation, and in any case there is no presumption that his movements must have been guided by that description, rather than by the more immediate description 'walking out of the room'.

These examples raise a question about error. The question is not whether the agent can make mistakes in this area, because it is obvious that he can make them. What is difficult to establish is whether there is any limit to the kinds of mistake that he might make. In general, it must be possible for him to make mistakes wherever crediting him with infallibility would be crediting him with an unbelievable amount of self-knowledge. Now, if the thesis that his statement, that his action issued from a certain desire, entails a general proposition covering other similar occasions in his life, is combined with the thesis, that his statement is infallible, there is a real risk that he will be credited with an unbelievable amount of self-knowledge. But a closer look at the examples will show that we grade his immunity from error according to the content of his claim.

When he describes his action under some immediate aspect – e.g. as 'walking out of the room' – and his impression is that it was guided by this description of it, we do attach very great weight to his impression. We still do not regard it as infallible, because neural surgery might have turned his normal achievement into a lucky success, or perhaps because there is the marginal possibility of other, psychologically produced, illusions. But such impressions are, for practical purposes, conclusive. However, these are not impressions of motivation, and less can be extracted with certainty from impressions of motivation. This is obvious when it is the agent's impression that a particular component desire was sufficient, or that it was necessary, and, though it is less obvious when he has either of these two impressions about the desire to do A merely because he wants to do A under the description 'A', it is still true. Even when he confines himself to giving his main motive, he may still make a mistake. The only marginal case would be one in which he made the minimum claim that a particular component desire made some contribution to the outcome.

So the difficulty is avoided by a distinction between knowing what one is immediately doing and knowing why one is doing it. If an agent is doing something intentionally, there will be some immediate description of what he does which guides his performance, and his impression that his action issued from the desire that matches this description will carry very great weight. But his impression of his motivation will carry less weight, and how much less it will carry will depend on its precise content.

There are, then, limits to the weight that can be attached to the agent's impression. But within these limits there are also favourable factors which explain why we attach more weight to it than to the observer's immediate awareness of physical causation. The limits are imposed by the logical constraint of the entailed general propositions, while the favourable factors are epistemological. One question remains: Is it possible to point to any favourable features of the meaning of rational explanations of actions? For instance, do they, perhaps, make a less ambitious claim than has been suggested so far? If so, this would be a favourable logical factor.

It is often said that the agent's own rational explanation of his action is immune from error. But this has been shown to be false. The most that can be claimed is that it provides him with a picture of his own agency which is important not only for his relations with others (e.g. it affects reward and punishment), but also for his relations with his own future self. But this kind of importance is not truth. Desires can operate outside the circle of light cast by consciousness. The fact, that, when they are caught in it, we build them into a useful structure, does nothing to show that they are always caught in it. Nor is this shown by the fact that an intentional action must be performed under the guidance of a description that matches some desire. It is true that motivation is usually channelled through consciousness. But even then it is a fact that the agent would not have performed the action if he had not been aware of the existence and tendency of a particular desire; he may not know this fact, and sometimes when he claims that his awareness of the desire was necessary, he will be wrong. It may be true that when his awareness does make a difference, it will often be reinforcing the tendency of a desire which exists independently of his awareness of it. But this too is not always so, and so it is impossible to extract from such cases any general argument for the correctness of an impression which makes a difference. It seems that it is wrong to ascribe infallibility to the agent even in these limited cases. Such infallibility is not guaranteed by the meaning of rational explanations of actions, and, if it did exist in certain cases, its existence would be contingent.

However, there is a feature of their meaning which does support another, less extreme claim. They are often vague about the contribution made by the desire adduced to explain the action. If the agent says that he did A in order to achieve B, he will be giving his main motive. But though a sincere claim of this kind can be falsified, its vagueness gives it considerable resilience. It allows us to interpret his statement in a way that reduces the claim made by it, and so to attach more weight to his impression.

This vagueness can also produce a misleading side-effect. It creates uncertainty whether we ought to reduce the claim, or whether we ought to interpret it in the maximal way and so treat a negative result as falsificatory, and this uncertainty can lead to a blurring of the difference between the agent's actual motivation and his picture of it. For when we cannot be sure of the effect of a negative result, we feel that it would be more practical to leave this question unanswered, and simply to accept the agent's picture of his motivation. But do we then accept it as true? It is easy to evade this question when we move from the point of view that includes the possibility of preconscious motivation to the point of view that excludes it. For the theoretical difference between the two points of view may be forgotten. But the fact is that when we move to the second and cease to consider the possibility that the agent may be mistaken, we do not deny the existence of that possibility. We only reject it as irrelevant to his picture, and perhaps as a tiresome theoretical appendage. But it is only too easy to misconstrue this move, and to imagine that we are actually excluding the possibility of agents' mistakes. Thus the illusion of the agent's infallibility arises from a misunderstanding of the theory underlying a move that is practically convenient.

Even when the agent says something more precise, such as 'I did A only in order to achieve B', there will still be a certain vagueness in the concept of 'a complete set of operative component desires'. This source of vagueness was mentioned earlier, but it is worth examining in more detail now. The example used earlier was the case of a person selecting candidates for a certain type of job. He is guided by a short list of requirements, and he says that he accepted a particular candidate because he met them. Then on a later occasion he rejects another candidate who meets the same requirements, but, he says, has a defect which the first candidate did not have. The question is: Does this falsify his explanation of his acceptance of the first candidate because it shows that it was incomplete? Or should we say that there is no falsification here, because there is no need for him to have mentioned the absence of the defect on the first occasion?

Assume that all the sources of uncertainty mentioned in this paper have been removed. So we really do know from the result of the test that, if the first candidate had had the defect (and it had been noticed), he would have been rejected. Furthermore, we know that this would have happened because on the earlier occasion too the selector wanted a candidate who did not have the defect. It follows that the desire to accept the candidate only if he lacked the defect was operating preconsciously if the agent's statement of his reason was sincere, and that it was operating consciously if his statement was insincere. It is unconvincing to object that it cannot have been operating in any way, because lack of a defect is something negative. For it is not always possible to draw a line between positive and negative characteristics, and in any case it is easy to find examples of characteristics which are clearly negative but which consciously influence a choice. Nor does there seem to be any other reason to deny that in this example the selector's desire to accept the candidate only if he lacked the defect was operating in one way or another.

But would we therefore say that his rational explanation of his action on the first occasion was incomplete? If he was guided by a set of agreed principles, which included the requirement of freedom from the defect, we would say that it was incomplete. But the matter is less easy to settle when the agent's criteria are not explicitly formulated. In such cases there seems to be no general answer to the question, what counts as a complete set of component desires. We have to make do with rough conventions which vary from one type of case to another. This does not mean that the assessment of completeness is arbitrary. There would usually be general agreement about the legitimacy of the agent's plea that a particular part of his reason was not worth mentioning. For instance, he would not need to say that he accepted the candidate because he was not fatally ill, but he would have to mention his race if it made a difference. So we can recognise clear cases of incompleteness when we encounter them. Nevertheless, there is some vagueness in the concept of a complete set of component desires.

This vagueness is another factor that produces the two effects already noted. First, it allows us to reduce the claim made by the agent's statement, that he did A only in order to achieve B, and so to attach more weight to his impression. But, second, it creates uncertainty whether we ought to do this, or whether we ought to take a negative result as falsification, and this uncertainty makes it easy for us to overlook the difference between the agent's actual motivation and his picture of his motivation. We move to the point of view that excludes preconscious motivation without thinking out the implications of this move.

6 Ifs and Cans

J. L. Austin's lecture on this topic contributes little to the problem of freedom of the will, and so in my discussion of his ideas I shall stop short of the difficult part of that problem. His most important positive suggestion is that hypotheticals should be divided into two classes, conditionals and pseudo-conditionals. He claims that neglect of this distinction has been the cause of mistakes in certain forms of the dispositional analysis of the statement that an agent could have acted otherwise, and he then goes on to criticise all forms of that analysis using arguments which do not depend on the difference between the two kinds of hypothetical.

This discussion will be in two parts. In the first I shall take up Austin's distinction between conditionals and pseudos and criticise it and develop it at length, because it seems to me to be the most important thing in his lecture. Since I shall not have space for comment on fortuitous errors made by defenders of the dispositional analysis of the claim that an agent could have acted otherwise, I shall concentrate on the essential features of that analysis. My investigation of the differences between the two kinds of hypothetical will lead to further distinctions which can be used in defence of the general idea expressed in dispositional analyses of ascriptions of powers, abilities and capacities. So in Part I of this discussion I shall develop Austin's main idea in a direction that is approximately the opposite of his line of argument.

In Part II I shall examine some general attacks on all forms of the dispositional analysis of such ascriptions. Most of these general criticisms are developed in Austin's lecture. But I shall also examine a criticism which has been produced more recently by K. Lehrer.[1] My disagreement with Austin in this field will

1. 'An empirical disproof of determinism?' in *Freedom and Determinism*, ed. K. Lehrer, New York, 1966.

be more direct than it is in Part I. But, though I shall try to show that his arguments do not support his complete rejection of the dispositional analysis, I think that one of them does lead to an equally important, if not quite so ambitious, conclusion.

Part I

Austin distinguishes conditionals from pseudos in the following way: a hypothetical is a conditional if and only if it entails its contrapositive – otherwise it is a pseudo.[2] E.g. the hypothetical 'I can pay you tomorrow if I choose' is a pseudo by this contrapositive test. This is a good way of drawing the distinction, because it is natural to call a hypothetical a conditional when and only when the truth of the antecedent is put forward as a sufficient condition of the truth of the consequent, and when and only when this is its point the hypothetical passes the contrapositive test for conditionality.

There is, of course, nothing wrong with a pseudo. The only reason for giving it this faintly pejorative name is that the conditional use of 'if' is its central and most frequent use. So those who argue, as I shall argue in this paper, that some pseudos contain a conditional 'if' in a special subordinate position, need not be suffering from the prejudice that all occurrences of 'if' have to be accounted for in some such way. The justification of this kind of account is its explanatory power, if it fits. It is based on the central and most frequent use of 'if', and so, when it can be extended to outlying cases, it will explain them very well.

After drawing this clear distinction, Austin complicates it by bringing in a second test of conditionality. According to the second test a hypothetical is a conditional if and only if it does not entail its detached consequent.[3] The hypothetical 'I can pay you tomorrow if I choose' also fails this second test for conditionality, and so comes out again as a pseudo. This test might be called 'the non-detachment test'. Naturally, the use of both

2. *Philosophical Papers*, Oxford, 1961, p. 157. All references to Austin's British Academy lecture 'Ifs and cans' (1956) will be to this reprint in *Philosophical Papers*.

3. ibid., p. 157.

tests should be restricted to cases in which neither the antecedent nor the consequent is analytic or self-contradictory.

There are difficulties about the use of these two tests for conditionality. First, it might be argued that they give divergent results for the hypothetical 'He can do it if he chooses'. This hypothetical is in fact used to ascribe ability and opportunity to the agent, but it might conceivably be made to include the implication that he can choose to do it – or, to put this in more natural English, that he can bring himself to do it. So someone might argue that it does not entail its detached consequent (in spite of not entailing its contrapositive), on the ground that it might be true that the agent had the ability and opportunity, but not true that he could bring himself to do it.[4] But against this argument we could defend Austin's simultaneous use of both his tests for conditionality by pointing out that he was not expanding the verb 'can' so as to include the implication that the agent could bring himself to do it. When 'He can do it' only ascribes ordinary ability and opportunity to the agent, it really is entailed by the original hypothetical. So Austin could have maintained that his two tests for conditionality do not diverge in this case, provided that the meaning of 'He can do it' is not expanded. This defence of his position amounts to interpreting the detached consequent in the following way: 'He can do it, whether or not, perhaps *per impossibile*, he chooses to do it.'

However, this is not a complete defence of his position, because the two tests for conditionality really would produce divergent results if we did pack the extra implication into the expanding suitcase 'can'. But we can complete the defence by making two further points. First, if the 'can' in the detached consequent included the extra implication, then so too would the 'can' in the original hypothetical. But, secondly, though the 'can' in the original hypothetical might conceivably be *given* this meaning, it certainly does not already have it. For, as I shall show later, 'He can if he chooses' is used to convey the information that the agent's choosing would close the gap between the existing situation and his performance. It goes as far as, and no farther than, an ordinary ascription of ability and

4. R. Chisholm emphasises this possibility in a different context in his review of *Philosophical Papers*, *Mind* 1964, part of which is reprinted in B. Berofsky (ed.), *Free Will and Determinism*, New York, 1966.

opportunity. Naturally the more difficult part of the problem of freedom of the will is not touched by these defences of Austin's thesis that 'He can do it if he chooses' entails 'He can do it'.

There is another kind of case in which it is difficult to apply Austin's two tests, not because they give divergent results, but because neither of them seems to be applicable. An example of this kind would be the hypothetical 'This van can do 70 m.p.h. if it is unloaded'.[5] If this hypothetical is taken as a conditional ascription of the unconditional power to do 70 m.p.h., there is no difficulty. For, on that interpretation it clearly passes both the contrapositive test and the non-detachment test for conditionality. The difficulty arises if we take it as an unconditional ascription of the conditional power to do, if it is unloaded, 70 m.p.h. For, on this interpretation, the questions whether it entails its contrapositive or its detached consequent do not seem to arise.[6] This is because, when the hypothetical is construed in this way, the antecedent is used in the specification of the ascribed power, and so is no longer available to fill the grammatical role of governing the main verb which ascribes it. It is therefore impossible to write down the contrapositive of the ascription, and impossible to regard its affirmation as the affirmation of a detached consequent. So here is an example of a pseudo for which Austin's tests for conditionality cannot be set up. Yet it seems quite legitimate to interpret the hypothetical as a pseudo, unconditionally ascribing a conditional power. In fact I shall try to show later that, when the antecedent in a hypothetical ascribing a power or ability introduces a factor which contributes to specifying that power or ability, we nearly always have an option between the two interpretations, conditional and pseudo, and that we sometimes have a good reason for choosing the pseudo interpretation. In such a case the explanation of the lack of a contrapositive is simple: we have chosen to put the antecedent of the original hypothetical to another use. It is not that we are forced to give it another use,

5. M. R. Ayers discusses examples of this kind in *The Refutation of Determinism*, London, 1968, Ch. 5. Though my treatment of them differs from his, I agree with his idea that Austin's concept of a pseudo ought somehow to be applicable to this kind of example too.

6. This point was made by Richard Malpas in discussion.

because the hypothetical does not pass the contrapositive test: rather, we choose to give it another use, and so there is no contrapositive test.

This, of course, is not a case in which Austin's two tests give divergent results, but one in which it is difficult to apply his tests at all. If, gratuitously, we placed the antecedent 'If it is unloaded . . .' in front of the ascription of the conditional power 'It can do, if it is unloaded, 70', the two tests could be applied, and would give the same result. For this new hypothetical would not entail its contrapositive (we would not deduce that, if the van lacks the conditional power, it is loaded), and it would entail its detached consequent (we would deduce that it possesses the conditional power, whether or not it is unloaded: for unloading it does not give it the power to do, if unloaded, 70). But in fact it is gratuitous to write in the antecedent a second time, and it is better to say that this kind of pseudo does not fail Austin's tests for conditionality, but, rather, fails to qualify to take them. The explanation of this radical failure is simply our choice of interpretation.

There is, however, another way of looking at the pseudo interpretation of this hypothetical. Without writing in the antecedent a second time, we could say that someone who takes the hypothetical as a pseudo is simply interpreting it as not entailing its contrapositive. Having taken that decision, he then asks himself what he should do about the antecedent, and his solution to this problem is to construe it as qualifying the complementary verb 'do 70'. Now this explanation has a point. The understanding of the hypothetical does involve two stages, the realisation that the antecedent does not govern the main verb, and the realisation that it does govern the subordinate verb, and this explanation takes these two steps separately in this order, whereas the other explanation takes them in one stride. But though there is a point in the stepwise explanation, which would allow us to write down the contrapositive of the original hypothetical, it is unclear and confusing. For if we split the application of the tests into these two stages, we get an incoherent account of the tester's process of thought. For how can he deny that the hypothetical entails its contrapositive unless he has already attached the antecedent to the subordinate verb? And, if he has attached it to the subordinate verb, how can he write down the contrapositive of the unconditional ascription of the conditional power? So let us adhere to the other explanation, which takes the two stages in one stride, and so achieves a more realistic account of what the tester does in cases like these in which he exercises an option.

The application of Austin's tests to this example suggests the question whether the subordinate phrase 'do, if it is unloaded, 70' passes Austin's two tests, and so comes out as a subordinate conditional. Or do his two tests perhaps give divergent results for this subordinate phrase? But this question may be deferred for the moment. Meanwhile let us look at a case in which the application of his two tests to the main part of a hypothetical clearly produces divergent results.

Consider the following example, in which the hypothetical does not pass the contrapositive test for conditionality, but in which the antecedent does not add a further specification to the task. A chess player says 'I can resign if I choose'. Here there is no option, and we have to say that the hypothetical does not entail its contrapositive. But the antecedent certainly does not add a further specification to the task – resigning. For there are not two ways of resigning, by choice and not by choice, as there are, for some people, two ways of shedding tears.[7] If we take this hypothetical and negate both the antecedent and the consequent, we get: 'I cannot resign if I do not choose to'. This hypothetical too fails the contrapositive test, and again we do not have the alternative option of construing it as the conditional denial of an unconditional power. However, this is denied by Lehrer, who uses a similar example in his article 'An empirical disproof of determinism?', but construes it as a hypothetical which may be allowed to pass the contrapositive test for conditionality. I disagree with his treatment of such examples, and I shall explain why I disagree later. At present, it is sufficient to point out that, if a chess player said 'I can not resign if I do not choose to', he would certainly mean it as a hypothetical which failed the contrapositive test for conditionality. Admittedly, it would be an odd thing to say, because there is only one way of resigning, by choice – or, to put this in a way that connects it with the hypotheticals about the van,

7. Norman Dahl pointed out in discussion the importance of this difference between verbs of action in the investigation of the logic of pseudos.

the words, 'by choice' do not add a further specification to resigning, but designate something which is already included in the meaning of that verb. It follows that the chess player would have to be making an *a priori* statement about resigning. No doubt, this is odd, but, if he made the remark, he would certainly mean it in this way. But equally certainly it would not fail the non-detachment test for conditionality. For from the fact that he cannot resign without choosing to, it evidently does not follow that he cannot resign. So here is a case which exhibits a clear divergence between Austin's two tests.

This example introduces some very complex considerations, which I shall try to unravel later. We may wonder how Austin's two tests can possibly give divergent results for hypotheticals of any kind. But I want to defer the explanation of this phenomenon. It is enough for my present purpose that the phenomenon exists, and that Austin's two tests really do give divergent results with this kind of hypothetical. This ought to make us very cautious about the simultaneous use of the two tests, and from now on I shall use only the contrapositive test. A hypothetical is a pseudo if and only if it fails the contrapositive test for conditionality. Some pseudos entail their detached consequents, while others do not – a difference which needs to be explained.

The antecedent in a pseudo does not govern the main verb. So perhaps in some cases it governs the subordinate verb.[8] For example, in the pseudo 'I can pay you tomorrow if I choose', since the antecedent does not govern the main verb 'can', perhaps it governs the subordinate verb 'pay'. This is a grammatical possibility. But it is closely linked with the semantic possibility that the antecedent in a pseudo combines with the subordinate verb to form a subordinate conditional – i.e. a conditional which somehow falls within the scope of the main verb. Such a suggestion is not unfamiliar. It is natural to treat 'It is possible that . . .' as an operator followed by brackets which sometimes contain a molecular proposition, and the suggestion that is here being put forward amounts to extending this treatment to ascriptions of power or ability. The difficulty is to see

8. As far as I know, this suggestion about pseudos in which 'can' is the main verb was first made by Don Locke in 'Ifs and cans revisited', *Philosophy*, 1962. Cf. Ayers, *The Refutation of Determinism*, p. 101.

exactly how such ascriptions would then be understood.

A clear case of a hypothetical with this structure would be the expression of a conditional intention – e.g. 'I intend to pay him if he asks me', which evidently means that I intend to, if he asks me, pay him. But is 'I can' amenable to this treatment? The fact that 'it is possible that . . .' may be treated as an operator might encourage us to treat 'I can' as an operator too. But it is notorious that the general claim 'I can do it' does not mean the same as 'It is possible that I should do it'. So, if the suggestion is going to work, some account must be given of the special semantics of conditionals subordinated to the main verb 'can' in pseudos ascribing powers or abilities.

It seems to me to be easier to give such an account for hypotheticals like 'This van can do 70 if it is unloaded' than it is for hypotheticals like 'I can pay you tomorrow if I choose'. So I shall begin with hypotheticals of the first of these two types.

'This van can do 70 if it is unloaded.' I pointed out earlier that we have an option between the two interpretations of this hypothetical: we can take it either as a conditional or as a pseudo. This option is explicable. For the hypothetical gives a general specification of what the van can do, and the antecedent contributes something important to the specification. Consequently we may read it in either of two ways: either as a conditional saying that lack of a load would give the van the unconditional power to do 70, or as a pseudo saying that it unconditionally has the power to do 70 without a load. Let me call lack of a load a 'performance-specifying factor' or 'S-factor' for short. Then an S-factor, introduced in the antecedent of a hypothetical ascribing a power or ability to a thing or person, may be regarded in either of two ways: either as something that pushes the power up to the level of a completely specified task – in this example, doing 70 – or as something that pulls the task down within reach of the power – i.e. pulls it down because the speaker adds it as a further specification which makes it easier – in this example, the task is then finally specified as doing 70 unloaded.

There are three features of this explanation which ought to be emphasised. First, the antecedent is always taken as offering a sufficient condition – of the power going up, on the conditional interpretation, and of the task coming down, on the pseudo interpretation. The word 'if' sometimes conversationally implicates[9] 'and only if'. But that is a complication which it would take too long to investigate.

Secondly, not all S-factors make the task easier. Lack of a load happens to be a facilitating S-factor. But presence of a load is an impeding S-factor. So the hypothetical 'This van can do 70 if it is loaded' needs a more elaborate explanation. The word 'if' in this case means 'even if', and so, when the hypothetical is taken as a pseudo, its point is that the load does not push the task up beyond the reach of the van's power – i.e. that it does not push it up out of reach although the speaker adds the fact that it is loaded as a further specification which makes it more difficult. But this too is a complication which lies off my route.

Thirdly, when the word 'if' does not mean 'even if', the S-factor need not be exactly facilitating. Facilitation is a matter of degree, and is often associated with a scale. But an S-factor might involve a difference of kind, which pushed the task over a sharp edge into the domain of feasibility.

My aim in this section is to show that, when the hypothetical 'This van can do 70 if it is unloaded' is taken as a pseudo, it contains a subordinate conditional: i.e. I hope to show that, on this interpretation, the antecedent governs the subordinate verb 'do 70', and that this grammatical partnership expresses an ordinary conditional connection between the S-factor mentioned in the antecedent and the action of the subordinate verb. If this is right, the only unusual feature of the example will be that the conditional is a subordinate one, falling within the scope of the main verb 'can'. Since I am using the contrapositive test for conditionality, it follows that, in order to establish this point, I shall have to demonstrate that the original sentence entails another which is derived from it by contraposing the subordinate phrase 'do, if it is unloaded, 70'. As I remarked at the beginning, we do not need to be prejudiced in favour of this theory. Its merit is its explanatory power, if it fits·

But before I develop this theory, more needs to be said about the option between the conditional and pseudo interpretations

9. See Paul Grice, 'The causal theory of perception', *Proceedings of the Aristotelian Society*, Supp. Vol. XXXV, 1961, pp. 126–32 for an early sketch of his theory.

of the hypothetical 'This van can do 70 if it is unloaded'. The option is puzzling, because it is not clear exactly what is at stake. It is evident that the truth-conditions of the hypothetical will be the same, whichever way it is taken. So the difference between the two interpretations can only be a difference between two ways of looking at the same facts – either as the conditional possession of an unconditional power, or as the unconditional possession of a conditional power.

But on what does the option depend? If I am right, it is open to us when and only when the factor introduced in the antecedent is an S-factor, like lack of a load. Choosing, on the other hand, is usually not an S-factor. In fact, choosing cannot be an S-factor when it is choosing to perform an action which is specified in a way that implies that it is a full human action, like paying a debt or resigning at chess. So choosing is not an S-factor in the hypothetical 'I can resign if I choose'. Consequently we do not have the option of treating this hypothetical as a conditional. It simply cannot mean that my choosing would push my ability up to the level of the specified task,[10] and so we are forced to take it as a pseudo. Moreover, when it is taken as a pseudo, it will not mean that my choosing, added as a further specificatory factor, would pull the task down within reach of my ability. When choosing is not an S-factor, as it is not in these cases, we are forced not only to adopt the pseudo interpretation, but also to understand the pseudo in a different way, which I shall try to explain later.

Choosing, if it is choosing to perform an action specified in a way that implies that it is a full human action, is not the only example of a factor that is not an S-factor, when it is introduced in the antecedent of a hypothetical which has 'can' as the main verb of its consequent. Another example would be wanting, as it occurs in 'I can pay you tomorrow if I want to'. The verbs 'can' and 'be able' need not occur in such sentences: for instance, neither of these two verbs occurs in the sentence 'He was clever enough to have been a doctor if he had wanted to be one', and yet it has the same structure. In these last two examples, it is, of course, conceivable that wanting is being put forward as an S-factor which would increase, or would have increased, the

10. See Part II for the discussion of Lehrer's view that it might have this meaning.

agent's ability. But it is much more likely that it is not being put forward as an S-factor, and so that the two hypotheticals are meant as pseudos to be understood in a way that will be explained later. I hope to show eventually that the contrast between S-factors and non-S-factors is closely connected both with the distinction between conditionals and pseudos and with certain problems in the dispositional analysis of ascriptions of power and ability.

It is evident that the application of the term 'S-factor' is relative to the kind of verb which designates the performance. It is also relative to the nature of the subject to which the power or ability is ascribed. Suppose, for example, that my car is a Morris Minor and I say 'It could do 150 if it were an E-type Jaguar'. Then, although being an E-type Jaguar makes that performance feasible, it cannot be classified as an S-factor. For the power to do 150 if it is an E-type Jaguar is a power whose specification involves a change of identity in the subject to which it is, as a matter of fact, being ascribed. If the antecedent were fulfilled, we would not say that my car had been changed into an E-type Jaguar; we would say, rather, that I had exchanged my car for an E-type Jaguar. So here we have an example of a factor which is similar to an S-factor – unlike choosing, which in the case specified above is quite dissimilar – but which is just beyond the limit of that classification.

But, to return to the option between the two interpretations of a single hypothetical, what is at stake? In cases which leave the option open to us, what inclines us to one interpretation rather than to the other? I do not want to answer this question in detail, because it lies off my route. It is evident that in general the choice is governed by two considerations, the kind of subject to which the power or ability is being ascribed, and the context of the ascription. Suppose, for example, that a salesman says 'This car can do 120 if it is filled with high-octane petrol'. This statement, in this context, would naturally be taken as an unconditional ascription of a conditional power. On the other hand, if he said 'This car can do 120 if its compression ratio is increased', this would naturally be taken in the other way, because the conversion of an engine is a big alteration to a car. However, in certain contexts, even this statement could be taken as an unconditional ascription of a conditional power –

e.g. in a conversation between two mechanics. As we have seen, the absolute limit to the possibility of this interpretation has been passed when the fulfilment of the antecedent would change the identity of the subject. Probably we ought to move this limit one step further inwards, and insist that the fulfilment of the antecedent should leave some basic determinant properties of the subject unchanged: e.g. in the conversation between the two mechanics the point is that the other properties of the car are such that it actually is capable of doing, if its compression ratio is changed, 120.[11]

Much more could be said about the option. But I must now develop the thesis that, when such hypotheticals are taken as pseudos, the antecedent governs the subordinate verb both grammatically and semantically, and that this partnership expresses a subordinate conditional.

I am not sure how important for my purpose it is to establish that the antecedent governs the subordinate verb grammatically, or how much can be done to establish this point without the support of a general grammatical theory. My thesis rests mainly on the plausibility of the semantic analysis which I am going to put forward. But there seems to be some fairly strong evidence to be collected from the grammar of these hypotheticals.

The first point to notice about their grammar is that the verbs 'can' and 'be able' belong to the class of auxiliary verbs which show some independence in their behaviour. For they are not used merely in order to form tenses and moods of other verbs. In the sentence 'He could have taken that trick if he had been leading'[12] the verb 'could' maintains a degree of indepen-

11. Ayers argues that our choice between the two interpretations follows the line dividing the subject's intrinsic properties from its extrinsic properties (*The Refutation of Determinism*, Ch. 5). But context also seems to exert an influence, and even, in some cases, to help us to answer the question, which properties of the subject should be treated as basic.

12. This sentence means that he had the capacity, and that if he had also had the opportunity nothing would have prevented him from taking the trick. But it could convey this message in either of two ways. Nowell-Smith suggests one of them in 'Ifs and cans' (*Theoria*, 1960, reprinted in Berofsky (ed.), *Free Will and Determinism*. See pp. 325–6): he takes the main verb to mean 'nothing would have prevented him', and then the hypothetical is inevitably interpreted as a conditional. However, if it is not contradictory to

dence, and does not lose its natural grammatical rights in slavery to the complementary verb 'take'. Of course it must have a complementary verb, and it is for this reason that it is classified as an auxiliary, but the relationship between it and its complement is on more equal terms than the relationship between the verbs 'will/would' and 'shall/should' and their complements. These verbs are usually slavish auxiliaries to their complements. E.g. in the sentence 'He would have taken that trick if he had been leading', the verb 'would' is totally used up in the task of forming a tense and mood of the complementary verb 'take'.

Although this is the usual lot of the verbs 'will/would', and 'shall/should', it is an interesting fact that they sometimes cast off their shackles and achieve the same degree of independence as the verbs 'can' and 'be able'. This certainly happens in emphatic statements of intention, like 'I will not pay that tax'. But even in this example we should not discount the possibility that an ordinary future tense statement is somehow implied. Austin argues that the verb 'would' achieves the higher degree of independence in the sentence 'X would have hanged him, but Y was against it'.[13] His idea is that the first part means that X actually wished to have hanged him. This may be an exaggeration of the force of the verb 'would' in this sentence, but there is no doubt that this element is an essential part of at least some statements of intention.[14]

It is an important fact that the verb 'can' always enjoys this degree of independence. For it makes it possible in certain cases

---

treat 'nothing prevented him' (i.e., 'all-in could') as an operator with a subordinate conditional in its scope – and I suppose that it is not contradictory – it would be possible to interpret the main verb as 'nothing prevented him', and the rest of the sentence as a subordinate conditional, 'from, if he had been leading, taking the trick'. The sentence would then be a pseudo. (This treatment depends, of course, on the validity of the theory of subordinate conditionals.) Austin interprets the sentence as a pseudo, but in a more natural way than this, because he takes the main verb to mean 'he had the capacity' (pp. 177–8). All these interpretations are viable, but Austin's needs some refinement, because he needs to explain the implication of the complementary phrase 'have taken'.

13. Austin, p. 168, footnote 2.

14. See Anscombe, *Intention*, passim, and Kenny, *Action, Emotion and Will*, Ch. 11.

for us to vary the moods of the main verb 'can' and of its complementary verb independently of one another, in order to convey a double message in an economical way. This can be illustrated by the previous example. The speaker wanted to convey two pieces of information in one hypothetical – that the player had the capacity to take the trick, and that he did not take it because he lacked the opportunity. The first piece of information is conveyed by the verb 'could', interpreted, as Austin interprets it, as a past indicative unconditionally ascribing a conditional capacity to the player (I am here following the pseudo interpretation of the hypothetical, although, as I said, it is not obligatory). The second piece of information is conveyed by the time-shifted perfect infinitive 'have taken' and the time-shifted quasi-subjunctive 'had been leading'.

If this account of the passing of the two pieces of information is going to work, it needs to be supplemented with an explanation of the function of the time-shift towards the past. The explanation is that in English it is possible to shift the tense of a verb one step backwards in time as a substitute for the true subjunctive mood. For example, we say 'If Hannibal had marched on Rome . . .' rather than 'If Hannibal marched on Rome . . .', and this is a way of implying that he did not march. The strength of this implication must not be exaggerated: sometimes we use the backward time-shift, like the true subjunctive mood, to express a lesser degree of remoteness from actuality – e.g. the case is problematical.[15] But whatever the exact strength of the implication, a time-shifted quasi-subjunctive when it is subordinated to a verb like 'can', automatically goes into the perfect infinitive. Thus we arrive at 'He could have taken that trick if he had been leading', and 'He was clever enough to have been a doctor, if he had wanted to be one'. In these cases the ability and cleverness are said to have been actual, but the implication, such as it is, of the perfect infinitives is that the performances were not actual. So the fact that the verb 'can' is an auxiliary with this degree of independence is a semantically important fact. It enables us in certain cases to vary the moods of the main verb and of its complement independently of one another, in order to convey a double message in an economical

15. See Chisholm, review of *Philosophical Papers*, in Berofsky (ed.), *Free Will and Determinism*, p. 343.

way. But it must be observed that 'could have' is not always analysable in this way. 'Could have' must mean 'would have been able to', when these hypotheticals are interpreted as conditionals, and sometimes they must be interpreted as conditionals (sometimes they cannot be, and sometimes there is an option).

The possibility of analysing the grammatical structure of these pseudos in this way provides some support for my thesis that they contain subordinate conditionals. But I am not sure how much support it provides. In any case, it is far more important for me to establish that a complementary verb-phrase like 'to, if it is unloaded, do 70' really does pass the contrapositive test for conditionality.

It seems that this phrase does pass the contrapositive test. For the hypothetical 'This van can do 70 if it is unloaded' gives the measure of the van's power, and, when it is taken as a pseudo, it does this by specifying the task in a way that is sufficient to bring it down within its reach. So on this interpretation it says that the van has a power such that the task, doing 70, if it is 70 without a load, is a task that it can do. Now this entails that the van has a power such that the task, doing 70, if it is a task that it cannot do, is 70 with a load. But in this entailed statement the hypothetical in the specificatory consecutive clause has simply been contraposed. Therefore, in this case the antecedent really does govern the subordinate verb, producing in this way a subordinate conditional. This result may be generalised to all hypotheticals which have 'can' or 'be able' as their main verbs and antecedents introducing S-factors. When a hypothetical of this kind is taken as a pseudo, the antecedent governs the complementary verb in the usual conditional way and this partnership may be bracketed to show that it falls within the scope of the operator 'X has a power such that . . .'. Such pseudos may be called 'integrated pseudos', because the antecedent is integrated into the structure of the sentence.

It is no objection to these paraphrases of integrated pseudos to point out that their main sentences contain the word 'power' and that their specificatory consecutive clauses contain the word 'can'. For the paraphrases are not intended to analyse ascriptions of power or ability. They are only intended to display the logical structure of those ascriptions that are pseudos. So it is no fault that each of them contains an occurrence – in fact, two correlative occurrences – of words in the 'can' family. This would be a fault only if they were intended as analyses.

However, it is necessary to say something about the meaning of the operator 'X has a power such that . . .'. It is, as I mentioned earlier, notorious that it means more than 'It is possible that X . . .'. For at least in cases of human agents and usable objects the ascription of a power, capacity or ability requires more than that its exercise should be consistent with all known facts and laws. Now it is plausible to suppose that the extra requirement is that there is some identifiable initiating factor (I-factor), given which and given opportunity, performance will ensue, or, at least, will ensue in a high enough proportion of cases. If this is right, the ascription will entail that, if this I-factor is present, then, given the opportunity, the performance will ensue, or at least that this will happen sufficiently often. Omitting the qualifications, we might say that *p* entails *If q then r*. This, of course, is the idea behind the attempt to analyse such ascriptions dispositionally. The attempt is not entirely successful, because it runs into difficulties more serious than the complications which have just been mentioned. *q* itself may be partly dispositional, and it may even entail *If p then r*. Moreover, the meaning of *p* may not be completely exhausted by its entailed hypothetical *If q then r*. In fact, if *q* does entail *If p then r*, it looks as if *p* and *q* will each require an attachment to the world that is independent of its entailed hypothetical. Nevertheless, it may still be true that *p* does entail *If q then r*.

If this is true, then the way to eliminate the word 'can' from the consecutive clause specifying the power of the van would be to insert a second antecedent introducing an appropriate I-factor: e.g. 'This van has a power such that the task, doing 70, if the task is doing 70 without a load, and if it is driven with the throttle fully open, is one which it will perform'. This more elaborate consecutive clause is at least part of the analysis of the ascription of the power to the van, because, given the opportunity, and allowing for an imperfect success-rate, it is entailed by it. But it is equally clear that this consecutive clause too passes the contrapositive test for conditionality. For the whole proposition now entails that this van has a power such that, if it does not do 70, then either the task is 70 with a load, or it is not being driven with the throttle fully open. Therefore, even when we change the consecutive clause to bring it closer to an analysis of the ascription of the power, it still passes the contrapositive test, and so the original hypothetical still contains a subordinate conditional.

Let me now pick up a question which I dropped earlier, the question whether Austin's two tests for conditionality sometimes give divergent results. I argued that, when they are applied to the hypothetical 'I cannot resign if I do not choose to', they inevitably give divergent results. Let us now ask whether they give divergent results when they are applied to the subordinate phrase in the hypothetical now under examination, 'do, if it is unloaded, 70 m.p.h.'.

It has just been shown that this subordinate phrase does entail its contrapositive. So the next question is: Does it entail its detached consequent? i.e. when the hypothetical is taken as a pseudo, unconditionally ascribing a conditional power, does it entail that the van can do 70? If it does, then the subordinate phrase will fail the non-detachment test for conditionality, in spite of passing the contrapositive test.

In fact, there is a strong case for saying that the original hypothetical, taken as a pseudo, does entail that the van can do 70. However, though the conclusion follows, and so, given the truth of the premise, must be true, it offers a misleadingly incomplete specification of the van's power. So we would never assert it in a context governed by a higher standard of completeness of specification. But the premise itself sets a higher standard. Therefore, we would never draw the conclusion unless we heavily emphasised the word 'can'. It seems, then, that though there is a strong case for saying that, when Austin's two tests are applied to the subordinate phrase in this hypothetical, they give divergent results, there is also something to be said on the other side.

It is, perhaps, worth while to look at the related example 'This van cannot do 70 if it is loaded'. When this hypothetical is taken as a pseudo, unconditionally denying a conditional power, its subordinate phrase passes the contrapositive test for conditionality. For if the van's power is such that the task, doing 70, if the task is 70 with a load, is one which it cannot perform, it follows that it is such that, the task, doing 70, if it is one which it can perform, is 70 without a load. But does the subordinate phrase pass the non-detachment test for conditionality? Unlike the subordinate phrase in the previous example, it passes it convincingly. For from the fact that it cannot do 70 when loaded, it does not follow that it cannot do 70. So the original hypothetical, taken as a pseudo, does not entail that the van cannot do 70, and in this case there is no need to bring in the context. Austin's two tests, applied to this subordinate phrase, give the same result in a straightforward way.

This lack of symmetry between the subordinate phrases in these last two examples can be explained. The explanation is that there is a disanalogy masked by an analogy. The analogy is that the positive hypothetical entails that there are some further specifications of the task, doing 70, which bring it within reach of the van's power; and, similarly, the negative hypothetical entails that there are some further specifications which push it out of reach of the van's power. So far the two cases are symmetrical, and we might suppose that in both cases the detached consequent of the subordinate phrase is entailed, and that in both cases the only odd thing about discarding the antecedent is the misleading omission of the further specifications of the task. But this would exaggerate the symmetry. For there is also an underlying disanalogy. Although the conclusion 'It can do 70' follows from the premise that there are circumstances in which it can do 70, the conclusion 'It cannot do 70' does not follow from the premise that there are circumstances in which it cannot do 70. For the statement that it cannot do 70 means that there are no circumstances in which it can do 70. The difference lies in the relationship between the two quantified corollaries of the original hypotheticals and the two conclusions that we draw when we discard the antecedents. In the positive case the conclusion does follow from the quantified corollary of the original hypothetical, but in the negative case it does not. So if we discard the antecedent in the positive hypothetical, and draw the conclusion, the only oddity is that the van's power is incompletely specified, whereas, if we discard the antecedent in the negative hypothetical, the conclusion is a *non sequitur*.

This explanation of the asymmetry between the positive and negative examples relies on the tacit assumption that to drive a van loaded and to drive it unloaded are both normal uses of it. For the range of values of the variable of further specifications of the task must be restricted in this way. In this case the two further specifications do fall within the restricted range, and so all is well.

It appears, then, that Austin's simultaneous use of his two tests for conditionality can be more or less vindicated in these cases, in spite of certain difficulties. But earlier we found an example in which it cannot be vindicated. For when the tests are applied to the hypothetical 'I cannot resign if I do not choose to', they clearly give divergent results – which is a surprising result. What is the explanation of the divergence in this outlying type of case?

First, it must be remembered that this hypothetical does not allow the tester an option between the two interpretations, conditional and pseudo. He writes down its contrapositive, finds that it is not entailed and draws the unavoidable conclusion that the hypothetical is not a conditional. The reason why he cannot avoid this conclusion is that choosing, in relation to resigning, is not an S-factor, but rather a logically necessary part of resigning.

Now, to develop a point that was made earlier, the stepwise account of the tester's process of thought is realistic in this case: i.e. first he finds that the hypothetical does not entail its contrapositive, and then he asks himself what he should do with the antecedent. The reason why this account is realistic in this case is that he is forced to interpret the hypothetical as a pseudo, whereas in cases which allow an option between the two interpretations, conditional and pseudo, the stepwise account is not realistic, because he has no reason to interpret the hypothetical as a pseudo unless he has already attached the antecedent to the subordinate verb.

When he asks himself what he should do with the antecedent of the hypothetical 'I cannot resign if I do not choose to', his solution may be to attach it to the subordinate verb, taking the pseudo as integrated. But, if he does take this line, he cannot interpret this pseudo exactly like the pseudo 'This van cannot do, if it is loaded, 70'. He may say that it means that my ability is such that the task, resigning, if it is not by choice, is a task that I cannot do, and that this entails that it is such that the task, resigning, if it is a task that I can do, is resigning by choice.

But he cannot treat this pseudo exactly like the pseudo about the van, because choosing in relation to resigning, is not an S-factor, and so this pseudo does not give the measure of my ability to resign, but, rather, offers an *a priori* truth about anybody's ability to resign. However, it does entail a statement in which the subordinate phrase has been contraposed. So though it does not entail its main contrapositive, it does entail its subordinate contrapositive.

This puts us in a position to explain the divergence of Austin's two tests in this case. They diverge, because the tester's unavoidable verdict is that the hypothetical fails the contrapositive test. He does not first choose to attach the antecedent to the subordinate verb, and then decide that the hypothetical is a pseudo which, like 'This van cannot do, if it is loaded, 70', does not really have a contrapositive or a detached consequent. At this stage he has to say that the detached consequent is 'I cannot resign', which is not entailed by the original hypothetical. Hence the divergence.

However, we can mitigate the paradox of this divergence by making two explanatory points. First, since choosing is a logically necessary part of resigning, it would be natural if the tester's first move were to attach the antecedent to the subordinate verb. Secondly, if he does make this attachment, Austin's two tests do give the same result for the subordinate phrase: we may replace it by its contrapositive, and we may not replace it by its detached consequent. So it seems that this queer case of divergence is produced by an unusual combination of circumstances. First, the hypothetical cannot be taken in a way that allows it to pass the contrapositive test. Secondly, in spite of this, there is a reason for immediately attaching the antecedent to the subordinate verb, and then applying both Austin's tests to the subordinate phrase. But thirdly, this reason is not very easy to perceive, because it involves the special relationship between resigning and choosing. What strikes us immediately is the failure to pass the contrapositive test, and then our course is set for the correct, but paradoxical conclusion that the two tests diverge in this case.

Integrated pseudos seem to be a fairly homogeneous class. But it is likely that non-integrated pseudos will exhibit more variety. Examples of non-integrated pseudos are 'There are biscuits on the sideboard if you want them', and 'He can run a mile in five minutes if you are interested'. In neither of these two cases does the antecedent govern the complementary verb – in the first case for the best possible reason, that there is no complementary verb. In both cases the antecedent is in some way attached to the passing of the message rather than to anything said in the message. Hence the lack of integration. But this explanation of the lack of integration is unlikely to work for all non-integrated pseudos. For example, Austin treats hypotheticals like 'I can pay you tomorrow if I choose' as non-integrated pseudos[16] and, though I shall attempt to show that in fact they are integrated, Austin may be right, and yet in such cases the antecedent is certainly not attached to the passing of the message as it is in 'He can run a mile in five minutes, if you are interested'.

I shall now try to show that the pseudo 'I can pay you tomorrow if I choose' is an integrated pseudo. But the attempt may not succeed. It must be remembered that the word 'if' need not always govern something inside the sentence. Sometimes, if it governs anything, what it governs will have to be supplied in thought. So there is no presumption that the integrated treatment must work.

Let me begin by asking what this pseudo means. I think that there is no doubt that it means, roughly, 'I can pay you tomorrow, and if I choose to I shall'. My not choosing is being put forward as the only thing that may stand between my unexercised ability and actual performance. To put this in another way, my choosing is being put forward as the only absent, or possibly absent necessary part of the total sufficient condition of performance. This implies that I shall have the opportunity, and so that there will be nothing to prevent me from paying you tomorrow. However, there is an important limitation on this last implication: as I argued earlier, this pseudo is used in such a way that it is non-committal about the possibility that I may be unable to bring myself to pay you tomorrow. The implication is only that, apart from this possibility – i.e. so far as ordinary ability and opportunity go – I can ('all-in') pay you tomorrow. In this implication the word 'can' is not being expanded to its limit.

16. p. 160. He calls them 'loose-jointed'.

We may characterise the meaning of this pseudo more briefly by saying that my choosing is being put forward as the 'performance-gap' – a convenient abbreviation of the long phrase 'the only absent or possibly absent necessary part of the total sufficient condition of performance'. This way of characterising its meaning is really a combination of two of Austin's semi-paraphrases:

'I can; *quaere* do I choose to?'
and 'I can; I have only to choose to.'[17]

The concept of a performance-gap is a familiar one. It is used in such sentences as 'The plane will arrive on time if there is no fog'. The only unusual thing about the hypothetical 'I can pay you tomorrow if I choose' is that the performance-gap is here introduced in the antecedent of a pseudo. Hence the natural tendency to suggest the paraphrase 'I can pay you tomorrow, and, if I choose to, I shall', which restores the performance-gap to its usual position in the antecedent of a straightforward conditional mentioning performance in its consequent.

It might be objected that this natural paraphrase cannot be reconciled with the thesis that 'I can pay you tomorrow' entails, roughly, that, if I choose to pay you tomorrow, I shall. For, if this thesis is accepted, the paraphrase will contain a pointless redundance: first, it says that I can, and then, quite needlessly, it adds something which simply follows from 'I can'.

The way to find an answer to this objection is to look more closely at the suggested entailment. It is inexact to say that 'I can pay you tomorrow' entails that, if I choose to, I shall. We must allow for possible lack of opportunity, and for possible lapses. Here it is the opportunity that is important. For the pseudo 'I can pay you tomorrow if I choose' says what I can do tomorrow, and so carries an implication about my opportunity tomorrow. The implication is that I shall have the opportunity, and this implication is secured in the way already explained by the addition of the antecedent 'If I choose'. My choosing is put forward as the performance-gap, thus indicating that, so far as ordinary ability and opportunity go, there will be nothing to prevent me from paying you tomorrow. So the sentence 'I can

17. p. 160.

pay you tomorrow' does not entail 'If I choose to pay you tomorrow I shall' until the antecedent has been added. The antecedent fixes the strength of the implied claim, and it is only after this has been done that the sentence 'If I choose to pay you tomorrow I shall' is entailed. So the alleged redundancy disappears.

The appearance of redundancy was an illusion produced by imprecision about the strength of the implied claim. A general ascription of a capacity, like 'I can buy any painting in the world' does not entail that, if I choose to, I shall. It is necessary to be more precise and to say that, if anything, it entails that if I choose to, and if I have the opportunity, I shall. On the other hand, 'I can pay you tomorrow if I choose' really does entail that 'If I choose to, I shall'. But this is only because the antecedent 'if I choose' has been added to 'I can pay you tomorrow', thus producing a pseudo strong enough to carry the entailment.

Some confirmation of this account of the meaning of 'I can if I choose' may be found in conversational usage. A asks B 'Can you be there at 5.00 tomorrow?', and B answers 'I can' – an answer which undoubtedly conveys the message that he will be there. But how is the message conveyed? One explanation is that here the verb 'can' has a secondary meaning, 'manage' or 'succeed', with no hint of mere potentiality.[18] But the objections to this explanation might well lead us to try to apply Grice's theory of conversational implicature to B's answer. We shall then get an explanation of this conversational phenomenon which connects it with the account just given of the pseudo 'I can pay you tomorrow if I choose', and so provides some confirmation of that account. For in a context in which B knows that A wants to discover whether he will do a particular thing, and in which A knows that B knows that A wants to discover this, A may merely ask whether B can do that thing, because B will be under an obligation to mention any performance-gap of which he is aware. So when B merely replies 'I can', A is justified in taking him to imply that he is not aware of any performance-gap. If B had regarded his choosing to be there as an absent or possibly absent necessary part of the total suffici-

18. This explanation is adopted by A. M. Honore in 'Can and can't', *Mind*, 1964, and by I. Thalberg in 'Austin on Abilities' in *Symposium on J. L. Austin*, ed. K. T. Fann, London, 1969.

ent condition of performance, then he ought to have added '. . . if I choose'. So the message that B will be there at 5:00 is conveyed as a conversational implicature governed by the general rule that information of the kind that is being sought should be maximised. This rule will not apply in every context, but only in the kind of context that has been specified. It is not necessary to add 'if I choose' to 'I can' in all cases in which my choosing is in fact the performance-gap, any more than it is always necessary to add 'if there were a cat around' to 'There is just enough room to swing a cat' (Groucho Marx's example). In the context specified above, the theory of conversational implicature seems to provide a better explanation of the message that B will be there than the theory that the verb 'can' has its alleged secondary meaning. But the generalisation of the theory of conversational implicature to all other cases of this phenomenon presents considerable difficulties.

It is one thing to observe that the performance-gap is introduced in an unusual position when it is mentioned in the subordinate phrase 'pay you tomorrow if I choose'; it is quite another thing to establish that this phrase really is a subordinate conditional. If this could be established, it would introduce some heterogeneity into the class of integrated pseudos. For in the present case the specificatory consecutive clause is 'such that, if I choose to pay you tomorrow, I *shall*', whereas in the case examined earlier it was 'such that the task, doing 70, if the task is 70 without a load, is one which it *can* perform'. But can the theory of subordinate conditionals be extended to the present case?

Now there is no difficulty in showing that the sentence 'My capacity is such that, if I choose to pay you tomorrow, I shall' entails the sentence 'My capacity is such that, if I do not pay you tomorrow, I shall not have chosen to', in which the subordinate conditional has been contraposed. The difficult thing is to explain how, if at all, this subordinate conditional falls within the scope of the main verb 'can' in the original pseudo. Austin may have been right to treat it as a non-integrated pseudo.

The difficulty is connected with the difference between the consequents in the two consecutive clauses. It is all very well to say that the verbs in the two consequents are different –

'shall pay' in the present case, and 'can perform' in the earlier case – and to observe that this difference would introduce some heterogeneity into the class of integrated pseudos. But is there not a fundamental difficulty here? For if 'I can pay you tomorrow if I choose' entails 'If I choose to pay you tomorrow, I shall', then 'I can pay you tomorrow' ought to entail 'I shall pay you tomorrow'. But 'I can pay you tomorrow' obviously does not entail 'I shall pay you tomorrow'. It carries this implication only as a conversational implicature in a special kind of context.[19]

The solution to this problem seems to lie in the peculiar function of the antecedent 'if I choose' in the pseudo 'I can pay you tomorrow if I choose'. Its function here is to fix the strength of the implied claim about what will be open to me tomorrow. 'I can pay you tomorrow' without the addition of this antecedent does not entail, even roughly, 'If I choose to pay you tomorrow, I shall'. It is only when the antecedent has been added that it carries the entailment. But from this it does not follow that you can remove the antecedent 'If I choose' both from the entailing statement, 'I can', and from the entailed statement 'I shall', as is done by the objector. For the function of the antecedent on the left-hand side of the entailment sign is quite different from its function on the right-hand side of it. On the left-hand side it is the antecedent of a pseudo, and its function is to fix the strength of the implied claim about what will be open to me tomorrow. But on the right-hand side it is the antecedent of a conditional, and its function is to give the sufficient condition of performance. Therefore the theory that 'I can if I choose' is an integrated pseudo is not open to the objection that in that case 'I can pay you tomorrow' would entail 'I shall pay you tomorrow'.

There might still be a complaint that the lack of homogeneity in the class of integrated pseudos is a weakness in the theory.[20] But there is no presumption that the verbs in the consequents of the two consecutive clauses ought to be the same. Moreover, the theory is capable of explaining the fact that they are different. So there is nothing arbitrary about the suggestion that

19. This difficulty was pointed out by Paul Grice in discussion.

20. A simpler theory would be preferable, if it fitted all the facts. But I cannot think of one.

'This van can do 70 if it is unloaded' should be paraphrased as 'This van has a power such that the task, doing 70, if the task is doing 70 without a load, is one which it can perform', whereas 'I can pay you tomorrow if I choose' should be paraphrased as 'My capacity is such that, if I choose to pay you tomorrow, I shall'. The explanation of this difference is that the first pseudo is a general ascription of power to the van, which, therefore, introduces an S-factor in its antecedent, but no I-factor: whereas the second pseudo does not put any limitation on my capacity to pay you tomorrow, but, on the contrary, assesses it as high enough to match tomorrow's opportunity, and, therefore, introduces an I-factor in its antecedent, but no S-factor. As I pointed out earlier, it is possible to rewrite the first paraphrase as 'This van has a power such that the task, doing 70, if the task is doing 70 without a load, and if it is driven with the throttle fully open, is one which it will perform'. This exhibits the relationship between the two species of integrated pseudo, but, naturally, it does not remove the differences between them.

It might still be objected that choosing is not really an I-factor, like depressing the accelerator of a van. But the answer to this objection is that the dissimilarities do not affect the similarity which justifies the classification of both as I-factors. Certainly, choosing is not always, or even typically, an event that is separate from the action. But the thesis that it is an I-factor does not require that it should be. It only requires that, if the claim implied by 'I can' is that, as far as ordinary ability and opportunity go, there is nothing to prevent me, then 'I can' entails, roughly, 'If I choose to, I shall' ('roughly', because there is many a slip between choosing and doing: strictly speaking, what is entailed is only a probability statement). So there is no implication about the categorisation of choosing, which may even be in many cases a sort of adverbial qualification of the action itself. In general, the classification of factors as I or S is correlated with, and only with, the semantics of the hypotheticals in whose antecedents they are introduced.[21]

I would conclude that 'I can pay you tomorrow if I choose' is an integrated pseudo, introducing an I-factor in its antecedent, and thereby implying that this I-factor is the performance-

21. This general thesis runs up against some difficult cases, which will be discussed in Part II.

gap. This would not be an isolated suggestion about 'I can if I choose'. It could be generalised to apply to cases in which the performance-gap is not an I-factor, but a stimulus linked to an I-factor: e.g. 'This rocket is programmed to shut down its engines if it reaches 90,000 feet', or 'He is prepared to hit you if you insult him'.

However, it must be observed that the pseudo 'I can pay you tomorrow if I choose' might introduce an I-factor in its antecedent, thereby implying that this I-factor is the performance-gap, *without* being integrated; i.e. if Austin's view about its structure were correct, the remainder of my account would still apply to it. In that case, I could still claim that the antecedent governs the supplied consequent 'I shall'. But since this consequent is not in the sentence, there would be another alternative available – to interpret the 'if' as a wholly non-conditional 'if'. I shall not investigate this last alternative. The drive behind Part I of this paper has been the desire to extend the unified theory of conditional 'if' as far as possible. If it has been extended too far, that will not affect my classification of factors as I and S, or the correlation of this classification with the semantics of the hypotheticals in which they are introduced. The only difference will be that, because 'I can if I choose' will be interpreted as a non-integrated pseudo containing a non-conditional 'if', a different account will have to be given of the way in which my choosing is introduced as the performance-gap. It is in fact difficult to see how this different account would go. Yet it seems certain that my choosing is introduced as the performance-gap. Perhaps this provides additional confirmation that, even if 'I can if I choose' is a non-integrated pseudo, the 'if' in it is still a conditional 'if'.

Part II

The dispositional analysis of sentences ascribing powers and abilities to things and people runs into many difficulties. The situation is especially complex and confusing when such ascriptions are brought to bear on particular occasions, and carry some implication about the opportunities available on those occasions. Some of these difficulties are produced by superficial confusions, but I shall concentrate on those that beset any version of the dispositional analysis. Three difficultie will be examined, one presented by Lehrer, and two by Austin.

Lehrer presents his difficulty as a refutation of Moore's dispositional analysis of 'X could have acted otherwise', which was 'If X had chosen, he would have acted otherwise'.[1] I shall introduce his objection by relating it to the distinctions drawn in Part I. Expressed in my terminology, his point is that Moore's analysis presupposes that choosing is not an S-factor, and yet it might conceivably be an S-factor. From this he deduces that it might conceivably be the case that, since X did not choose to act otherwise (this is implied by the *analysandum*), he could not have acted otherwise, in spite of the truth of Moore's *analysans*, that, if he had so chosen, he would have acted otherwise. For if choosing were an S-factor, it could be regarded as a necessary condition of X's ability to act otherwise: i.e. it would be possible to interpret the hypothetical 'X could not have acted otherwise unless he had chosen to' as a conditional. Lehrer's conclusion is that Moore's analysis should be rejected, because the *analysandum* might conceivably be false in spite of the truth of the *analysans*.

This objection may be expressed in the symbolism introduced in Part I. It is an objection to the thesis that *If q then r* entails *p*. Now there may be other objections to this thesis, but for the time being I shall concentrate on this one. Bruce Aune has shown[2] that it is related to a much more widely used objection to Moore's analysis.[3] According to Lehrer's argument, the following triad is consistent:

(1) Moore's *analysans*.
(2) 'X could not have acted otherwise unless he had chosen to' (interpreted counter-intuitively as a conditional).
(3) 'X did not choose to act otherwise.'

According to the more widely used argument, the following triad is consistent:

1. 'An empirical proof of determinism?'.
2. 'Hypotheticals and can, another look', *Analysis*, 1968. See also Lehrer's rejoinder, 'Cans without ifs', and Aune's 'Reply to Lehrer', both in *Analysis*, 1970.
3. See Chisholm, review of *Philosophical Papers*.

(1) Moore's *analysans*.
(2) 'X could not have acted otherwise unless he could have chosen (brought himself) to act otherwise.'
(3) 'X could not have chosen (brought himself) to act otherwise.'

The objection based on the consistency of the second triad was discussed briefly in Part I. It is, of course, connected with the more difficult part of the problem of determinism. It certainly points toward something important, but it does not refute Moore's analysis of ascriptions of ordinary ability and opportunity. The objection based on the consistency of the first triad will now be examined.

But first it is necessary to say something more about the distinction between S-factors and I-factors, because this distinction is relevant to the disagreement between Lehrer and Moore. It was presented in Part I as if it could never happen that a single factor could ever belong to both types. But that was only because simple examples were being used in order to get the distinction demarcated, and its general connection with the distinction between conditionals and pseudos established. So nearly all the factors considered were either S or I but not both. However, there are cases in which the factors introduced in the antecedents of hypotheticals, which have 'can' as the main verb of their consequents, fall under both concepts, I and S. These cases must now be examined, because the theory put forward in Part I ought to be capable of explaining them too, and because they throw some light on the disagreement between Lehrer and Moore.

One case of a factor which is both I and S was mentioned in Part I – the rather unusual case in which choosing is introduced as an S-factor after 'I can . . .', because the complementary verb leaves it open whether the action is to be done by choice or not. The example was 'I can shed tears if I choose', which was contrasted with 'I can resign if I choose'. In the first of these two cases, choosing might be an S-factor – for example the hypothetical might be uttered by an actor who might happen to be unable to shed tears naturally. In the second case, choosing is not an S-factor, because it is already included in the concept of resigning, and so cannot be meant as a further specification of that performance. The point that needs to be added now is that in the first case, in which choosing is an S-factor, it will still retain its usual I character. It will therefore be an I-and-S-factor.

This may seem unacceptable for two distinct reasons. First, choosing in 'I can . . . if I choose' nearly always functions as a pure I-factor. Secondly, it might be thought that, if it did simultaneously function as an S-factor, it would have to be regarded as something which gave the agent the capacity by bringing about some change in him: but Moore was quite right when he assumed that we do not regard choosing in this way; therefore, choosing cannot ever function as an S-factor.

But neither of these two arguments destroys the suggestion that choosing is sometimes an I-and-S-factor. Against the first, it is enough to observe that the exceptional can happen, in this case explicably. The second argument is more interesting, but it is based on a mistaken assumption. For it is a mistake to assume that choosing could function as an S-factor only if it gave the agent the capacity by bringing about some change in him. It could equally well give him the capacity by 'bringing about some change' in the performance. In the example that is being considered, when the performance is shedding tears naturally, the actor lacks the capacity to shed them; but when it is shedding them by choice, he has the capacity to shed them. This difference may be described as 'a change in the performance', but perhaps it is better to characterise it, as I did in Part I, by saying that the S-factor, choosing, is added as a further specification of the performance. Cf. 'I could reach that book if it were two feet lower'.

There is, however, a more troublesome objection to the suggestion that choosing may sometimes be an I-and-S-factor. It might be admitted that it could function as an S-factor in the exceptional cases described, but denied that it could simultaneously function as an I-factor. For it might seem impossibly strained for a speaker to introduce it once only in the antecedent of a hypothetical in order to make the two, quite different, points, that it is enough to bring the task, shedding tears, down within reach of his capacity, and that it is the performance-gap. Moreover, if anyone did introduce it with these two functions, S and I, the theory that has been put forward here could not be applied to the hypothetical. For, according to that theory, the hypothetical 'I can shed tears if I choose', has to be interpreted as a pseudo when choosing is an I-factor, and may be interpreted as a conditional when it is an S-factor. So, when choosing is an I-and-S-factor, the theory could not be applied to the hypothetical without generating a contradiction.

But there seems to be a way of avoiding the contradiction without abandoning the theory. The paraphrase of 'I can if I choose' may be refined in order to accommodate this special case. Let us use the letters I and S as subscripts under the verbs in the antecedents of hypotheticals of this kind. Then the two functions of the factor introduced in the antecedent of 'I can if I choose' may be exhibited in the following, more elaborate paraphrase: 'If I choose_s I can . . .' (this part may be interpreted as a main conditional), '. . . shed tears if I choose_i' (this part must be interpreted as a subordinate conditional if this antecedent is integrated into the structure of the sentence).

Naturally, the verb 'choose' appears twice in this paraphrase, because it has the two different functions indicated by the two subscripts. This is perfectly all right. However, this feature of the paraphrase will remind us that the residue of the objection – that it would be intolerably strained for the speaker to introduce choosing once only in order to make the two distinct points – remains unanswered. Would it be intolerably strained?

Perhaps the best way to answer this question would be to look at some other, less unusual, examples. But, first, the following tentative conclusions may be drawn from the hypothetical about the actor.

(1) If choosing is already included in the meaning of the verb of action, it cannot be an S-factor, and must be a pure I-factor.
(2) When choosing is an S-factor, it still retains its I-character, and so may be introduced to make two points simultaneously – that it is sufficient to bring the task down within reach of the subject's power, and that it is the performance-gap.
(3) In such a case, if we focus on its S-function, we may construe the hypothetical as a conditional, but from this it does not follow that we must regard choosing_s as

something which gives the agent the capacity by bringing about a change in him.

Anyone who reads Lehrer's objection to Moore's analysis of 'X could have acted otherwise' will immediately be struck by the importance of the first of these three points. But this point alone is not a sufficient basis for an answer to Lehrer, because choosing is not always included in the meaning of the verb of action.

Let me now take up the question whether there are any parallel examples, less unusual than the hypothetical about the actor, in which the speaker introduces a factor once and once only with the two different functions, I and S. The verb 'try', which is, incidentally, a more effective I-factor, provides the most convincing examples. For this verb means, roughly, 'attempt', and sometimes includes the additional meaning 'make an effort'. So if someone says 'I can solve this problem if I try', he might mean that he could solve it if he made an effort (a real effort), and in that case the factor introduced in the antecedent would have the two distinct functions. The two messages would then be that an effort would be sufficient to bring the task down within reach of his ability, and that an effort is the performance-gap. The elaborate paraphrase, with the two subscripts I and S, under the verb-phrase 'make an effort', would exhibit the two functions of the factor that it designates. There is nothing mysterious about the message that making an effort_i is the performance-gap. The point is that for this agent it is the appropriate kind of attempt, because making an effort_s is needed as an additional specification of the task. The more usual case would be one in which attempting (without the extra qualification) could be put forward as a pure I-factor which is simply the performance-gap.

This example suggests a further development of the theory of factors. It is possible that in this case, when we focus on the S-function of making an effort, we should regard it as something which gives the agent the ability by bringing about a change in him.[4] If it is a fact that we could regard it in this way, it is an important fact. For it would provide us with an example of an ordinary pre-action verb (i.e. a verb like 'choose' or 'want',

4. This possibility was suggested by Philippa Foot in discussion.

taking the agent as subject) which produces two effects in the agent: first, it gives him the ability by bringing about a change in him, and then it activates this newly bestowed ability. The suggestion that making an effort might be regarded in this way, which goes beyond the thesis that it has an S-function (see point (3)), is obviously relevant to the disagreement between Lehrer and Moore.

Is the suggestion correct? It is difficult to answer this question, partly because the answer would need to be based on the neurophysiology of making an effort, which would presumably differ from case to case. But for my purpose it is sufficient to provide a general schema for answering it.[5] The general answer is that making an effort may be regarded as a factor which produces a capacity in a subject by bringing about a change in that subject, and which also activates that capacity. But if a single factor is to have these two functions, it must have two distinct aspects, each connected with one of the two functions in a way that, ideally, ought to be intelligible. Otherwise, when we attributed the two functions to the factor, we would, in effect, be postulating two capacities where there is really only an adequate basis for one. If the requirement is not met, there is only an adequate basis for the capacity to achieve performance A, and so what we ought to say is that, *so far as changes in the subject go*, the factor is only an I-factor which produces performance A. If we also regard it as an S-factor, we cannot regard it as an S-factor which gives the subject the capacity to do A by bringing about a change in him. If we claimed that this same factor, with no difference of aspect, is not only an I-factor but also an S-factor which gives him the capacity to do A by bringing about a change in him, we would be postulating a second capacity in the subject, the capacity to achieve the capacity to do A, without an adequate basis in fact or theory. That would be like maintaining that the space occupied, as we now say, by one material object, e.g. a table, is really occupied by two indiscernible tables. This would violate the principle of counting material objects, and similarly the attribution of a second capacity to the subject, when the requirement was not met, would violate the principle of counting capacities.

5. The argument that follows is a development of a suggestion made by George Myro in discussion.

It is, as I said, difficult to answer the question whether making an effort meets the requirement that it should have two distinct aspects. A case in which the requirement is clearly met is provided by the following mechanical example: someone manufactures a car in which the accelerator pedal starts the engine with the first part of its angular movement, and also continuously opens the throttle in the usual way. In this case the factor, depressing the pedal to a certain point, does meet the requirement, and so may be regarded both as an S-factor which gives the car a certain power by bringing about a change in it, and as an I-factor which activates this newly bestowed power.

It might be thought that the imposition of this requirement contradicts something that was said earlier. For in a hypothetical like 'I could reach that book if it were two feet lower', the factor introduced in the antecedent was said to be an S-factor, and so the hypothetical was said to be interpretable as a conditional, meaning that the S-factor would give me the ability to reach the book. But making an effort was also said to be something that the agent does, and so, presumably, like other actions, something that he is capable of doing. It seems to follow that making an effort might be regarded as something which gives him the capacity to solve the problem by bringing about a change in him, even if the requirement is not met. But the apparent contradiction vanishes if we distinguish between the statement that a factor is something that happens in a subject and the statement that, when it happens, it brings about a change in the subject and in this way gives him the capacity. It is indisputable that making an effort is a factor which may be characterised in the first of these two ways, and that is all that follows from what was said earlier. It is a debatable question whether it should also be characterised in the second way, and there is no contradiction in maintaining that an affirmative answer cannot be given to this question unless the requirement is met. But even if the requirement is not met, making an effort will still be an S-factor.

So it seems legitimate to add a fourth point to the previous three:

(4) When an S-factor is also an I-factor, it cannot be regarded as something which gives the subject a capacity

> by bringing about a change in the subject, unless the following requirement is met: the factor must have two distinguishable aspects, each connected, preferably in an intelligible way, with one of its two effects.

The theory of factors, with these additions and qualifications, may now be applied to Lehrer's objection to Moore's analysis of 'X could have done otherwise'.

Lehrer's objection is based on the suggestion that it might conceivably be true that X could not have acted otherwise unless he had chosen to. It is superficial, but worthwhile to make the point that this hypothetical is naturally taken as a pseudo, meaning that X could not have acted otherwise without choosing to; in which case, as was pointed out earlier, if acting otherwise is specified in a way that includes choosing in its meaning, it would be an understatement to say that the hypothetical might conceivably be true, because it would be true *a priori*. But, of course, Lehrer is suggesting that choosing might conceivably be an S-factor, and that the hypothetical might conceivably be a contingently true conditional.

One way of understanding this suggestion is the way that was appropriate to the hypothetical about the actor. i.e. we only need to suppose that acting otherwise is not specified in a way that includes choosing in its meaning, and then it is easy to accept the suggestion that choosing might be an S-factor, and that the hypothetical might be a contingently true conditional. Notice that the acceptance of this suggestion would not commit us to the counter-intuitive idea that choosing would be an S-factor which would give the agent the capacity by bringing about a change in him. However, again it is obvious that this is not Lehrer's interpretation of the hypothetical. For his objection to Moore's analysis is offered as an entirely general one, which is not confined to cases explicable in the special way appropriate to the hypothetical about the actor. He really is suggesting that, quite generally, choosing might be an S-factor, and – what is more – an S-factor which, by bringing about a change in the agent, produces in him, as nothing else does, the capacity to do A.

So his suggestion raises the question whether the requirement in point (4) is in fact met by choosing. But, before this question is tackled, it would be as well to take a broader look at his strategy, and at the obstacles to its success. His strategy is to argue that his hypothetical might conceivably be true in the way just specified at a moment when it was also true that X did not choose to act otherwise. It would follow that at that moment X could not have acted otherwise, in spite of the fact that Moore's *analysans* 'X would have acted otherwise if he had chosen to' might well be true.

One obstacle to the success of this strategy is that the hypotheticals 'I can resign if I choose to' and 'I cannot resign if I do not choose to' are not in fact used in this way. This obstacle is not made less formidable by its superficiality. For when Lehrer deduces from the second and third members of his triad that at that moment X could not have acted otherwise, a defender of Moore's analysis can reply with a dilemma: either this proposition does not have the same meaning as the negation of the *analysandum*, or else the two premises are not consistent with Moore's *analysans*, which is the first member of the triad.[6] The second horn of this dilemma is likely to provoke the dogged assertion that the triad really is consistent, and then this part of the controversy will have reached an impasse of the same tedious kind that Moore himself reached in one of his arguments with ethical naturalists in *Principia Ethica*. But the first horn of the dilemma needs closer scrutiny. What, if anything, is the difference between the meaning of the proposition which Lehrer deduces from the second and third members of his triad and the negation of Moore's *analysandum*?

To deny Moore's *analysandum* is to deny that X had the ability and opportunity to act otherwise. The proposition which Lehrer deduces from the second and third members of his triad seems at first sight to have precisely the same meaning as this denial. But, if Moore is right, the two propositions differ in meaning – indeed, according to him, they necessarily differ in meaning, if the triad is consistent (i.e. according to him, the first horn of the dilemma must be rejectable if its second horn is not rejectable). Moore takes this view because he retains the fundamental assumption which we all make in this matter – that choosing is a pure I-factor, or else, occasionally, not only

6. This reply is very effectively developed by Aune in his two criticisms of Lehrer, 'Hypotheticals and can, another look', and 'Reply to Lehrer'.

an I-factor, but also an S-factor, which, because it does not meet the requirement in point (4), cannot give the agent the capacity by bringing about a change in him. This is the rationale supporting his claim that his *analysans* entails his *analysandum*. Lehrer, on the other hand, is suggesting that our fundamental assumption may be mistaken, in which case, as we have seen, choosing would have to be an S-factor which met the requirement in point (4). This is the rationale supporting his counter-claim that Moore's *analysans* does not entail his *analysandum*. But, as Aune has shown,[7] Moore would not have to defend his analysis by arguing that the assumption which supports it could not conceivably be mistaken. The superficial point, that in fact we make the assumption and, on that basis, use the *analysandum* with the meaning that he ascribes to it, is a sufficient defence of his analysis. He only has to show that, against the background of things as they are – or, rather, as we assume that they are – we treat the hypothesis, that his *analysans* might be true, without the *analysandum* being true, as inconceivable. He does not carry the additional onus of proving that it is inconceivable that we should ever reject the assumption, and, as a result, treat the hypothesis as conceivable. No analysis *has* to be defended in that way.

This point may be reinforced by asking what characterisation of the agent would be projectable into the intervals between his choices, if our fundamental assumptions about choosing turned out to be mistaken. The answer which involves the smallest change in our conceptual scheme is that, instead of projecting the ability to do A, as Moore rightly claims that we do, we would start projecting the ability to achieve the ability to do A. For choosing would be regarded as a factor which gave the agent the ability to do A by bringing about a change in him (S-function), and then immediately activated it (I-function). Moore can hardly be criticised for not anticipating this new usage with his analysis.

In practice the change introduced by the new usage would be small. But from a theoretical standpoint, it would be large. For, as we have seen, the new conceptual scheme for choosing and ability would be viable only if choosing met the requirement in point (4) – that it be a factor with two distinguishable

7. ibid.

aspects, each connected, preferably in an intelligible way, with one of its two effects. It is not enough for the innovator to suggest that it might be a mistake to assume that choosing is either a pure I-factor or else occasionally not only an I-factor but also an S-factor which does not give the agent the ability to do A by bringing about a change in him. The innovator must add that it might be the case that choosing met the requirement in point (4).

Does choosing meet this requirement? This is a big question, and I do not see how it can be answered at present. For it seems to be a question which lies on the borderline of two incompletely explored fields, the conceptual analysis of pre-action verbs, like 'want', 'choose', and 'try', and their underlying neurophysiology.

But, whatever the answer to that question, it is clear that there are faults in the strategy of Lehrer's objection to Moore's analysis of 'X could have acted otherwise'. So I conclude that his objection to this particular thesis of the form '*If q then r* entails *p*' is invalid. Of course, it does not follow from this that there are no valid objections to theses of this form.

Austin, in fact, makes a suggestion which might be used as a basis for criticising theses of this form from a different angle. He is examining Nowell-Smith's version of the dispositional analysis of the general ascription of ability 'X can do A', which is 'If X has the opportunity to do A, and a preponderant motive for doing it, he will do it'.[8] Austin applies this to the example 'Smith can run a mile', and he observes that in this case, though it is true that *p* follows from *If q then r*, the antecedent *If q* is redundant, because *p* follows from *r* alone.[9] It is not clear how far he is prepared to generalise this suggestion, because he also remarks that there are good reasons for not saying that 'I can lift my finger' is directly verified when I proceed to lift it.[10] But

8. *Ethics* (Harmondsworth, 1952), Chs. 19 and 20.

9. p. 175.

10. p. 171, footnote. Thalberg argues that this footnote appears to contradict the passage on p. 175, and that the way to remove the contradiction is to observe that 'Smith will run a mile' entails 'Smith can run a mile' only because the verb 'can' here has its secondary meaning 'succeed', so that the two sentences mean the same ('Austin on abilities', pp. 182 ff.). But it is not clear what point Austin is making in the footnote, and there is an alternative to Thalberg's remedy. *(Footnote continued overleaf)*

in a case in which the suggestion is valid, it seems that it could be used as the basis of a new criticism of theses of the form '*If q then r* entails *p*'. For if *r* alone really does entail *p*, we could discard *If q*, or keep it and give *q* any value under the sun.

It seems that Austin's suggestion could also be used as a basis for criticising theories of the form '*p* entails *If q then r*'. Ayers puts it to this use in *The Refutation of Determinism.*[11] He argues that, if the entailment really did hold in this direction, then anything that was evidence for *p* would also be evidence for *If q then r.* But the truth of *r* alone is evidence for *p* without being evidence for *If q then r.* Therefore, *p* does not entail *If q then r.* He appears to use this argument quite generally, and not to mark any restriction on the validity of Austin's suggestion.

The two criticisms both use Austin's suggestion as a basis, and the second one is also based on the further assumption that *If q then r* is something more than a material implication. In fact, Austin does not develop the criticism of theses of the form '*If q then r* entails *p*'. But Ayers does develop the related criticism of theses of the form '*p* entails *If q then r*'. I shall now examine the basis that is common to both criticisms. I shall not give *q* the rather complex value that Nowell-Smith gives it, nor even the value 'he chooses', which I gave it earlier. For even when a person can do a thing, there is many a slip between the I-factors wanting and choosing and actual performance. I shall, therefore, give *q* the value 'he tries', so that the I-factor introduced by *If q* will be a more effective one. Also, in order to simplify

---

When Austin claims that *r* alone entails *p*, his claim can be defended without interpreting *p* as 'Smith succeeds in running a mile'. For Smith's running a mile proves that it is possible that he should run a mile, and, since running a mile involves trying to do something which is at least closely related to running a mile, it also proves that he has the capacity to run a mile, even though the truth of this last statement requires the truth of *q*. This is a characteristic of cases in which we do not commonly need to draw the distinction between doing A as the full action A, and doing A not as the full action A.

This explanation will be developed in what follows. Thalberg's explanation, that the verb 'can' here has its secondary meaning 'succeed', will not be discussed. It would need to be worked out in detail, and pitted against the rival theory that, when there is an implication of success, it can be explained as a conversational implicature.

11. pp. 125–35.

the discussion that follows, I shall assume that the opportunity is perfect. These tactical conventions will not affect the main issue in this controversy.

Is Austin's suggestion, that *r* alone entails *p*, correct? That seems to depend on the kind of performance that is in question. 'Smith can run a mile' really does seem to be entailed by 'Smith has just run a mile'. But, by way of contrast, suppose that *p* is 'X can hit a bull's-eye with a .22 rifle at 150 yards'. In this case it is easy to imagine situations in which *r* is true, *q* is false and *p* is not established. For example, X shuts his eyes and sweeps the rifle round in a series of random arcs, and while he is doing this squeezes the trigger, and hits the bull's-eye 150 yards away. This does not establish that he has the ability ascribed to him by *p*. It only establishes that it is possible that he (or anyone else) should hit a bull's-eye (or anything else) 150 yards away, because an object at that distance is within the range of a .22 rifle, and, if it is not behind cover, may be hit. What is lacking in this case is the truth of *q*: he was not trying to hit the bulls-eye.

It is true that in this case there would also be something else wrong with the claim that the truth of *r* established *p*. For, whatever counts as success, one success is usually not enough to support the ascription of a capacity or ability to a person.[12] But though this deficiency is important, it does not detract from the importance of the other deficiency that has just been noted in this way of trying to establish *p*. For suppose that we multiply the instances of the truth of *r* without the truth of *q*: i.e. X repeats his movements with his eyes shut again and again, and very often gets the same amazing result. We would then decide that more was being established than that it was merely possible to hit something at 150 yards with a .22 rifle. At the very least it would begin to look probable that the target assigned to X before he shut his eyes would be hit.

But this is not the only conclusion that could be drawn from these surprising facts. We might put forward the more ambitious hypothesis that X had a remarkable gift which made the usual fussy style of marksmanship unnecessary. This hypothesis could

12. Thalberg makes this point about rifle-shooting, and also the related point that different abilities require characteristically different success-rates ('Austin on abilities', pp. 187 ff.).

be tested in other places, and with other rifles, and it might be confirmed. If so, X would be credited with a new ability, the ability to hit targets without squinting down the sights of his rifle, and, when *p* was given this new value, it might seem that it really would be established by repeated instances of the truth of *r* without the truth of *q*.

However, this would be an illusion. It is, no doubt, likely that in the circumstances X would be credited with a new ability. But if this conclusion were drawn from the facts, his new technique – shutting his eyes and the rest – would have become for him another way of trying to hit the target. He would be like a person who begins by trying to predict future events in the usual inductive way, collecting and assessing evidence, but then discovers that what he sees in a crystal ball always happens later. Looking into a crystal ball would soon become for such a person another way of trying to predict future events. Similarly, X would have replaced the old technique of marksmanship with a new one. During the transition the antecedent *If q* may seem to drop out as irrelevant, but in fact, if *p* is going to remain the ascription of an ability, the old value of *q* must be replaced by a new one.

It hardly matters in this case whether we would think that we were also giving *p* a different value, or whether we would regard the ability ascribed to X after the transition as the same old ability based on a new technique. The important point is that we cannot expel the antecedent while *p* remains the ascription of an ability. This reveals the logical structure of ascriptions of abilities to persons. It was claimed in Part I that such an ascription means more than that the performance is consistent with all known facts and laws. For its truth requires that there should be an identifiable I-factor, given which (and given, as I am now assuming, the opportunity), the performance will ensue, or, at least, will ensue in a high enough proportion of cases. Some confirmation of this claim can be extracted from the present discussion. For I am arguing against a suggestion which serves as the basis of a criticism both of the thesis that *p* entails *If q then r*, and of the thesis that *If q then r* entails *p*. The suggestion is that the truth of *r* alone is sufficient to establish *p*. But this suggestion misleadingly discards the increment of meaning which is essential to ascriptions of abilities to people, because it distinguishes them not only from statements beginning 'It is possible that . . .' but also from statements beginning 'It is probable that . . .'. The increment contributed by the antecedent *If q* will be the requirement that there should be a definite technique, as in the present example, or else basic trying, as it would be if *p* were 'He can move his ears'. Naturally, this does not imply that there is no other characteristic difference between the meaning of an ascription of an ability to a person and the other two types of statement.

It is interesting to observe how the two deficiencies in the original method of establishing 'He can hit a bull's-eye with a .22 rifle at 150 yards' cooperate with one another. At first, when X had only done it once with his eyes shut, the evidence for ascribing the ability to him was inadequate in both ways: it was the wrong kind of instance, and it was only a single instance. So all that was established at this point was a statement beginning 'It is possible that . . .'. When the instances were multiplied with frequent success, the inference was a statement beginning 'It is probable that . . .'. At this point there was a choice in the telling of the story and the final conclusion would depend on what happened next – i.e. on the type of case in which experiment discovered a high rate of success. It might have turned out that it did not make any difference who spun the rifle, and that it was not even necessary that it should be spun by a person, but that it had to be that particular rifle. In that case a mysterious power would be ascribed to the rifle, and the ascription would entail a hypothetical mentioning a specific I-factor in its antecedent. But the story was developed in a way that was favourable to the ascription of an ability to X, and it emerged that it was essential to this development that X should come to regard his antics as a new technique for achieving the same performance, or, to put the point in a way that connects it with the theory of factors, that he should regard them as a new I-value for *q* in the hypothetical *If q then r*. In short, the ascription of an ability or power is an extract from the total situation – an extract which can be made only if the appropriate I-factor is there.

However, there are gaps in this account. Suppose that at the point where there was a choice in the development of the story, things had taken a different turn, and experiment had shown that X only needed to be near the rifle, and then, if it were spun or fired mechanically, the same score of bull's-eyes would be achieved. This seems to be a case in which we would not ascribe an ability to X, in spite of the fact that, if he placed himself near the rifle (verb of action), then given the opportunity (the mechanical rotation of the rifle), the bull's-eye would often be hit. What we would ascribe to X would be a usable power, based presumably on his physical properties.

It would be a lengthy business to explain this difference fully. The salient point seems to be that X would be using his body just like any other material object, so that it is unduly narrow to give *q* the value 'he places himself near the rifle', which is a verb of action. What we ought to say is that X's body has a certain power which manifests itself in the way specified provided that it is near the rifle (I-factor), and the rifle is rotated (opportunity). No doubt, this is a fantastic example, but it is easy to find everyday cases in which a power of this kind is ascribed to a person's body rather than an ability to the person. For example, an expert in acoustics might say that human bodies can absorb sound; or someone might say 'X can sink a canoe', meaning that he can sink one by the mere weight of his body.

In general, given facts structured as they are in this last development of the story, it is possible to ascribe either an ability to X, or to X's body the kind of physical power which is independent of the fact that X is a self-mover. Which of the two ascriptions we make will depend on the way in which X uses his body, if indeed he does use it. In the last case mentioned, if X did use his body to sink canoes, we might say that he sank them (verb of action), and we might also ascribe the corresponding ability to him. Evidently, the distinction between the proper evidence for an ascription of a power of this kind and the proper evidence for an ascription of an ability is not an exclusive distinction. A thorough investigation of it would lead far afield into the concepts of action, consequence and skill, and would require a long discussion of different possible theoretical backgrounds.

There is also another gap in my argument against the thesis that in this kind of case the truth of *r* alone is enough to establish *p*. For when *p* is 'Smith can run a mile', it seems that the truth of *r* alone really is enough to establish *p*. So I have to explain what marks off this kind of example from the last one. This gap too would take a long time to fill adequately, but I can make a start.

The salient point here seems to be that we do not commonly need to distinguish between running a mile as a full human action and running a mile not as a full human action. For the verb of action 'run a mile' nearly always includes trying to run a mile, or, at least, trying to do something that is closely related to running a mile (cf. the parallel point about resigning and choosing in Part I). So when Smith actually runs a mile, we do not need to stipulate, as something extra, that he must be trying to run a mile, before allowing that it has been established that he has the ability or capacity to run a mile. The truth of *r* in this case involves the truth of *q*. So Austin's original suggestion about this example needs to be taken with some scepticism. It is true that here the verification of *r* alone is enough to establish *p*. But it is misleading to express this truth in this way, and a plain *suggestio falsi* if the point of expressing it in this way is to eliminate the antecedent *If q*.

To put the same point in a different way, Smith may be lucky to run his mile, but his luck cannot be like the luck of a man who hits his target without even trying to hit it. On the rifle-range we do need to distinguish between hitting the target as a full human action and hitting it without even trying to hit it, and the second of these two performances does not support the ascription of an ability. But on the race-track we do not have to guard against the possibility of a performance of the second kind. For it is not possible for a runner to have the good luck to run a mile, when, for example, he thought that he was marking time, like a car with its engine running in neutral.

When this point was made earlier (p. 179 footnote 10), I said that the truth of *q* makes the difference between a case of the truth of *r* which supports 'X has the ability' and a case of the truth of *r* which only supports 'It is possible that X should . . .'. This is roughly correct, but it needs qualification in the light of the intervening discussion. For sometimes, when the truth of *q* is not required, what is established will be that X's body has a power of the kind that is independent of the fact that he is a self-mover rather than the non-ascriptive proposition that it is possible that X should . . . These seem to be cases in which Austin's suggestion is true, and not misleadingly expressed provided that it is only meant to exclude antecedents containing pre-action verbs like 'try'. But if it is also meant to exclude antecedents introducing other kinds of I-factor, then it is misleading. For powers like the power to sink a canoe by one's own weight involve factors which, though they are not designated by pre-action verbs like 'try', are none the less I. If we wish to find examples which do not involve I-factors, the best way to find them is to go all the way down to cases where the evidence only supports non-ascriptive statements of possibility. Perhaps there are also cases where the evidence supports non-ascriptive statements of probability but does not support any ascription of power or ability, but this is more doubtful.

It appears, then, that when p is an ascription of an ability, Austin's original suggestion, even when it is true, cannot be used as the basis of a criticism either of the thesis that p entails *If q then r* or of the thesis that *If q then r* entails p. A full development of the argument against these uses of it would involve a lengthy investigation of the concepts of ability and power. But perhaps two minor points may be added before this topic is left.

I have been arguing that, where p is the ascription of an ability to a person, the truth of r without the truth of q is not sufficient to establish p, and that this is not merely because one confirmatory instance is not enough, but also because it is the wrong kind of instance. This is not the same as saying that, in order to establish p, we need to establish that the truth of q is a necessary condition of the truth of r. That would be an absurd thing to say, because a person who has the ability to hit the bulls-eye at 150 yards with a .22 rifle may happen to do that very thing accidentally. As we have seen, an accidental performance is not enough to establish that he has the ability. But neither does it establish that he lacks the ability. To insist that the truth of r without the truth of q is not sufficient to establish p is not the same thing as requiring that the truth of q should be a necessary condition of the truth of r. In fact, the reason for insisting on the former point is precisely that in cases in which the I-factor introduced in *If q* is not included in the meaning of the verb of action, r may be true without q being true.

It might be objected that, though I am not saying that trying is a necessary condition of successful performance, I am saying that it is a necessary – in fact, a logically necessary – condition of the kind of successful performance that is required to support *p*, and this may seem to be incompatible with the thesis that it is a contingently sufficient condition of successful performance. But the appearance of incompatibility is an illusion. Someone might say that 'This is safety-glass' entails 'If it breaks, it breaks into tiny fragments'.[13]

As I said, Austin does not develop either of these two criticisms of Nowell-Smith's analysis of ascriptions of abilities to people. The criticism which he does develop is more damaging, but perhaps not so damaging as he takes it to be. It is developed in two closely related stages.[14] First, he points out that from the fact that *p* entails *If q then r*, it does not follow that *If q then r* entails *p*. Secondly, he argues that from the fact that, if *p* and *q* are true, then *r* must be true, we cannot infer that *p* simply means that, if *q* is true, *r* will be true. If this inference were valid, we could also argue that *q* simply means that, if *p* is true, *r* will be true. But when *p*, *q* and *r* are given the values that they have been given here, this is absurd. According to him, these are not two different stages in the development of his criticism, but simply two different ways of making the same point. But in fact we shall find that the second goes further than the first.

There are also some unimportant differences between the way in which he presents his criticism and the way in which it is being presented here. He mentions opportunity in his formula, but I have omitted it, on the assumption made earlier, that it is perfect. Also he gives *q* the value 'he has a preponderant motive', but I am giving it the value 'he tries', because trying is a more effective I-factor. These differences will simplify the discusssion of his criticism without affecting the main issue.

It can hardly be doubted that the point made in the first stage of his criticism is correct: the thesis, that *p* entails *If q then r*, does not entail its converse. It is, therefore, invalid to argue in this way for the dispositional analysis of ascriptions of abilities or powers. The truth of the premise of this argument

13. An example used by Ayers, *The Refutation of Determinism*, p. 134.
14. ibid., pp. 173–7.

would leave it an open possibility that such an ascription might mean more than *If q then r*.

Perhaps it would be helpful to fill in some more details. From the premise, that *p* entails *If q then r*, we really may infer that *q* entails *If p then r*. Austin does not mention this, because his concern is to point out that neither the premise of this inference nor its conclusion entails its converse. But it is worth mentioning, because it provides some confirmation for the view that in each case the dispositional formula on the right-hand side does give at least part of the meaning of the proposition on the left-hand side. For, after inferring that *q* entails *If p then r*, we may notice that, with the values already assigned, this conclusion seems to be true. It really does seem to be part of the meaning of 'He is trying to do A' that, if he has the ability, he will do A – or, at least, that he will do A in a sufficiently high proportion of cases in which his contribution to the outcome is the same.

Although the two converse statements do not follow from the direct statements, it is worth enquiring whether they are true. For if they were true, then, given the truth of the two direct statements, the dispositional formulae on the right hand side would be complete analyses of *p* and *q* respectively. Some philosophers have maintained that this is indeed the case with *p*, but they can hardly take the same line about *q*, because, as was observed in Part I, at least one of the two propositions, *p* or *q*, will need sufficient conditions independent of the dispositional formula. Otherwise both dispositional formulae will be unusable. For example, we might want to use them in order to establish that X lacked the ability to do A, because, though he often tried, he always failed; but we would be unable to establish that he often tried, if our only resource was the two-way dispositional formula that, if and only if he tries, then, if he has the ability, he will succeed. A single equation with two unknown quantities is insoluble. So at least one of the two propositions, *p* and *q*, needs an independent sufficient condition, and certainly *q* seems to have one. This feature of *q* allows us to establish *via* the truth of *q* that X has the ability to do A, and then on a particular occasion when we doubt his claim that he really is trying to do A, we may rely on the truth of *p* and use the formula '*q* entails *If p then r*'. But then this independent sufficient condition has a claim to be included in the meaning of *q* which is as strong as the claim of the dispositional formula. If there is also an independent sufficient condition of *p*, it too will have a claim to be included in the meaning of *p* which is as strong as the claim of the dispositional formula *If q then r*.

This argument, though largely convincing, leaves much unexplained. We need a detailed account of the breakdown of the two converse statements '*If p then r* entails *q*' and '*If q then r* entails *p*', if indeed they do break down. Certainly, they do not follow from the direct statements, but this does not show that they are incorrect. However, the first is in fact incorrect, for a reason that has already been discussed. X may have the ability to do A and yet do it accidentally, and then it need not be true that he tried to do A: i.e. *p* and *r* may be true without *q* being true.

The case against the converse statement, '*If q then r* entails *p*' is more complex. Two points have already been made in this area. First, because *p* ascribes an ability, which has temporal spread, its verification requires repeated instances of the truth of *q* and *r*. In this respect *p* is to be contrasted with *q*, which reports an event and obviously does not require any repetition of instances for its verification. Secondly, when *r* is true in a sufficiently high proportion of cases of the truth of *q*, that is enough to verify *p*. The second point now needs to be amplified and qualified. A lot was said about the fact that, for many values of *p*, instances of the truth of *r* that are favourable to the truth of *p* require the truth of *q*. But there was no discussion of the related question, whether the general statement 'Whenever X tries to do A he succeeds' (or an appropriate statistical general statement) actually entails *p*. It is one thing to say that a run of instances favourable to this general statement is enough to verify *p*, but quite another thing to say that the general statement entails *p*. Transference of verification is a less exacting relation than entailment.

The reason why a qualification needs to be added is that X might try to do A, and do A, in spite of the fact that his attempt was totally inadequate. In such a case, the explanation of his success would be luck: he was aided by some unforeseen and perhaps unforeseeable factor. Now this might conceivably happen often and, if it did, he might become superstitious, and we might mistakenly ascribe the ability to him. The existence of this possibility is enough to show that the general hypothetical does not entail *p*. It is also necessary that X's trying should really produce his successes. The theoretical background must be right. This requirement is easily forgotten, because in cases where the success is repeated again and again we naturally take it for granted that the theoretical background is right, perhaps without even knowing what it is, and so hold that *p* has been verified.

This is a perfectly reasonable attitude in practice, particularly when the sequence of successes has been so prolonged that the alternative hypothesis would be a fantastic coincidence, but it does not justify the thesis that the general hypothetical entails *p*. However, it might seem to justify the thesis that *p* is more dispositional than *q*. But this thesis needs to be treated with caution, and even with some scepticism. For the extra element that has to be added to the general dispositional formula in order to produce a proposition that really does entail *p* is important, and its claim to be included in the meaning of *p* really does seem to be as strong, or, at least, nearly as strong, as the claim of the dispositional factor to which it is added. Moreover, the addition will usually amount to more than the stipulation that X did not achieve his successes by luck. His own contribution, which we call 'trying', ought to be seen to produce his successes in an appropriately direct way. For example, it must not be the case that a demon always corrects his bungling attempts. But it is not enough that there should be no evidence that anything extraneous produced his successes. The extra requirement, in its most complete and satisfying form, will include an account of the structure of X and of the function of whatever is designated by the verb 'try' in the relevant instances.

It is easy to exaggerate this point in reaction against the excessive claims that have been made in the past for the dispositional analysis of ascriptions of powers and abilities to things and people. So it would be as well to cut it down to life-size. Although knowledge of the extra element is desirable, it is often lacking. We often simply do not know the theoretical basis of the performances, and yet in many cases of this kind we are justified in making the ascription. Moreover, in a case in which we can fill in the extra requirement, it will be an element in the meaning of p that is less important than the dispositional formula. For if the general hypothetical were repeatedly falsified in generously varied circumstances, it would simply be a mistake to maintain p on the ground that the subject satisfied the accepted theoretical requirement. In such a case we would reformulate the theoretical requirement because the dispositional formula always remains the dominant partner in this syndicate of meaning. So, though it would be an exaggeration to say that the dispositional formula entails p, it would be an even greater exaggeration to say that the other partner entails p. This, of course, raises the much discussed problem of multiple criteria. In what sense of 'sufficient' do we sometimes have a sufficient condition of p which is independent of the dispositional formula? This question needs to be answered by anyone who wants to assess the force of the earlier argument that either p or q needs an independent sufficient condition which will have as strong a claim to be included in its meaning as the claim of the dispositional formula. But I shall not attempt to answer it.

Let us look, finally, at the suggestion that q is less dispositional than p. There are several reasons for making this suggestion. First, it has already been pointed out that q entails the singular hypothetical *If p then r* – or rather, since this has to be qualified to allow for cases of fallible ability, that at least it entails that if p is true, then r will be true in a sufficiently high proportion of cases. Naturally, the generality in this necessary condition of q does not involve temporal spread, because X's trying is a single event, even if the ascription of power to this event entails a general hypothetical. Incidentally, this characterisation of trying presupposes that it is also characterised in another, non-dispositional, way. Otherwise it would be impossible to specify the cases in a high proportion of which r must be true. They must be specified as cases in which X's contribution to the outcome is the same again. However, the generality in the dispositional characterisation of trying does not involve temporal spread, and this seems to be one of the considerations supporting the idea that q is less dispositional than p. Another is that the converse thesis, that *If p then r* entails q, breaks down for the reason mentioned earlier, that, even if X has the ability to do A, he may do it accidentally.

This raises the same question about q that has just been

answered for *p*: what more has to be added to the dispositional formula in order to produce a proposition which entails *q*? Here two distinct but related extra elements are available: there is X's sincere report that he did try, and in certain cases there is physical evidence that he did try. If we lacked both these extra elements, we could not even bridge the gap between the verification of *If p then r* and the verification of *q*. So these are not merely desirable, but dispensable additions, like the extra element in the meaning of *p*. On the contrary, they are dominant partners in their syndicate of meaning, because they are sufficient to establish that X tried to do A even on those possibly rare occasions when he failed in spite of possessing the relevant ability. This is a third consideration supporting the idea that *q* is less dispositional than *p*.

These considerations show that in various ways it is more absurd to maintain that *If p then r* entails *q* than it is to maintain that *If q then r* entails *p*. So the second stage in Austin's criticism of Nowell-Smith, when its implications are worked out in detail, evidently does go beyond the first stage. He has produced an effective *reductio ad absurdum* of one way of arguing from the thesis that *p* entails *If q then r* to the converse thesis. However, if the question is whether the dispositional analysis is true, his argument is not so effective as he supposed. For, first, it only attacks the converse thesis, that *If q then r* entails *p*, leaving the direct form of the thesis unscathed. Secondly, it only undermines one argument for the converse thesis, leaving it an open question whether the converse thesis is true. Thirdly, the case for saying that the converse thesis that *If q then r* entails *p* is not true, is not nearly so strong as the case for saying that the converse thesis that *If p then r* entails *q* is not true. So Austin's criticism of the dispositional analysis of ascriptions of abilities to people is blunted by the very thing that makes his *reductio ad absurdum* of the argument that he attributes to Nowell-Smith so effective.

7 Hume's Empiricism and Modern Empiricism

In the *Enquiry concerning Human Understanding* Hume said:

> If we take in our hands any volume; of divinity or school metaphysics for instance; let us ask: *Does it contain any abstract reasoning concerning quantity or number?* No. *Does it contain any experimental reasoning concerning matter of fact or existence?* No. Commit it then to the flames, for it can contain nothing but sophistry and illusion.[1]

In *Language, Truth and Logic* Professor Ayer quoted this passage, and asked:

> What is this but a rhetorical version of our own thesis that a sentence that does not express either a formally true proposition or an empirical hypothesis is devoid of significance?[2]

Hume realised that his philosophy provided a criterion of significance. For in *An Abstract of a Treatise of Human Nature* he said about himself:

> When he (our author) suspects that any philosophical term has no idea annexed to it (as is too common), he always asks *from what impression that idea is derived?* And if no impression can be produced, he concludes that the term, is altogether insignificant.[3]

1. *Enquiry concerning Human Understanding*, § XII, pt. iii.
2. *Language, Truth and Logic*, 2nd ed., 1950, p. 54.
3. *An Abstract of a Book Lately Published, Entitled A Treatise of Human Nature* in *Hume: Theory of Knowledge*, ed. D. C. Yalden-Thomson, Edinburgh, 1951, p. 251. The *Abstract* is also included in the Fontana edition of *A Treatise of Human Nature*, Book 1, ed. D. G. C. MacNabb, London, 1962, p. 337.

This principle is closely related to the principle that Russell formulated in *The Problems of Philosophy*:

> Every proposition which we can understand must be composed wholly of constituents with which we are acquainted.[4]

Hume's system even contains a psychological version of logical atomism. For example, in the *Enquiry* he compares his kind of analysis to microscopy:

> Complex ideas may, perhaps, be well known by definition, which is nothing but an enumeration of those parts or simple ideas that compose them. But when we have pushed up definitions to the most simple ideas, and find still some ambiguity and obscurity; what resource are we then possessed of? By what invention can we throw light on these ideas, and render them altogether precise and determinate to our intellectual view? Produce the impressions or original sentiments from which the ideas are copied. These impressions are all strong and sensible. They admit not of ambiguity. They are not only placed in a full light themselves, but may throw light on their correspondent ideas, which lie in obscurity. And by this means, we may, perhaps, attain a new microscope or species of optics, by which, in the moral sciences, the most minute and most simple ideas may be so enlarged as to fall readily under our apprehension, and be equally known with the grossest and most sensible ideas that can be the object of our enquiry.[5]

Russell was thinking of a similar analogy when he said:

> The reason that I call my doctrine *logical* atomism is because the atoms that I wish to arrive at as the sort of last residue in analysis are logical atoms and not physical atoms. Some of them will be what I call 'particulars' – such things as little patches of colour or sounds, momentary things – and some of them will be predicates or relations

4. *The Problems of Philosophy*, 16th imp., 1936, p. 91.
5. *Enquiry concerning Human Understanding*, § VII, pt. i.

> and so on. The point is that the atom I wish to arrive at is the atom of logical analysis, not the atom of physical analysis . . . The process of sound philosophising, to my mind, consists mainly in passing from those obvious, vague, ambiguous things, that we feel quite sure of, to something precise, clear, definite, which by reflection and analysis we find is involved in the vague thing that we start from, and is, so to speak, the real truth of which that vague thing is a sort of shadow.[6]

These are striking similarities, and it would be easy to add to the list. But how deep is the affinity between Hume's empiricism and modern logical empiricism? Perhaps the most obvious difference is that the analysis practised by Hume was psychological or phenomenological, rather than logical. Consequently when he applied his theory of meaning to some difficult problem, like the idea of causal necessity, he searched his mind for an impression or set of impressions from which the idea could be derived. For he held that, if it were a genuine idea, it would either be derived directly from a single impression, which it copied, or else it would be built up by definition out of other ideas, each of which would itself have been derived from an impression. The result of his search in this case was that the idea is derived not from any sensory impression, but from an interior impression of inevitability. When someone makes a causal inference, he cannot help making it, since he is drawn along by the association of ideas. That, according to Hume, is the origin of the idea of causal necessity.

Few modern empiricists have taken over Hume's positive solution of this problem, but many have taken over his more important negative contention, that there is no sensory impression of causal necessity. They have taken it over and transformed it into a logical thesis. According to them, the connection between a cause and its effect is not a third thing that is observable in the particular situation, and so every singular causal statement must imply some general causal statement. This is clearly a logical version of Hume's thesis that an inference from cause to effect depends on the association of the two ideas, which is

6. 'The philosophy of logical atomism', in *Essays in Logic and Knowledge*, ed. R. C. Marsh, London, 1956, pp. 179–80.

itself produced by the constant conjunction of the two impressions to which they correspond.

But how much difference does this transformation really make? Certainly, at first sight, it seems to make a great difference. For the way in which Hume conducts his search for an impression of causal necessity makes it appear to be only a contingent fact that no such impression is yielded by the senses: and he sometimes talks as if it were only a contingent fact that the only possible connection between distinct impressions is constant conjunction. The modern version, on the other hand, makes it quite clear that it is logically impossible that any third thing that might be observed between the cause and its effect should be the desired causal connection, since any such third thing would merely lead us to ask how the cause was connected with it, and how it was connected with the effect, so that the problem that originally remained unsolved at one point would now remain unsolved at two points. It also demonstrates that a logical connection between two events, which, according to it, is the only form of connection that is stronger than constant conjunction, is simply ruled out by the requirement that the two events must be distinct. However, Hume was aware that his negative thesis is more secure than he sometimes makes it appear. For he says that those who object that there must be something more to causal necessity do not really know what they want; and here he comes very close to arguing that no sensory impression could conceivably be the desired impression of causal necessity, and that no connection stronger than constant conjunction could conceivably link the two impressions.

Perhaps it is not so very important that Hume examined the contents of the mind, whereas modern empiricists examine language. It may be a more important difference that Hume's psychological system contains an over-simplification which is avoided in their logical system. For he often treats a thought as if it were merely an idea: but, in fact, if the word 'idea' is used in his sense, a complete thought can never be reduced to a single idea, since it is necessarily composed of at least two ideas. Similarly, a sentence, which expresses a complete thought, cannot be reduced to a single element (a word is usually a single element, but there are exceptions to this: e.g. 'Ambulo' is a complete Latin sentence). Modern empiricists, who start with sentences, are careful to observe the distinction between them and the elements out of which they are composed. Unlike Hume, they do not treat the composite product as if it were a single unit.

An example of Hume's over-simplification can be found in his account of memory. According to him, all that happens when a person remembers something is that a strong and vivacious idea (i.e. image) of it occurs in his mind. This simple account seems to fit a case in which an image just comes into my mind, for example, an image of a house that I visited as an infant, and I myself am unaware that it is a memory, but others assure me that it is. But suppose that we take another, more frequent type of case, for example, a house that is later in my life, and I try to remember what kind of tree it was that stood on the lawn in front of it. Perhaps my effort of recollection would be rewarded by an image of a tulip-tree. Then this image would not be an isolated picture, which just came into my mind, as Hume suggests. On the contrary, it would be deliberately summoned up by me as part of a complete thought, the thought that a tulip-tree stood in front of that house. If the remainder of the thought consisted of images (and Hume has no other material to offer), the whole thing would be a proposition expressed in images, just as a sentence is a proposition expressed in words. When he reduces it to a single image, he is unable to explain what makes it a memory about a particular place. If he tried to meet this objection by saying that everything could be got into one image of the front view of the house, he would still have to admit that this image was divided into parts which were taken in a specific order, the order in which the thought would be expressed in words.

The same over-simplification can be seen at work in his account of existence. 'To reflect on anything simple', he says, 'and to reflect on it as existent are nothing different from one another. The idea of existence, when conjoined with the idea of any object, makes no addition to it. Whatever we conceive, we conceive to be existent.'[7] This does not mean that whatever we conceive we believe to exist, since believing, as he was well aware, is more than conceiving. His point is that, when I

7. *Treatise*, Bk. I, pt. 2, § vi.

consider the possibility that there is a weather-vane on top of that house, I think of the weather-vane as existing, without yet believing that it does exist. It is easy to see why he takes this view. For the original impression, to which the idea of the weather-vane corresponds, was not accompanied by a separate impression of existence.

However, this is not enough to establish his point. For, though existence is not a separate impression – i.e. not a property that things in the world are seen to possess – it might still be a separate idea. Indeed, if it were not, it is hard to see how anyone could have a negative existential thought, for example, the thought that God does not exist (whether he believed it or not). But Hume does not think of this. He uses the example of God's existence in order to reduce all complete thoughts to single ideas.

> It is a vulgar error [he says] to distinguish conception from judgment; to define conception as the simple survey of one or more ideas, and to define judgment as the separating or uniting of different ideas. This distinction and these definitions are faulty. For it is far from true that, in every judgment that we form, we unite two different ideas; since in the proposition *God is*, or indeed any other which regards existence, the idea of existence is no distinct idea which we unite with that of the object, and which is capable of forming a compound idea by the union.[8]

But the error is Hume's. The idea of existence must be a separate idea, since otherwise nobody could have a negative existential thought. Admittedly, it is a peculiar idea, because it adds nothing to anything in the world, and so is not a predicate (an ambiguous thesis), and, no doubt, this peculiarity was one of the things that led Hume to conclude that complete thoughts are single ideas. But we can avoid this conclusion if we treat existence as an idea of a higher order – *viz.*, the idea of an idea's having a correspondent impression or impressions,[9] or the concept of a concept's having an instance or instances. This, in effect, is how Kant and Russell treat existence. If we follow

8. *Treatise*, Bk. I, pt. 3, § vii, footnote.
9. Hume says that we have ideas of ideas, ibid., Bk. I, pt. 1, § i.

them, there will be no reason to expect the idea of existence to be derived from an impression in a straightforward way, and the absence of such an impression will be explained.

In any case, there seems to have been no good reason why Hume should have extended his over-simplified account of existential thoughts to other thoughts. For other ideas do not possess the peculiarity of the idea of existence. Why, then, did he not treat existential thoughts as exceptional, and admit that other thoughts cannot be reduced to single ideas? Perhaps the reason is that he believed that he could treat all thoughts as if they were existential in form. For example, he may have regarded the thought that the tree in front of that house might be a tulip-tree as a single complex idea or image of something whose existence in the real world is automatically conceived with it. But there are many objections to this, the most obvious one being that it does not bring out the specific thing that the person is thinking (and would say, if he put his thought into words).

How is Hume's maxim, that all ideas are derived from impressions, related to Russell's maxim, that every proposition that we can understand must be composed wholly of constituents with which we are acquainted? Russell's point is that every proposition contains some terms whose meaning depends on their denotation, and that anyone who understands it must be acquainted either with the denotations of those terms or with the denotations of other terms into which they can be analysed. If Hume had not reduced complete thoughts to single ideas, his maxim would have come close to being a psychological version of Russell's: *viz.*, in a significant thought every idea must either be derived directly from a single impression, or else it must be built up by definition out of other ideas, each of which would itself have been derived from an impression. But Hume did reduce complete thoughts to single ideas, as has been shown. In any case, even if he had not done so, his maxim would not have been an exact psychological counterpart of Russell's. For Hume's ideas are not unspoken words that denote impressions, as Russell's spoken words do, but images that copy impressions (though the extent to which general ideas can do this is limited).

Hume's psychological system has another deficiency, which

is connected with his over-simplified account of complete thoughts, and that is that it does not allow for singular references that are not explicitly descriptive. For example, a proper name or a demonstrative pronoun may occur as the subject of a singular sentence, and a corresponding psychological element ought to occur in the thought that the sentence expresses. But all Hume's singular ideas have descriptive content, naturally enough, since they are copied from sensory impressions. Consequently, a singular thought, for example the thought that Richmond is on the river, will achieve its reference by means of an idea of Richmond, i.e. by means of an image which functions as a kind of description of the place.[10] The result is a thought which is rather like a proposition in which, according to Russell's recommendation, a definite description has been substituted for a proper name; except that in Russell's analysis it is clear which is the subject of the proposition and which is the predicate, whereas in Hume's over-simplified account of thoughts the specific order in which their parts are to be taken is not clear.

But what about demonstrative pronouns? There seems to be no trace of them in Hume's system. The explanation of their disappearance is that they usually occur in sentences about things that are being perceived at the moment, and in his system there is no room for thoughts about things that are being perceived at the moment. Even if there had been room for such thoughts, they would have achieved their singular references in the usual Humean way, by means of ideas with descriptive content, and so there would still have been no exact psychological counterpart of demonstrative pronouns, which have no descriptive content, or almost none. But in fact there is no room at all for such thoughts, because, though ideas can function, albeit inadequately, as thoughts that are not about contemporaneous sensory impressions, they cannot function at all as thoughts that are about contemporaneous sensory impressions. For, according to Hume, an idea can refer to an impression only by copying it, and what, for him, would be the point of copying a sensory impression that was being received at that moment? So demonstrative pronouns vanish without trace. It is not merely that

10. cf. his remarks about the idea of Paris. *Treatise,* Bk. 1, Pt. 1, §1.

their psychological counterparts are subjected to analysis, which is what happens with proper names, but rather, in their case there is no room in the system for their psychological counterparts, so that there is nothing there to be analysed.

His exclusion of all singular references that are not explicitly descriptive produces an important difference between his version of atomism and Russell's version. Of course, his version is psychological, and Russell's is logical. But, in addition to that difference, it is important that Hume develops an atomic theory only about general ideas, whereas Russell extends the theory so that it covers not only general terms but also singular terms. The explanation of Hume's restriction of his theory is that his system contains no psychological counterpart of non-descriptive singular terms, or – to put the same thing from a logical point of view – that it is more like Quine's system than Russell's. Consequently, his atomic theory can be applied only to general ideas. It may sound paradoxical to say this, since all his ideas are particular in their existence, and achieve generality, if they do achieve it, only by being given a general signification. But, though paradoxical, it is true. For generality and singularity are not intrinsic properties of ideas, but depend on the way in which ideas function in thinking. Now the function of one of his singular ideas, for example, the idea of Richmond, is to refer to a particular. But it will always perform this function through its descriptive content, and, since it must always be possible to describe a particular in more than one way, it follows that all singular ideas must be complex, and so the only ideas that could possibly be simple are general ones.

A general idea is simple, according to Hume, if it can be acquired only from a corresponding impression, and complex if it can also be built up by definition out of other ideas (singular ideas, because they can always be built up in this way, are always complex). Russell's distinction between simple and complex general terms runs parallel to this: a general term is simple if its meaning cannot be learned without acquaintance with its denotation, and complex if it can be defined, because in that case there will be an alternative way of learning its meaning, *viz.* acquaintance with the denotations of the terms that occur in its definition. Russell's extension of this theory to singular terms produced his theory of logically proper names, a theory which is fraught with interesting difficulties, but which has no analogue in Hume's system.

Hume never looked closely enough into the internal structure of thoughts, and he believed that he could treat them as single ideas. But he examined the connections between them with great care, and his account of causal inference is the most important thing in the first book of the *Treatise*. However, it is not matched by an equally thorough account of *a priori* inference, and it relies too heavily on the fact that it is natural for human beings to form habits of thought. These are two striking differences between Hume's philosophy and modern analytic philosophy.

When Hume uses habit to explain inference, he is, of course, not writing about *a priori* inference, but only about causal inference.

> To consider the matter aright, reason is nothing but a wonderful and unintelligible instinct in our souls, which carries us along a certain train of ideas, and endows them with particular qualities, according to their particular situations and relations. This instinct, it is true, arises from past observation and experience; but can anyone give the ultimate reason why past experience and observation produces such an effect, any more than why nature alone should produce it? Nature may certainly produce whatever can arise from habit: nay, habit is nothing but one of the principles of nature, and derives all its force from that origin.[11]

This paradox is not meant to apply to *a priori* reasoning. It is true that he allows himself to say that 'the necessity which makes two times two equal to four, or three angles of a triangle equal to two right ones, lies only in the act of the understanding by which we consider and compare these ideas.'[12] But he also says that such connections between ideas are invariable so long as the ideas themselves remain the same.[13] So, when someone makes an *a priori* inference, the psychological process can be

11. *Treatise*, Bk. I, pt. 3, § xvi.
12. ibid., § xiv.
13. ibid., § i.

justified by the internal structure of the ideas themselves. In fact, his perfunctory account of *a priori* inference is a psychological version of the theory of analytic propositions. The central contention of the first book of the *Treatise* is, as Ayer says, that *a priori* propositions are empty, and that any significant proposition that is not empty must be based on experience.[14]

Hume's account of causal inference is a subtle paradox. He is not proposing the naïve thesis that the association between the idea of the cause and the idea of the effect always works instantly and blindly in the mind of the person making the inference. Perhaps this does happen in simple and obvious cases, but even then people can recall and review the evidence which supports their inferences, the constant conjunctions of the correspondent impressions. But in complicated cases the evidence is often conflicting, and, according to Hume, reflection on it is essential. He even allows that, when people pause to assess the evidence in such cases, they invoke rules, and he gives a list of rules by which to judge of causes and effects.[15] So his paradox is not a piece of naïveté: he is not simply failing to allow for the fact that people often reflect on the evidence that supports their causal inferences, and consciously follow rules when they assess its direction and strength.

But, if he allows all this, is there any room left for his paradox, that causal inference depends on the association of ideas? There is, but only if he uses association to explain other operations of the mind, instead of denying their existence. This, in fact, is what he does. His rules – or at least those of them that do not simply follow from the definitions of cause and effect – are themselves based on experience, but on experience of a wider and more general kind. But in his system this means that they too are based on constant conjunctions of impressions. Consequently, he can appeal in the usual way to the association of ideas in order to explain the fact that people accept rules – or, at least, those rules that are not guaranteed by definitions.

So the subtle point of his paradox is that the operations of the mind that assist causal inference, however various they may be, all depend for their justification on the same kind of evidence, constant conjunctions of impressions. This point, is of course,

14. cf. *Enquiry concerning Human Understanding*, § IV, pt. i.
15. *Treatise*, Bk. I, pt. 3, § xv.

the negative thesis that many modern empiricists have taken over from Hume. But it is highly debatable whether the right way to make this point is to try to use one operation of the mind, association, to explain the others, as he does in his paradox. For why should there not be several irreducibly different operations, all based on the same kind of evidence? And, if his explanation were worked out in full psychological detail, could it possibly retain any plausibility? These are some of the considerations that have led most modern empiricists to reject his positive solution of the problem of causal necessity.

But Hume does not attempt to give any detailed justification of his contention that even people who are following a rule are merely being drawn along from one idea to another associated idea. In fact, as he implacably extends the word 'association' to cover more and more operations of the mind, it becomes clear that he is simply applying it to all connections between ideas that are not justified by the internal structure of the ideas themselves. Then, having collected all the problematical phenomena under one heading, he says that the tendency to associate ideas is just a feature of human nature that has to be accepted without explanation. Or he sometimes allows that it might be worth looking for a physiological explanation of it.[16] Either way, it is a brute fact about human beings that they record constant conjunctions in their experience.

A rational man (in the loose sense of that phrase) is a man who makes sure that the operations of his mind that cannot be justified *a priori* will always match the constant conjunctions in his experience. For obviously an operation is not justified merely by being one of those that Hume grouped together under the heading 'association': it also needs to match a constant conjunction. But, since the operations to which he gave this title do not in themselves provide a justification of inferences, there is no obvious reason why he should not have extended it still further to cover operations that assist *a priori* inferences, which are justified in an entirely different way. For such an extension would not have produced a collision between two incompatible justifications. Why, then, did he not make it? Perhaps he would have done so if his account of *a priori* infer-

16. *Treatise*, Bk. I, pt. 2, § v.

ence had been less perfunctory, and if he had included an examination of complicated cases where the mind gropes from stage to stage in an argument, instead of confining himself to simple cases where the inner connection between two ideas is grasped immediately. Or it may be that even then he would not have extended the operation of association to *a priori* inferences. For possibly it would have seemed to him absurd to say that a person had learned to associate a series of ideas each of which had an *a priori* connection with the next one. But, in fact, it would not be absurd. For *a priori* inferences can become habitual no less than causal inferences: and, given his paradoxical extension of association to cases where someone is following a rule, there is no reason left why it should not be said to be at work even in cases where an *a priori* inference is accompanied by insight.

However, it may be that there is another, more interesting explanation of his refusal to extend association to *a priori* inferences. For he certainly believed that the theory of the association of ideas not only belongs to the descriptive psychology of human beings, but also provides part of the justification of causal inference. Of course, it could not possibly provide the whole justification, since associations have to match constant conjunctions: but it might well provide part of it, because it might be impossible to find a justification that did not appeal either to it or to some other very general fact about human beings. Now the fact that people tend to associate is a contingent fact: it might have been otherwise. But Hume may have thought that the 'act of understanding', which is needed in *a priori* inference, and which is elicited in most people by certain pairs of ideas, is something that could not conceivably have been lacking in all people. If he thought this, his refusal to extend association to *a priori* inferences would be explained. For it would be natural for him to refuse to apply the same name to something that human nature might conceivably have lacked and to something that it could not conceivably have lacked.

But is it really true that human nature could not conceivably have lacked the capacity for Hume's 'acts of understanding', or – a less radical question – is it really true that they could not have been elicited by entirely different pairs of ideas from those that do in fact elicit them? Anyone who took the extreme conventionalist view of logical necessity would answer these questions, or at least the second one, in the negative. It is interesting to observe that when Wittgenstein takes this line in *Remarks on the Foundations of Mathematics,* he suggests that it is just an ultimate fact about human beings that they find certain *a priori* inferences natural. Thus he extends Hume's appeal to human nature from causal necessity to *a priori* necessity. Whether this extension of the appeal is correct or not, one thing at least is certain: the substitution of rules for habits does not do anything towards justifying an inference, unless it can be shown that the rules that people actually do follow are their own justification; but if this could be shown, it could equally be shown that their natural habits are their own justification.

Few modern empiricists would allow Hume to effect his extension of the word 'association' by vaguely diluting its meaning until it covers the following of rules. For they would have a precise objection to this: namely, that he says that, when someone is drawn along from one idea to another associated idea, this process is itself causal, whereas the following of a rule is not a causal process. This objection was frequently used by Hume's British Idealist critics. If its point were simply that there is a clear difference between drawing a conclusion after careful reflection and drawing a conclusion automatically without reflection, it would be valid, but not a very damaging criticism of Hume. If the point is to be really damaging, it must be that the following of a rule cannot be regarded as a causal process from any point of view, not even from the point of view of an observer, who might be a psychologist or a neuro-psychologist. But this is not nearly so plausible and probably false.

8 Hume's Account of Personal Identity

Hume's account of personal identity is superior to most other accounts because it is more penetrating. It is given in two parts. First, there is the reductive theory set out in the main body of the *Treatise*, and then in the Appendix there is the recantation of that theory. Since the two parts cancel out, it is unrealistic to ask whether the whole account contains more truth, or less error, than other accounts. But we can assess it in another way. We can ask whether the trip was a good one, and whether we learned anything from the arguments which Hume uses, first against rival theories, and then against his own. When his discussion is assessed in this way, it should get high praise. It made a permanent difference to the subject.

The theory offered in the body of the *Treatise* was intended to explain the fact that a person is a single unified being, persisting through time. It is a theory based on several axioms, and Hume builds it up on this basis very carefully and very scrupulously, never allowing himself to slip extra material into the structure, or extra assumptions. But in the end he finds that the theory does not fit the fact which it was designed to explain. So he is faced with a dilemma: either he must argue that the fact is not really what he had taken it to be, or else he must abandon the theory. He chose to abandon the theory, and he confessed that he was unable to find a better one to put in its place.

That is a summary description of an investigation which is lengthy and complex. I shall now go back to the starting-point and explain the axioms on which Hume based his supposedly unsuccessful theory. These may be divided into two groups. The first group is concerned with the conditions of perfect identity; and the second is concerned with the nature of the connection between the components of a composite thing.

The axioms in the first group are the following:

(1) An incomposite thing enjoys perfect identity so long as it lasts.

(2) A composite thing enjoys perfect identity so long as there is no change in the identity of its incomposite components.

(3) There is no third way of achieving perfect identity through time.

Axiom (3) is directed against any third way that might be suggested. But the suggestion which Hume had chiefly in mind, and on which he spends a lot of argument, is the suggestion that a composite thing might achieve perfect identity through a constant substrate. This substrate would be a substance in one sense of that word, but not in the sense in which Hume allows that an incomposite thing would be a substance. That is a different use of the word. An incomposite thing would be a detectable substance, but a substrate would be an undetectable substance, and so, according to Hume, even if its nature were intelligible, its existence would be dubious. An incomposite thing is a kind of substance which avoids these disadvantages, but has another disadvantage instead; it selfishly refuses to extend perfect identity to anything other than itself.

Let us now look at the axioms in the other group, which is concerned with the nature of the connection between the components of a composite thing. I give these in Hume's words:

(4) 'All our distinct perceptions are distinct existences.'[1]

(5) 'The mind never perceives any real connection among distinct existences.'[2]

These two axioms are stated for the special case in which the composite thing is a person's mind. But Hume really subscribes to generalised versions of them, which apply to composite material objects as well as to minds.

The next thing is to ask how he proceeds to build up his supposedly unsuccessful theory on the basis provided by these axioms. But before tackling that question I want to divide his discussion of personal identity into two layers, in order to make it more manageable. On the surface there is his elaborate

1. *A Treatise of Human Nature*, Appendix, p. 331. Page references in this paper are to the Fontana edition, ed. D. G. C. MacNabb, London, 1962.

2. ibid.

argument about identity, diversity and change, leading to the conclusion that persons do not enjoy perfect identity through time. Let me call this 'the surface plot', meaning not that it is superficial or unimportant, but only that it is explicit. Beneath the surface plot, and largely hidden by it, there is what I shall call 'the underplot'.

This division of Hume's discussion may be pictured as a horizontal line, whereas the other division that I mentioned, between the theory itself and the recantation of it, would be drawn as a vertical line. Above the horizontal line the surface plot is played out. The distinctive mark of the surface plot is that it treats persons like ordinary composite material objects. I do not mean that Hume treats persons *as* material objects. Far from it. After a few allusions to human bodies, he turns his back on them, and addresses himself to the narrower task of explaining the unity of human minds rather than human beings. What I mean is that, having restricted himself to human minds, he treats them *like* ordinary material objects. e.g. when he asks whether the impressions and ideas, which go to form a mind persisting through time, are organised in a way that confers perfect identity on that mind, he construes this question like the question posed by William James in his discussion of this subject: Are the individual beasts in a herd of cattle persisting through time organised in a way that confers perfect identity on that herd?[3] Both these questions get a negative answer based on Axioms (2) and (3), according to which, whenever there is any change in the identity of the components of a composite thing, physical or mental, it loses its title to perfect identity through time.

I am not yet in a position to give a detailed characterisation of the underplot. But what can be said in general is that it takes account of factors which are peculiar to persons and certain other animals, and perhaps some machines. This, of course, is only a schema for describing the underplot, and different people will fill in the details in different ways. My way of filling them in will be based on Hume's text. I am interested only in those peculiarities of embodied minds which almost break the surface of his discussion of personal identity, but which do not quite

3. William James, *Principles of Psychology*, London, 1891. Vol. 1, pp. 333 ff.

succeed in breaking it. It would, of course, be possible to broaden the scope of the inquiry, so as to bring in factors such as intentions and actions which lie entirely outside the drama as Hume presents it in Book I of the *Treatise* and in the Appendix. But I prefer to keep the inquiry more narrowly focussed on to those two texts, because I want to exhibit the tensions between his surface plot and his underplot.

I shall not say much about the surface plot, because the general pattern of it is tolerably clear. It is important to notice that right from the start Hume turns his back on the human body, and concentrates on the unity of the human mind. He easily shows that a mind does not satisfy either of the two conditions of perfect identity laid down in Axioms (1) and (2). Then he dismisses the third suggestion, that it might achieve perfect identity through a substrate. This is dismissed by an appeal to Axiom (3). Anyone who claims to have a distinct impression of his self as a separate entity is guilty of 'a manifest contradiction and absurdity'.[4] I take it that the absurdity that he means is the absurdity of identifying an enduring substrate with any of the components which go to make up the composite thing whose substrate it is. At least, that is how the absurdity is presented in the surface plot. Just as the substrate of a lump of rock cannot be identified with any of its physical components, so too the substrate of a mind cannot be identified with any of its mental components.

But here I must interrupt the exposition of the surface plot in order to glance at the underplot. For the surface plot does not exhaust the richness of the absurdity which Hume is trying to expose. In the case of a material object, such as a table or chair, it is absurd to identify the suggested substrate with any detectable component. But in the case of a mind there is an extra dimension to the absurdity. There is, first, the parallel absurdity of identifying the substrate with any detectable component of the mind, i.e. with any impression or idea. Then there is the additional complication that, if we did make such an identification, the impression of the self would be an impression of another impression, and, therefore, in Hume's terminology, an impression of reflection. Now this complication

4. *Treatise*, Bk. I, pt. 4, § vi; p. 301.

is not enough, in itself, to lead to any further absurdity. For it would have been possible to argue, as William James did later, that consciousness simply consists in the fact that one component of the mind reflects another.[5] But Hume's adversaries required the self to be a single subject, and such a subject could hardly get an impression of itself. James's theory that the subject is the passing thought, which apprehends earlier thoughts but not itself, avoids this absurdity, but only by abandoning the requirement of a single subject. Thus something which is simple enough in the surface plot carries richer implications in the underplot.

Let me return to the surface plot. The next step in its development concerns the relations between the mental components which go to form a single mind enduring through time. According to Hume, these relations are resemblance and causation. As demonstrated, they do not produce perfect identity, but they do produce the inferior substitute with which we have to rest content when we leave the philosopher's study. In other words, when Hume wrote the text of the *Treatise* he believed that his theory of personal identity, founded on resemblance and causation, was an adequate theory, in spite of the fact that it does not satisfy philosophers' dreams about perfect identity. He believed, as we say nowadays, that his analysis of the concept of personal identity was correct.

Since he had ceased to believe this by the time that he wrote the Appendix, it might be a good thing to mention two relations which have a strong claim to be included on his list, but which are not included on it. He does not include contiguity, in spite of the importance of temporal contiguity in the mental life of a person, and in spite of the fact that causation, which he does include, is said by him to involve contiguity. Another equally striking exclusion is the memory relation. This is the relation which holds between a memory impression and the earlier mental component of which it is a memory impression. When I say that he excludes the memory relation from his list, I mean only that he does not treat this relation as part of the basis of personal identity. Naturally, he thinks that memory is indispensable, but only as a means of acquiring knowledge of one's

5. *Principles of Psychology*, Vol. I, p. 342.

own identity. For without memory, how could anyone discover that a series of mental items really were related by resemblance and causation, which, according to the theory, are the two basic relations? How could he even discover the existence of the mental items? But this does not make the memory relation into a third basic relation. It is true that he allows it a minor role in producing personal identity, as opposed to discovering it. Because he thinks that memory impressions are replicas, the memory relation multiplies resemblances and so helps to produce personal identity as a sort of side effect. But this work is done through resemblance, and resemblance is a basic relation already on the list, and so the memory relation does not acquire a title to a place of its own on the list.

It might be argued that Hume was right to refuse to put the memory relation on the list of relations that constitute personal identity. Perhaps memory does only discover personal identity. This is a difficult matter to settle, and the difficulty can be exhibited in the following way. Suppose that he had said that the memory relation also helps to produce personal identity by multiplying causal connections between mental items. This would have been a much more important point than his suggestion that it multiplies resemblances. As far as I know, he never says that memory helps to produce personal identity in this way. But if he had made this point, he could have argued very plausibly that it locates the most important thing that memory contributes to constituting personal identity. But would this give the memory relation a title to a place of its own on the list of basic relations? Probably not. For if he had made the point about memory and causality, he could still have defended his refusal to give the memory relation a place of its own on the list. Memory would play its further role only through causation, which is already on the list. So perhaps his refusal to add the memory relation to the other two is not wrong, and the only fault in this part of his argument is that he does not offer a full justification of his refusal.

What then is the *dénouement* of the surface plot? If we do not include the Appendix, the story ends with Hume's acceptance of a reductive theory. A human mind is composed of impressions and ideas related by resemblance and causality. He argues that there is no real alternative to this theory. Those who say that a human mind enjoys a tidier type of identity have simply made a mistake about the nature of the scale of better and worse types of identity. When we place various kinds of thing on this scale, we are merely applying Axioms (1), (2) and (3) to the empirical phenomena. If the result is that a physical atom exhibits perfect identity through time, while cabbages and kings do not, that is a final result, and there is no appeal beyond it. Of course, someone might challenge Hume's account of the empirical phenomena, and claim that the identity of a physical atom, or of a cabbage, is not as he describes it. Or someone might make the more radical suggestion that we should not use the three axioms to define perfect identity; or even that we ought to give up talking about perfect identity altogether, because each kind of thing has its own appropriate criterion of identity, and there is no competition between them. But if we do construct the scale in the way sketched by Hume, and if we cannot find any mistake in his description of the empirical phenomena, then that result is final. It is a misunderstanding of the nature of the scale to bring in the un-empirical concept 'substrate', and to try to use it as the basis of a third type of perfect identity, which would be a sort of consolation prize for those who fail in the empirical competition.

So Hume is satisfied with his reductive theory, and he has an explanation of his adversaries' dissatisfaction with it. His adversaries are obsessed with perfect identity, and try to find it where it does not exist. But when we follow the surface plot into the Appendix, there is a dramatic change. All his satisfaction with his theory vanishes. He still refuses to accept the suggestion that we have an unempirical concept of substance. But when he reviews his account of the connections between the impressions and ideas of a single person, he finds it defective. Since philosophers' recantations are not too common, let me quote some of this one: 'If perceptions [i.e. impressions and ideas] are distinct existences, they form a whole only by being connected together. But no connections among distinct existences are ever discoverable by human understanding. We only *feel* a connection or determination of the thought to pass from one object to another. It follows, therefore, that the thought alone feels personal identity, when reflecting on the train of past perceptions that compose a mind; the ideas of them are felt to be connected together, and naturally introduce each other. . . . But all my hopes vanish when I come to explain the principles that unite our successive perceptions in our thought or consciousness. I cannot discover any theory which gives me satisfaction on this head.'[6]

This really is a recantation. It is not just a case of Hume's common flirting with his adversaries' feelings. His treatment of causal necessity contains several examples of this kind of insincerity – or, it may be, irony. I am thinking of the passages in which he expresses the fear that his reductive account of causal necessity may not only look too sceptical, but actually be too sceptical. But on the whole he is satisfied that that theory is adequate because it covers everything that is empirically accessible. So his settled conclusion about that matter is that his adversaries are misled by the mind's 'great propensity to spread itself on external objects, and to conjoin with them any internal impressions which they occasion'.[7]

Why, then, is he not equally satisfied with his reductive theory of personal identity? We may suspect that he is influenced by something in the underplot. For example, minds are self-reflexive, and so, though it may be a good explanation of causal necessity to say that the mind spreads itself on external objects, it does not sound so good an explanation of personal identity to say that it spreads itself on internal objects. However, Hume does not mention this difficulty at this point. Nor does he explicitly introduce any other motifs from the underplot. He sums up his reasons for rejecting his theory of personal identity in the following words: 'In short, there are two principles which I cannot render consistent, nor is it in my power to renounce either of them, viz. *that all our distinct perceptions are distinct existences*; and *that the mind never perceives any real connection among distinct existences*. Did our perceptions either inhere in something simple and individual, or did the mind perceive some real connection among them, there would be no difficulty in the case. For my part, I must plead the privilege of a sceptic, and confess that this difficulty is too hard for my understanding.'[8]

This is not irony. Hume was a subtle writer, capable of irony

6. *Treatise*, Appendix, p. 331.
7. ibid., Bk. I, pt. 3, § xiv; p. 218.
8. ibid., Appendix; p. 331.

which often passes undetected. So it could have been irony. But it is not in fact irony, and the proof of this is that it is entirely different from his later reaction to his reductive theory of causal necessity. In his *Abstract* of the *Treatise* he admits the sceptical character of that theory but claims that it is correct.

Why, then, did he recant about personal identity? In the remainder of this paper I shall go through the underplot trying to show that his real reasons for recanting are to be found there. But, naturally, I shall start from the reasons that he himself gives in the Appendix.

The explicit reasons, given in the Appendix, belong to the surface plot. He does not say anything that is not also true of ordinary material objects, and his argument could equally well be applied to the identity of cabbages. This is a very striking fact. An even more striking feature of his recantation is that he sums it up by repeating Axioms (4) and (5) and saying that he cannot renounce either of them and yet that he is unable to render them consistent. Now Axioms (4) and (5) belong to the second group that I distinguished at the beginning of this paper. They are concerned with the nature of the connections between the components of composite things, and they stipulate that these connections are always contingent. What then can he mean when he says that he cannot render them consistent? They do not even look inconsistent with one another. In fact, it would be plausible to argue that (5) merely gives the definition of the word 'distinct' as it is used in (4).[9] If this is correct, Hume's point is that there are *a priori* connections between ideas, and associational connections between ideas produced, e.g., by constant conjunctions of impressions, but no third kind of connection called 'real connection'.

I think that the solution to this problem of interpretation is that Hume means not that the two axioms are inconsistent with one another, but only that taken together they are inconsistent with the fact that a person is a single unified being persisting through time. In other words, he takes this fact to imply a greater degree of unity than the two axioms allow. If he had been prepared to revise his interpretation of the fact, he would not have had to recant. But he found himself unable to accept

9. G. H. von Wright, *The Logical Problem of Induction*, in *Acta Philosophica Fennica*, Fasc. 3, 1941; revised edition, Oxford, 1957, ch. 2.

a more reductive interpretation of the fact, and so he recanted.

As far as the text goes, this interpretation fits the whole tenor of the passage. Moreover, he never says that the two axioms are inconsistent with one another, but only that they are inconsistent. But I must admit that even this is an odd way of expressing the view that I am attributing to him, and possibly the explanation is that the brevity of the Appendix has made it very inexplicit at this point.

In any case, this interpretation will be convincing only if it can be explained why the lack of a real connection between the components of a mind left Hume dissatisfied. After all, the two axioms only require the connections to hold contingently. So if I have a taste impression followed by a memory idea of Paris, it will only be a contingent fact that the second followed the first. But what is wrong with that? He can hardly have supposed that such a connection ought to be non-contingent. Admittedly, in this example the connection happens to be causal, but then his main thesis about causal connections is that they only hold contingently. In any case, non-causal examples could easily be found.

It seems that the only way to answer this objection and to give an intelligible reconstruction of his reasoning is to draw on the underplot. Minds differ from ordinary composite material objects in more than one way, and it is likely that some of these differences will provide clues to his line of thought.

For example, the ownership of impressions and ideas has several well-known peculiarities. If I have a sense impression, there is no room for any question about its owner – the owner must be myself. Nor can I speculate that the sense impression might have been yours instead of mine, or that it might have existed on its own, not belonging to anybody. Such speculations lack sense. Now these peculiarities of the ownership of mental objects have to be accommodated in any viable theory of personal identity. But how was Hume to accommodate them in his theory? How was he to weave these threads from the underplot into a surface plot whose dominant pattern was set by the analogy between mental objects and ordinary material objects?

One would expect that there would be some distortion at this point, and in fact there is. Instead of saying that, if I have an impression, it must be mine, could not have belonged to anyone else, and could not have existed on its own, he wants to be able to say that, if I have an impression, it could not have failed to occur in the series that is myself. But that would not be the same thing. I think that it seemed to him to be the same thing because he pushed the analogy between mental objects and material objects too far. If a cow belongs to a particular herd, it need not have belonged to it, and it – the very same cow – might have belonged to a different herd, or even lived on its own. This may have suggested to him that, if he had allowed that a certain sense impression which occurs in the series that is myself might not have done so, then he would have been forced to allow that it – the very same sense impression – might have occurred in a series that is someone else, or even existed on its own. In fact no such concession would have been forced from him. He could have pointed out that there is a limit to the analogy between mental objects and material objects. But because he failed to see the limit, he thought that the only way to accommodate the peculiar features of the ownership of mental objects would be to say that, when a series contains a particular mental object, it could not have failed to contain it. In short, he confused the following two modal propositions:

(i) This series might not have included S.

(ii) S might have occurred outside this series.

The thesis, that Hume is here exaggerating the analogy between mental objects and material objects, must not be taken to imply that all types of material object have criteria which make their numerical identities independent of the numerical identities of material objects of any other type. That is not so. Although most types of material object are not identity-dependent in this way, some types are. For example, a particular brick is not dependent for its identity on the wall in which it has been incorporated, and it could have been incorporated in a different wall. But suppose that I point to the branch of a tree, and say that it – the very same branch – might have grown on a different tree. Here we have a material example of identity-dependence, and my speculation would lack sense. All that I can imagine is that another tree might have grown a branch exactly like this one, and that, at the same time, this tree might not have grown this one. So this kind of identity-dependence is not confined to mental objects.

However, it does seem to extend to all types of mental object, and it is, perhaps, especially puzzling in this area. Its puzzling character may be brought out through a contrast between a branch of a tree and a sense impression. An explanation of the identity-dependence of a branch would go something like this. In the case of a branch we could always adopt a new criterion, according to which its numerical identity would be tied to the matter out of which it is formed. Then the speculation that lacked a sense could immediately be given one. It would mean that that matter might have been absorbed by a different tree, and might have grown out of it in the form of a similar branch. Of course, someone might object that this would still not be a case of the very same branch growing on a different tree, because he might persist in treating the numerical identity of the tree as a necessary condition of the numerical identity of the branch. But there would be no mystery about this. We would have three discernible things to juggle with, the matter of the branch, its form, and its relation to a particular tree. These three things could be used in various ways to produce alternative criteria of numerical identity for branches. The relation to a particular tree is only one thing, and it is easy to see what is going on when someone refuses to allow the numerical identity of a branch to be independent of this relation.

But the whole affair is more mysterious in the case of a sense impression. For though two of the things are used in this case – the form (or quality) of the sense impression and its relation to a particular person – the third thing, its matter, is not used. Consequently, we do not have such a clear idea of what we would have to do in order to give a sense to the senseless speculation. Would we merely collapse the concept of the numerical identity of a sense impression into exact similarity? Or would we have to wait until we were in a position to base a new criterion of numerical identity on the matter of the nervous system?

To return to Hume – it may seem hard to believe that he could have exaggerated the similarity between sense impressions and material objects, such as bricks, to quite such an extent. For the facts about the ownership of mental objects are familiar, and so they might seem to be less malleable than this. But half-thought-out analogies are very powerful in philosophy, and there is ample evidence in the *Treatise* for this account of what was going on in his mind. For example, in the chapter on the Immateriality of the Soul, he says: '. . . since all our perceptions are different from each other, and from everything else in the universe, they are also distinct and separable, and may be considered as separately existent, and may exist separately, and have no need of anything else to support their existence. They are, therefore, substances, as far as this definition explains substance.'[10] This is not an isolated passage, and it marks out a line of thought which Hume was prepared to follow in the text of the *Treatise*, but not in the Appendix. The analogy with bricks, or perhaps with physical atoms, is being openly pushed to the extreme. In this way sense impressions seem to acquire a degree of independence which makes it impossible to explain the fact that one of mine could not have been one of yours.

This strange way of treating mental objects is connected with his account of the way in which memory helps a person to answer a question about his own earlier identity. He says that memory discovers, but does not constitute, personal identity, except in so far as it multiplies resemblances between a person's mental objects. This suggests that my memory puts me in touch with a number of mental objects, about which I then ask whether they belong to the series that terminates on myself at the present moment, and that I am supposed to answer this question by applying the criteria of resemblance and causation. But this description of my procedure presupposes that memory is an impersonal way of collecting data, which are then examined and assigned to myself or some other person. Did Hume then deliberately use 'memory' to signify a faculty which puts me in direct touch with earlier mental objects that belong to any person, myself or another? Apparently not. For there is no evidence to support the view that in his discussion of personal identity he is intentionally presupposing a predicament that is not ours. Of course, he allows for errors of memory, but not for what Shoemaker calls 'quasi-memory'.[11] On the other hand, in this discussion he does not even mention any of the ordinary ways in which we discover the objects in other people's minds. So

10. *Treatise*, Bk. I, pt. 4, § v; pp. 283–4.

11. Sydney Shoemaker, 'Persons and their pasts', *American Philosophical Quarterly* 7, 1967.

there really is an unintentional presupposition that memory is an impersonal way of collecting data. How should we interpret it?

It should probably be connected not with any carefully thought-out theory about the way in which the data are, or might be, acquired, but, rather, with his general picture of the world of mental objects. When he pushed the analogy between mental and material objects too far, it was natural for him to write as if we could establish the existence of mental objects without prejudice to the question of their ownership, as can be done with cattle. Then, if he retained his uncritical assumption that memory is the only source of the relevant data, it would be assigned a role which it could not possibly perform. For how could I rely on my memory for the existence of an earlier mental object, while rejecting the inference that it was mine?

Only too easily, it might be retorted, if the concept of memory is changed. But since there is no evidence that Hume was deliberately changing the concept in the required way, it is more likely that he slipped into the impersonal treatment of memory because he exaggerated the analogy between mental and material objects without fully realising the consequences.

So much for the second of the two possibilities whose unrealisability he laments in the Appendix: 'did the mind perceive some real connection among them (our perceptions) . . .'. The first one still remains to be considered: 'did our perceptions . . . inhere in something simple and individual . . .'. Why did he say that, if this possibility were realised, 'there would be no difficulty in the case'? What made him wish that he had been able to accept this kind of theory?

This question is unlikely to be answerable in as straightforward a way as the question about his other wish. The theory that a mind is 'something simple and individual" is such a panacea that the wish that it were an acceptable theory is likely to be over-determined. Nevertheless it is surprising to find how very general Hume's stated reasons are. The considerations that he adduces apply not only to minds but also to composite material things. According to him, the only kind of identity enjoyed by all these composite things is the inferior, fictional kind. But if the problem is so widespread, why does he confess his inability to solve it only in the case of minds? Here too there must be something at work in the underplot. But what?

There are two things that may have been working in his mind at this point. He may have felt that, if he could not show that the impressions and ideas of a person were presented to a single thing, consciousness would remain unexplained. Or, alternatively, he may have felt that, if he could not show that a mind is a simple continuant, he could not give an adequate account of the way in which it acquires and retains knowledge of the world in which it is placed. The first of these two problems is concerned with the phenomenology of what happens within a mind, while the second is concerned with its mechanism and its place in nature. Unfortunately, Hume does not say which of the two problems was exercising him. He gives clear reasons for rejecting the theory that the mind is 'something simple and individual'. If he had identified the self with any detectable component of a mind, the impression of the self would have been an impression of that component, and, therefore, an impression of reflection. But it is absurd to identify a composite thing with any of its components, and a single subject could hardly get an impression of itself in that way. Why, then, did he find this theory so attractive? He does not tell us, and the choice between the two interpretations must be based on indirect evidence.

The prevalent interpretation is the first one, which claims that he was hoping to find a way of explaining the phenomenon of consciousness. But there is strong circumstantial evidence against this interpretation. He never shows any sign of thinking that he needs to point to a single subject in order to explain consciousness. He took it for granted that one component of a mind can reflect another, and apparently did not feel that impressions of reflection posed any problem. He allowed himself to make use of intentionality without trying to explain it, and he felt no doubts about its range because he treated impressions of memory as unproblematic. In short, he did not see that there might be difficulties about the synthetic unity of consciousness, and his course appeared to be set towards the kind of theory that was later developed by William James. In fact, he did not go so far as to identify the self with the passing thought. But without violating the principles of his empiricism, he could have explained the idea of the self as an idea of an expanding series of mental components. These components would be identified through their positions in the series, and if a number of them were all tokens of the same type-idea, their contents would be identical. But the content of the idea of the self would increase as the series expanded. No doubt this is a complicated theory, but at no point does Hume show any signs of being troubled by the general problem of consciousness or by the special problem of reflexivity.

His difficulty seems to begin when he has to explain how a mind acquires and retains any knowledge of the world and of its place in it. For how can he explain the working of memory in his system? If I wonder whether a man sitting opposite me in a train is the one who sat opposite me yesterday, I would take my own identity for granted. But if he questioned whether I was the man who had occupied the same seat on yesterday's journey, I would have to verify my claim that I was, perhaps by producing memory impressions which could be checked. Similarly, the identity of a star could be established through a photograph taken by a rocket-borne camera, or the identity of the camera could be established through the images on its film. In both cases it is necessary that we should be able to argue either from the identity of the recorder to the identity of what it records, or in the reverse direction. This evidently requires that there should be general agreement between the record and the recorder's independently established history. But how could memory meet this requirement in Hume's system?

That depends on how liberally his system is constructed. He occasionally speculates about the physical basis of the mind, and, if he had allowed himself to use that kind of material in his discussion of personal identity, he might have given an adequate account of memory. But in fact he does not use it, and the implication is that he can solve the problem entirely from the resources of the mind. This restriction puts memory in an impossible position. Just as I, body and mind, am related to the two appearances of the man in the train, so too I, the remembering subject, ought to be related to any sense impressions that occur in my mind. But this will not work. For in the train there are independent ways of checking my identity, but there are no independent ways of checking the identity of the remembering subject in Hume's restricted system. His wish that the subject were single is merely the wish that this did not matter. Another reason why the analogy does not work is that there is no material left over for incorporation in an account of the causal mechanism of the remembering subject. His wish that the subject were simple is merely the wish that this too did not matter. However, it does matter that his picture of the mind impels him towards a theory which makes the identity of the subject independent of any checks and its operation independent of any mechanism. He knows that such a theory is a philosopher's dream, but he does not retrace his steps in order to find out which of them led him into the impasse.

9 Russell's Theories of Memory

Russell produced one theory of memory in 1912 in *The Problems of Philosophy* and another, quite different one nine years later in *The Analysis of Mind*. Theory I relies on acquaintance with particulars observed in the past, while Theory II relies on images occurring in the present. This bald statement of the difference suggests that Theory II is a representative theory. But that would be only a half truth. For though the images that it involves sometimes function as representative data, they often function as elements in memory propositions. In fact, one of the things that gives Theory II its interest is Russell's attempt to keep these two functions of images distinct from one another. In general, Theory II gives propositions more work than they are given by Theory I. True, they do something in Theory I, but acquaintance plays the major part. In fact, it is not easy to see how they cooperate with acquaintance in Theory I, and Russell has difficulty in explaining their contribution. Of course, the move from Theory I to Theory II is a large one, and it was not made suddenly, because it was connected with several changes of doctrine which did not all occur simultaneously. *Theory of Knowledge*, which he wrote in 1913 but never published in its entirety,[1] shows that he was beginning to move away from Theory I only one year after its publication in *The Problems of Philosophy*.

There are various kinds of memory, and we need to know which kind the two theories are intended to explain. They are

1. The typescript of this book is in the Bertrand Russell Archives at McMaster University. Its first six chapters appeared in the *Monist* in 1915. Three deal with the nature of acquaintance and have been included in Russell's *Essays in Logic and Knowledge*, London, 1956, by the editor, R. C. Marsh. The two which throw most light on his ideas about memory, 'Sensation and imagination' and 'On the experience of Time', have not been reprinted.

concerned not with immediate memory, which spans the specious present, but with remote memory, which takes over at the limit of the range of immediate memory, i.e., according to Russell, after about thirty seconds. Furthermore, they are not concerned with all cases of remote memory, but only with what he calls 'genuine memory'.[2] By this he means 'paradigmatic memory' rather than 'correct memory', but it is not too easy to discover which kind of remote memory he regards as the paradigm, because he tends to specify it in a way that involves his current theory about it. Thus in *The Problems of Philosophy* he specifies it in terms of Theory I: 'There is some danger of confusion as to the nature of memory, owing to the fact that memory of an object is apt to be accompanied by an image of the object, and yet the image cannot be what constitutes memory. This is easily seen by merely noticing that the image is in the present, whereas what is remembered is known to be in the past. Moreover, we are certainly able to compare our image with the object remembered, so that we often know within somewhat wide limits how far our image is accurate; but this would be impossible, unless the object, as opposed to the image, were in some way before the mind.'[3] This is clearly a description of the kind of case in which a person is related to his past in the most direct possible way, and so can check his first impression or supplement it using only the resources of his own unaided memory. Theory I, that we are acquainted with particulars perceived in the remote past, provides an apt description of this kind of case.

But Theory II makes no use of acquaintance, and according to it the only things that are immediately before the mind in the memory situation are images. So when Russell adopted Theory II, he had to specify the same kind of case in a different, and less vivid way. In fact, he specifies it negatively, by contrasting it with what he calls 'habit-memory': 'The recollection of a unique event cannot, so Bergson contends, be wholly constituted by habit, and is in fact something radically different from the memory which is habit. The recollection alone is true memory.'[4] But when Russell takes over Bergson's distinction and

2. *The Problems of Philosophy*, London, 1959, p. 117.
3. ibid., pp. 144–5.
4. *The Analysis of Mind*, London, 1961 (8th imp.), p. 166.

uses it to specify the paradigm case of memory, he runs into difficulties. It is evident that memory in the paradigm case achieves the maximum directness. But why should it be supposed that habit produces indirectness? In a paradigm case one checks and supplements one's first impression without drawing on any resources except those of one's own memory, but why should not the checks and supplementations themselves be the effects of habit? Russell is not in a position to answer this objection, because he gives no criterion for distinguishing between the habitual and the non-habitual. He suggests that paradigm memories never come in words,[5] but though a frequently repeated story may, in a sense, get between the raconteur and his original experience, this does not happen in all cases of remembering in words. Moreover it must also happen in some cases of remembering in images. This possibility certainly exists in Theory II, which allows that images often function as elements in propositions.

Theory I

If paradigm memories are those that put one in the most direct possible relation with one's past, does Theory I provide an adequate explanation of them? Certainly it provides a vivid description of such cases. But it seems to be vulnerable to two objections. First, it might be argued that the suggestion, that we remain acquainted with particulars perceived by us in the past, is either false or non-explanatory. Second, the theory could be criticised on the ground that it leads to a misunderstanding of the part played by propositions in cases of this kind.

There is no doubt that until 1919, when Russell abandoned the doctrine of acquaintance, he allowed acquaintance with both particulars and universals to outlast the perception of them. But though he set no general limit to the duration of acquaintance with universals, by 1917 he had come to the conclusion that acquaintance with particulars does not extend beyond the limit of the specious present.[6] But it is less easy to

5. *The Problems of Philosophy*, p. 116; *The Analysis of Mind*, pp. 175–6.

6. 'The philosophy of logical atomism', reprinted in *Essays in Logic and Knowledge*, pp. 201–3.

establish what he thought about the limits of acquaintance with particulars between 1912 and 1917.

However, there are remarks in *The Problems of Philosophy* which prove that at least in 1912 he applied Theory I to paradigm cases of remote memory; e.g. the passage already quoted continues in the following way: 'Thus the essence of memory is not constituted by the image, but by having immediately before the mind an object which is recognised as past. But for the fact of memory in this sense, we should not know that there ever was a past at all, nor should we be able to understand the word "past" any more than a man born blind can understand the word "light". Thus there must be intuitive judgments of memory, and it is upon them, ultimately, that all our knowledge of the past depends.'[7] True, it is tempting to read this as a statement about immediate memory. For only three years later, we find him saying that immediate memory is the source of our understanding of the word 'past' and the foundation of all our knowledge of the past.[8] But this interpretation of his remarks in *The Problems of Philosophy* is ruled out by the examples that he then proceeds to give. They are examples of recent and vivid memories, but the interval between perceiving and remembering starts at half a minute and increases. This proves that, when he refers to 'the fact of memory in this sense', he does not mean immediate memory, but paradigmatic remote memory. It is true that he does not mention acquaintance in this passage, but his phrase 'immediately before the mind' leaves no doubt about his meaning, which must be that it is acquaintance that relates the ego and the remembered particular.

But he soon began to lose confidence in this doctrine. This is why in 1915 he transfers the two important functions, making the past intelligible and making it accessible, from remote memory to immediate memory. The article in which he makes this move is part of *Theory of Knowledge*, and in the unpublished part of that work he poses the question whether we are ever acquainted with particulars in remote memory, and his answer is that he is inclined to think that we are not, but that he is not quite sure. In 1917 his agnosticism turned into certainty that we are not. So he gradually abandoned Theory I about para-

7. *The Problems of Philosophy*, p. 115.

8. 'On the experience of time', *Monist*, 1915, pp. 224–5.

digmatic cases of memory before he ceased to believe in the existence of the ego.[9]

If we are reluctant to attribute the theory to him even in 1912, the reason may be that it seems to entail that the remembered particular somehow persists as it was when perceived, so that now, when it is remembered, the relation between the act and the object does not need to span the interval of time. But, though he treats paradigmatic remote memory rather like perception, he does not go so far as to update its object to the time of remembering.

This is made quite clear in two remarks about Theory I which belong to the period when he no longer maintained it. 'Take . . . the remembering of a past event. The remembering occurs now, and is therefore necessarily not identical with the past event. So long as we retain the act, this need cause no difficulty. The act of remembering occurs now, and has on this view a certain essential relation to the past event which it remembers.' 'If we had retained the "subject" or "act" in knowledge, the whole problem of memory would have been comparatively simple. We could then have said that remembering is a direct relation between the present act or subject and the past occurrence remembered: the act of remembering is present, though its object is past.'[10] His refusal to update the object is made even clearer in a passage which belongs to the period of his agnosticism about Theory I: 'We are told (*sc.* by Meinong) that it is impossible the presentation should exist now, if its content does not exist now. But if presentation consists wholly and solely, as we have contended, in a relation of subject and object, then a memory-presentation is a complex of which one constituent is present while the other is past. It is not clear that such a complex has any definite position in the time-series: the fact that the remembering subject is in the present is no

9. In my book *Bertrand Russell and the British Tradition in Philosophy*, London, 1967, I said that he maintained Theory I until 1919, when he ceased to believe in the existence of the ego. J. O. Urmson, in a review of the book (*Philosophical Review 78*) proves that he could not have held Theory I in 1917. Urmson's further contention, that he never held Theory I, seems to be mistaken. There is a discussion of this controversial question of interpretation by R. K. Perkins in 'Russell on memory', *Mind*, 1973.

10. *The Analysis of Mind*, pp. 21, 163.

sufficient reason for regarding the whole complex as present.'[11]

But if no updating of the object is implied why did he feel any doubts about Theory I? Why did he not regard it simply as a descriptive theory which does justice to two important facts, that all memory is immediate or non-inferential and that in paradigm cases of remote memory one can check and supplement one's first impression as if one still had the original object under observation?

There seem to be several things that made that position too unstable for him to hold for long. Consider, for example, the reason for describing paradigmatic remote memory as acquaintance. It is supposed that it must be acquaintance because the impressions are under a continuous constraint. Of course, all memory impressions are under a constraint, which seems to be external, because the person who has them cannot alter them at will. But paradigmatic remote memories can be checked and supplemented, and so in such cases the constraint is continuous. Now this continuous constraint is explicable as the effect of the mechanism of memory, given the previous experience. But it is natural to externalise it in the present moment and to regard it as the direct contemporary effect of the remembered object. Certainly, that is what it feels like. This is the first step towards assimilating this kind of memory to perception. The second step is to exploit the fact that the remembered object supplies further impressions after the first one, all apparently under its direct control. This makes the remembering so like scanning a perceived object that the time-gap hardly seems to matter. Now at this point the assimilation ought to stop because nothing more can be added to the analogy. But Russell evidently felt that, if the analogy holds up to this point, it ought to hold beyond it. His phrase 'immediately before the mind' suggested that it ought to be possible to find more introspectable evidence for Theory I. But this is the demand that breaks the bank. No doubt there is much that is introspectable in paradigm cases of remote memory. One always finds oneself under constraint, and often there are images, which are the most conspicuous example of introspectable objects. However, it would be a mistake to expect more introspectable evidence. But he did

11. 'On the nature of acquaintance', in *Essays in Logic and Knowledge*, p. 171.

expect more, and, when he failed to find it, he gradually became convinced that Theory I is false.

It would be a superficial verdict that he simply pushed the analogy with perception too far. Certainly, that is what he did, but the interesting question is, why he did it. The reason seems to be that he required a philosophical theory to be too like a scientific theory. He apparently wanted Theory I to be more than an apt description of certain features of paradigmatic remote memory. It had to provide an explanation by suggesting the way in which that kind of memory works, and the suggestion had to be verifiable. But this demand led only too rapidly to the final dilemma, that either Theory I is non-explanatory or it is false.

Another source of instability in Theory I is Russell's treatment of propositions. For at the time when he assimilated paradigmatic remote memory to perception, his account of perceptual knowledge exaggerated its intuitiveness and underrated the contribution made by propositions. Perception, immediate memory and remote memory were all treated as examples of acquaintance, yielding truths which he regarded as self-evident. Of course, there is a decrease in certainty as the object recedes into the past, but there is no sharp break, and the scale of self-evident truths is continuously graded into the remote past so far as it is accessible to paradigmatic memory.[12] This part of Russell's epistemology is based on his logical analysis of acquaintance, which can best be gathered from his remarks about perception.

In 1917–18 he said that sense-data are simple particulars and that they are the meanings of the logically proper names that we attach to them on first acquaintance with them.[13] But this leaves it unexplained how it is possible to extract a truth about a sense-datum from acquaintance with it, and he discusses this problem at many places in his writings between 1910 and 1914. For instance, in 'The relation of sense-data to physics' he says:

> There is some difficulty in deciding what is to be considered *one* sense-datum: often attention causes divisions to appear when, so far as can be discovered, there were no divisions before. An observed complex fact, such as that

12. *The Problems of Philosophy*, pp. 137–8.
13. 'The philosophy of logical atomism', p. 200.

> this patch of red is to the left of that patch of blue, is also to be regarded as a datum from our point of view: epistemologically it does not differ greatly from a simple sense-datum as regards its function in giving knowledge. Its *logical* structure is very different, however, from that of sense: *sense* gives acquaintance with particulars, and is thus a two-term relation in which the object can be *named* but not asserted, and is inherently incapable of truth or falsehood, whereas the observation of a complex fact, which may be suitably called 'perception' is not a two-term relation, but involves the propositional form on the object side, and gives knowledge of a truth, not mere acquaintance with a particular.[14]

Evidently, this kind of sense-datum is not simple, and we need to know how he supposed that acquaintance with it generates awareness of its complex structure and so yields a truth about it. He describes this process in *Principia Mathematica*:

> Let us consider a complex object composed of two parts *a* and *b* standing to each other in the relation *R*. The complex object '*a*-in-the-relation-*R*-to-*b*' may be capable of being *perceived*; when perceived it is perceived as one object. Attention may show that it is complex, we then *judge* that *a* and *b* stand in the relation *R*. Such a judgment, being derived from perception by mere attention, may be called 'a judgment of perception'. This judgment of perception, considered as an actual occurrence, is a relation of four terms, namely *a* and *b* and *R* and the percipient. The perception, on the other hand, is a relation of two terms, namely '*a*-in-the-relation-*R*-to-*b*' and the percipient. Since an object of perception cannot be nothing, we cannot perceive '*a*-in-the-relation-*R*-to-*b*' unless *a* is in the relation *R* to *b*. Hence a judgment of perception, according to the above definition, must be true.[15]

If there is any doubt that perception is being treated as acquaintance in this passage, it is removed by the parallel discussion in *The Problems of Philosophy*, which he sums up in

14. Included in *Philosophical Essays*, London, 1910, p. 147.
15. Cambridge, 1910–13; Vol. 1, p. 43.

these words: 'In all cases where we know by acquaintance a complex fact consisting of certain terms in a certain relation, we say that the truth, that these terms are so related, has the first or absolute kind of self-evidence.'[16] Here acquaintance with a fact has taken the place of acquaintance with a complex object, but this is understandable in view of the transition from objects to truths which he is striving to achieve.

His way of effecting the transition tends to make judgments about sense-data infallible. The tendency is very clear in the last two passages. Admittedly, he distinguishes perception from judgment, just as in the parallel passage in *The Problems of Philosophy* he distinguishes acquaintance from judgment. But in each case the first thing seems to lead automatically to the second, and the second seems to be credited with infallibility.

However, in fact, he did not take this step so precipitately. It is true that it is required by his doctrine 'that error can only arise when we regard the immediate object, i.e. the sense-datum, as the mark of some physical object'.[17] For this implies that we cannot go wrong so long as we confine ourselves to describing our sense-data without saying anything about their causes. But in fact he was more cautious, at least in the passage quoted from *Principia Mathematica*, which continues: 'This does not mean that in a judgment which *appears* to us to be one of perception we are sure of not being in error, since we may err in thinking that our judgment has really been derived merely by analysis of what was perceived.' So there is a proviso attached to the thesis that these judgments of perception are infallible: when I make the judgment I must confine myself to what can be extracted by analysis from the complex object – or, as he sometimes calls it, 'the complex fact' – with which I am acquainted. When I try to analyse the complex fact and 'separate out its constituents', I may fail to carry our the task properly.[18]

So he never really took the third step. But his pre-1919 theory of judgment pushed him in that direction. For, according to that theory, when someone makes a judgment, the self is acquainted with the particulars and universals which are men-

16. *The Problems of Philosophy*, pp. 137–8.
17. ibid., p. 110.
18. ibid., pp. 136, 137.

tioned in it or in its analysis. To judge is to arrange these things in thought.[19] If the author of the judgment is confronted with an array of the same things in a perceived fact, it might well seem that he could hardly go wrong. But really this would be an illusion, produced by neglect of the question, how he identifies the things, and by concentration on the question, how they are arranged. It is no accident that so many of Russell's examples in this period involve spatial relations. Such examples focus attention on to the internal structure of the perceived fact and suggest that the percipient can analyse it and report it without drawing on his memory of anything outside it.

The best antidote to these examples is to consider so-called 'simple' sense-data, such as patches of colour. For, contrary to what he suggests, the same problem arises about such truths as 'This is red'. But in cases like this we are not tempted to treat analysis of the internal structure of the perceived fact as an entirely self-contained affair.

Russell's logical analysis of acquaintance was worked out for perception, but extended to immediate memory and paradigmatic remote memory. It underrates the contribution made by propositions, because it suggests that acquaintance can extract truths from its objects immediately and without calling on any external resources. So, though Theory I does not go so far as to attribute infallibility to paradigmatic judgments of remote memory, it does exaggerate their intuitiveness. Under the influence of Moore's early realism, Russell construed the mind's contact with its objects as if it always touched them with a fine point. Theory II attempts to correct this error by disentangling propositions from the doctrine of acquaintance, which is abandoned, with the ego, in 1919. But the attempt is not entirely successful, because in *The Analysis of Mind* Russell still finds it difficult to keep propositions distinct from the data with which they are concerned. Moreover, in this period the data are not objects outside the mind, but images. So, though the difficulties with which he struggles in Theory II are of the same general character, their specific form is different.

19. See 'On the nature of truth and falsehood', 1910. This paper in *Philosophical Essays* was substituted for the third part of his earlier paper, 'On the nature of truth' (Proceedings of the Aristotelian Society, VII, 1906–7).

Theory II

By 1917 Russell had come to the conclusion that Theory I is false. But he still believed that in immediate memory acquaintance with perceived particulars lasts as long as the specious present. The next step towards Theory II was taken in 1919, when he ceased to believe in the existence of the ego and so could no longer treat acquaintance as a dual relation between subject and object. This led to a general change in his epistemology, because it was no longer possible for him to suppose that the mere occurrence of data was enough to produce knowledge. It was now obvious that interpretation is always needed, and interpretation requires comparison and so must rest on a point of support outside what is immediately given. He ceased to treat perception and immediate memory as direct cognitive relations with particulars, and, since he had already rejected this treatment of paradigmatic remote memory, his rejection of it was now over-determined. He also had to work out a new theory of judgment. For in his previous theory (i.e. the theory published in 1910 in 'On the nature of truth and falsehood') the central role was played by the direct relations, acquaintance and judging, which related the ego to the objects outside the mind that were the constituents of the proposition judged true. If images or any other symbolic go-betweens occurred, they were a luxury. But according to the new theory, developed in 1919 in 'On propositions' and in *The Analysis of Mind*, judgment can not occur without symbols, and, very paradoxically, the symbols are always images.

This is a complex series of changes, and the last one led to some confusion in Russell's mind. For it gave images two distinct roles to play in paradigmatic remote memory. It is obvious that in that kind of memory they often function as representative data. If they are also required to function as the elements out of which memory-propositions are formed, that is an entirely different role. Anyone who does not keep these two roles of images carefully separated, will confuse two opposed directions of fit. First, there is the case described by Wittgenstein: 'But it is also possible for a face to come before my mind, and then for me to be able to draw it, without my remembering whose it is or where I have seen it.'[20] Here the image would be a datum, and, if it struck me as familiar, it would raise the question, 'Who is this?', and I would then try to fit a name to the image. But this direction of fit would be reversed if I started with the question, 'What does Mr. A look like?' In this case, if I got an image, it would not lead to a question, but would come as the answer to a question already asked, and so the direction of fit would be reversed. Now Russell did not simply confuse these two cases with one another when he developed Theory II. But he did not distinguish between them sufficiently clearly, and this produces flaws in Theory II at several points.

Theory II can be understood only against the background of the new account of judgment that Russell gives in 'On propositions'. His rejection of the subject made it necessary to find something else to put in its place. He puts what he calls 'the content of the belief' in this position. The content is what is believed, if it is a case of belief, and it is the same thing as the proposition. It is made up of words, images or both. But images are the gold, and words are only paper currency, because we understand the meanings of words only if we are able to get the right images.[21] When words 'operate without the medium of images, this seems to be a telescoped process. Thus the problem of the meaning of words is reduced to the problem of the meaning of images'.[22] The meaning of an image depends partly on resemblance, but it is partly 'within the control of our will. . . . The image of a triangle may mean one particular triangle or triangles in general'.[23] Finally, in addition to words and images, sensations may occur as parts of propositions:[24] i.e., when someone makes a judgment about a sensation, the sensation itself may occur autonymously in the proposition. In such a case, the sensation functions in two different ways simultaneously, as a datum, and as a symbol of itself or autonymously. This account of propositions is repeated in *The Analysis of Mind*, and the possi-

20. *Philosophical Investigations*, Pt. II, § iii.

21. 'On propositions', reprinted in *Essays in Logic and Knowledge*, pp. 307, 308, 302. Cf. Berkeley, *Principles of Human Knowledge*, Introduction, § xx.

22. 'On propositions', p. 303.

23. ibid., p. 303.

24. ibid., p. 311.

bility of the autonymous occurrence of sensations is explained at greater length.[25]

The resulting account of memory has two layers. First, Russell analyses the general phenomenon of memory in animals as well as in human beings. Then, on this basis, he builds up a theory about what only human beings can achieve. One explanation of the superiority that he attributes to images is that, like Aristotle, he wants to show that there is a continuous development from animals to human beings. 'It would seem that image-propositions are more primitive than word-propositions, and may well antedate language. There is no reason why memory-images accompanied by that very simple belief-feeling which we decided to be the essence of memory, should not have occurred before language arose; indeed, it would be rash to assert positively that memory of this sort does not occur among the higher animals.'[26]

Another explanation of the supposed superiority of images is that, according to him, they express paradigmatic remote memories, whereas words express habit-memories. This view is connected with his failure to maintain a clear distinction between cases in which images function as data and cases in which they function as symbols. Suppose that it is conceded to Russell that, when a person has an image functioning as a datum, he is in the most direct possible relation with his past. It still would not follow that, when images function as elements in memory-propositions, they have any lesser tendency than words to get between the raconteur and his original experience. Now it might look as if it were possible to offer a rather subtle defence of Russell's view that images, unlike words, express paradigmatic remote memories. For could we not interpret him to mean that images, unlike words, can occur autonymously in memory-propositions, and so combine the two different functions? But this defence will not succeed. For in a memory of that kind the image will be a representative datum, and so, if it is simultaneously taken as an element in the memory-proposition, it will be referring not to itself as representative datum, but rather to the past object which the representative datum represents. It cannot, therefore, occur autonymously. In this it

25. *The Analysis of Mind*, pp. 201, 237–9.
26. ibid., p. 242.

is quite unlike a sensation, which can occur autonymously, precisely because the proposition is about it and not about something else which it represents.

When Russell applied his new account to the propositions of paradigmatic remote memory, he modified his earlier thesis that pastness is one of their constituents.[27] His view now is that a proposition of this kind consists of a tenseless core of images and that pastness is not signified by anything in its content. Pastness is introduced in an entirely different way, as a specific modification of the feeling of belief, which he now takes over from Hume. This feeling, which attaches to propositions, has not only a generic form, bare non-temporal assent, but also two specific temporal forms, memory and expectation.[28] When he develops this theory of belief in *The Analysis of Mind*, he takes care to point out that, when a proposition about the past is believed on inductive grounds, pastness is signified by something in its content, and the attached feeling is non-temporal assent. Analogously, when a proposition about the future is believed on inductive grounds, futurity is usually signified by something in its content. The specific past-oriented feeling of belief is only needed for paradigmatic remote memories, and the specific future-oriented feeling of belief is only needed for what he calls 'expectations'. We might have supposed that he would have said 'precognitions', but he says 'expectations', and he is referring to a particular kind of inductively grounded belief, the kind of expectations that are unhesitatingly formed, and immediately and personally verified, like the expectation of thunder and lightning.[29]

After he had abandoned Theory I he might have been expected to put great emphasis on his 1915 thesis, that immediate memory is the origin of the concept 'past' and lays the foundations of all our knowledge of the past, because it alone puts us in a position to verify the correspondence of image to original. But the curious thing is that he says very little about those two points in *The Analysis of Mind*. He says that 'there may be a specific feeling of "pastness", especially where immediate memory is concerned', and that 'immediate memory is important

27. 'On the experience of time', pp. 224 ff.
28. 'On propositions', pp. 308 and 311.
29. *The Analysis of Mind*, pp. 176, 251–2.

because it bridges the gulf between sensations and the images which are their copies'.[30] However, there is no development of these points in *The Analysis of Mind*, and it might appear that he believed that the concept 'past' can be acquired through remote memory.

If that was his view in *The Analysis of Mind*, the concept 'past' would have had to be derived from some property of the images that occur in remote memory. He mentions two such properties which he might have regarded as the source of the concept. One is familiarity, and the other is the property 'which makes us regard them as referring to more or less remote portions of the past',[31] and which he actually calls 'pastness'. But it is implausible to suppose that these properties of images, or any others, could play this role. No doubt, familiarity is a felt property of certain images. But it suggests the proposition, 'I have experienced something like this before' only to someone who already possesses the concept 'past'. Presumably, the same is true of whatever property Russell means by the 'pastness' of an image. In general, such properties of images get their names from the propositions which they suggest, and they suggest propositions containing the concept 'past' only to those who have already learned the meaning of the word 'past' at closer quarters. In some cases it seems actually to be an illusion to suggest that there is a property, or at least to suggest that it can be identified independently of the proposition which it suggests.

If all such theories about the origin of the concept 'past' are implausible, and if Russell has in reserve a more plausible theory, according to which we acquire it in a less remote way, it is natural to suppose that he is relying on that theory in *The Analysis of Mind*. But there are two passages which seem to go against this interpretation. So if it is going to be adopted, the two passages must be reconciled with it.

One of them occurs in *The Analysis of Mind*: 'It might be contended that a memory-image acquires meaning only through the memory belief, which would seem, at least in the case of memory to make belief more primitive than the meaning of images'.[32] This is paradoxical, because, if belief requires a pro-

30. ibid., pp. 162, 175.
31. ibid., pp. 161, 162.
32. ibid., p. 235.

position, and if the proposition is formed out of images, there would not be anything to believe until the images had acquired meanings. However, the paradox is put forward tentatively. But in the second passage in 'On propositions', which was written earlier, he puts it forward without any reservations: '. . . it is clear that, when we remember by means of images, the images are accompanied by a belief, a belief which may be expressed (though with undue explicitness) by saying that they are felt to be copies of something that existed previously. And, without memory, images could hardly acquire meaning. Thus the analysis of belief is essential even to a full account of the meaning of words and images – for the meaning of words, we found, depends on that of images, which in turn depend on memory, which is itself a form of belief.'[33]

These obscure remarks amount to a suggestion that in the case of certain memory-propositions belief comes before understanding. But how could that be so? It is just possible that what Russell meant was that among the propositions of remote memory there are some which function like ostensive definitions and produce understanding of the concept past in much the same way that 'This is red' produces understanding of the concept 'red'. But he never says this, and in any case there is another interpretation which fits his remarks better.

What they probably mean is that there is a certain property of images which leads us to give them a past reference and to believe that they correspond to experiences that we have had. This would only happen to us when we already possessed the concept 'past'. So in these passages, he is not trying to explain our acquisition of the concept, but only the fact that after we have acquired it, we give certain images a past reference. The paradox is then less extreme. He is not saying that belief is more primitive than understanding in such cases, but only that it is more primitive than past reference. His idea is that an image occurs as a datum and strikes me as familiar, and so produced a belief in me, and then, in order to express this belief, I put the image into a proposition in which it has a reference to the past. This interpretation allows us to suppose that Russell still adhered to his 1915 theory that we acquire the concept 'past' through immediate memory.

33. 'On propositions', p. 306.

Although this is less paradoxical than the other thesis, it is still very paradoxical. For when we scrutinise the details of the complex process, described by him, several difficulties appear. First, consider the function assigned to familiarity. It must be remembered that Theory II has to explain the transition from the common achievements of higher animals and human beings to those that are peculiar to human beings. He begins with the common achievements, and builds up his theory from them. He points out that a person's belief that a particular image corresponds to a past experience of his, 'must, in fundamental cases, be based on a characteristic of the image itself, since we cannot evoke the past bodily and compare it with the present image'. The characteristic is familiarity which, according to him, is a feeling which need not involve a proposition. 'The judgment that what is familiar has been experienced before is a product of reflection, and is no part of the feeling of familiarity, such as a horse may be supposed to have when he returns to his stable.' It is a feeling capable of degrees: 'In an image of a well-known face, for example, some parts may feel more familiar than others; when this happens we have more belief in the accuracy of the familiar parts than in that of the unfamiliar parts. I think that it is by this means that we become critical of images, not by some imageless memory with which we compare them.'[34] Here he is rejecting the central tenet of Theory I that we can by-pass the image and achieve acquaintance with the object experienced in the past.

But how much can be extracted from the feeling of familiarity? Does it really provide a general explanation of the fact that we refer certain images to the past, and believe that they correspond to past experiences of ours? Or does it explain these two facts only in the special case described by Wittgenstein, where the image does not come in response to a question, but comes first, and the name or description is then fitted to it? And even in this special case we might feel doubts about the function that Russell assigns to familiarity. For he seems to import into this kind of case a definite reference to the past, which is only appropriate to the other kind of case, where the definite reference is supplied by the prior question. If an image strikes me as familiar, I only give it an indefinite reference to my past.

34. *The Analysis of Mind*, pp. 161, 169, 161–2.

Now he does not actually confuse the two opposed directions of fit. For he says that in human beings a familiar image suggests the claim 'I have experienced something like this before', whereas recollection usually produces a claim such as 'I had two eggs for breakfast', which expresses the attachment of the past-oriented feeling of belief to an image.[35] There are several differences between his descriptions of these two situations. In the first, the claim is indefinite, the feeling is familiarity, and presumably no attempt at recollection has yet occurred. But in the second, the claim is definite, the feeling is past-oriented belief, and there has probably been an attempt at recollection. However, he never explicitly draws the distinction between the two directions of fit, and he tries to show that the second type of case develops smoothly out of the first, without any sharp discontinuities. This is understandable, because his theory is an attempt to build up human memory out of elements that exist at the lower level of animal memory, and so it is natural for him to blur certain differences between the first case, which may be quite like what happens when an animal remembers something, and the second case, which is not.

The fundamental reason for his lack of clarity about the differences between the two cases is his adoption of an image theory of propositions. The image which occurs in the situation described by Wittgenstein may be exactly like the image which would have occurred if the direction of fit had been reversed. Hence, it is only too easy to minimise the difference between the first situation, in which the image is a datum, and, perhaps, a sign, in the sense in which a colossal bang is a sign that something catastrophic has happened, and the second situation, which exhibits the reversed direction of fit, because the image is a symbol which is part of my propositional answer to the question about the appearance of an absent person. This difference would not have been minimised by anyone who treated words rather than images as the usual elements of propositions.

There are several other factors which join in the conspiracy to keep the difference between datum and symbol out of sight. The most important one is Russell's well-known assimilation of remote memory to sense-perception. 'If (a sensation) is part of

35. ibid., p. 175.

a perception (of a person), we may say that the person presented is an object of consciousness. For in this case, the sensation is a sign of the perceived object in much the same way in which a memory image is a sign of the remembered object.'[36] General assent to this account of memory-images is unlikely to be revoked even when they are evidently functioning as symbols.

His theory that sensations may occur autonymously in propositions may also play a part at this point. For when a sensation occurs autonymously in the judgment '—— is of Jones', where the blank is filled by the sensation itself, the difference between datum and symbol is very inconspicuous. It would be equally easy to miss if an image could occur autonymously in the judgment '—— has occurred before in my experience'. Now he never actually says that a memory-image ought to be regarded as the past experience itself occurring autonymously in the present judgment. Even when he held Theory I he did not update the past experience so that it – the very same one – could function as the present object of remote memory, and he was even further from being in a position to take this line after he had given up the Theory I. However, in *The Analysis of Mind* he does take a step in that direction. He says, 'We might be tempted to put the memory-belief into the words: "Something like this image occurred". But such words would be very far from an accurate translation of the simplest kind of memory-belief. "Something like this image" is a very complicated conception. In the simplest kind of memory we are not aware of the difference between an image and the sensation which it copies, which may be called its prototype. When the image is before us, we judge rather "This occurred". The image is not distinguished from the object which existed in the past: the word "this" covers both, and enables us to have a memory-belief which does not introduce the complicated notion "something like this".'[37] To say 'This occurred' when confronted by a memory-image, with no distinction made between the image and its prototype is as close as he can get to saying '—— occurred' where the blank is filled by the prototype itself.

An auxiliary role is played by the fact that in certain cases the feeling of familiarity really does seem to develop quite

36. ibid., p. 292.
37. ibid., p. 179.

smoothly into the past-oriented feeling of belief (though he never identifies the two feelings). In the situation described by Wittgenstein the image of the face strikes me as familiar, and, since I am a human being and not a horse, this is equivalent to saying that it strikes me that I have seen it somewhere before, even if only in a dream. But, according to Russell, if I accept this, I have a past-oriented feeling of belief directed onto the tenseless proposition, 'I see this'. So in this case it seems natural to say that the feeling of familiarity develops into the propositional attitude.

But when we look more deeply into the differences between the two so-called 'feelings', it turns out to be much more plausible to say that they are quite different in kind, and that the second occurs after, and as a result of, the first.

Consider familiarity. If we call it 'a felt property of certain things', we must take care to add that the proposition that it suggests is part of the criterion of identity of the feeling. Now the proposition that it suggests is a memory-claim with an indefinite reference to the past. But Russell neglects this part of the criterion of identity of the felt property, because he concentrates on the feeling of familiarity rather than on the judgment that a thing is familiar, and, according to him, the indefinite memory-claim expresses a kind of recognition which 'differs from the sense of familiarity by being cognitive: it is a belief or judgment, which the sense of familiarity is not'.[38] But although, of course, the judgment is not identical with the sense of familiarity, it is part of its criterion of identity. For even if a person does not formulate an indefinite memory-claim, we say that something struck him as familiar only because he would formulate it, or, at least, that he has a basis for formulating it: and though a horse could not formulate it, we say that something struck it as familiar only because it would have a basis for formulating it, if it could. So it is a mistake to speak of the feeling of familiarity as if its criterion of identity were independent of the fact that it suggests, or would suggest, or would suggest if it could, a justified indefinite memory-claim. Provided that this error is avoided, we may say that to feel the familiarity of a thing is to experience one of its properties. Naturally, the pro-

38. ibid., p. 170; cf. the remark already quoted about the horse and its stable.

perty will be relational, because the thing may not be familiar to another person.

But those who hold that belief is a feeling can hardly classify it in the same way. For in this case the so-called 'feeling' is the person's reaction to a proposition. When he considers it, he feels bound to assent to it. So in this case the proposition comes first and elicits the feeling, whereas in the other case the feeling comes first and suggests the proposition.

Another, connected difference is that the feeling of belief is directed onto the whole proposition and not onto any part of it. If it had been directed onto a part of it, we might have been able to regard it as the experience of a property of that part, like the feeling of familiarity. But this road is blocked, and the obstacle explains the development of Hume's account of the difference between 'ideas of memory' and 'ideas of imagination'. Hume supposes that the former are distinguished by their vivacity. But if he meant 'vividness', his theory would be destroyed by the objection that it excludes the possibility of a memory-image of a foggy scene. This objection can be generalised: no pictorial property can serve to distinguish memory-images from the rest without excluding some class of memory-images which ought not to be excluded. The object of the feeling of belief must be a whole proposition, and, if we say that it is an image, that will only be a brief way of referring to the proposition of which the image is an element, and so the feeling cannot be the experience of a pictorial property of the image.

When Hume appealed to vivacity, he really meant the force with which an image imposes itself on a person either immediately, as in memory, or mediately, as in causal belief. This suggestion obviously requires the image to be an element of a proposition. In the case of memory the requirement would be met if, for example, I tried to recall the appearance of an absent friend. I might say that my image felt right, meaning that it felt right to me as the answer to a question, and, therefore, as an element in a proposition. It would, of course, be a mistake to treat this as a cast-iron criterion of accuracy. For there is also the question of credentials: 'How good is my memory?' But Hume's theory is correct to this extent: I am subjected to the force exerted by the mechanism of my memory, whatever that mechanism may be. This point is not substantially altered by

Russell's suggestion that the indication of time is in the feeling rather than in the proposition.

It is clear that Russell's account of the way in which images function in memory cannot be applied to the case in which an image occurs in response to a question. Why then did he not explicitly restrict its scope to the type of case described by Wittgenstein? The explanation seems to be that, when he develops his account of familiarity, he quietly imports into that kind of case a definite reference to the past which really belongs only to the other kind of case that exhibits the opposite direction of fit.

This comes about in a rather complex way. The first point to notice is one that has already been mentioned. According to Russell, familiarity immediately suggests a memory-proposition to us, and leads us to believe it. Now this memory-proposition is, as he says, an indefinite one, such as, 'I have seen (something like) this window before'. But without seeming to notice what he is doing, he substitutes a definite claim of the kind that I might, but need not, be able to make next. 'In the bedroom in which I slept as a child, the window was like this' (and here an image occurs). This cannot be correct because the feeling of familiarity, by itself, can neither suggest nor lead me to believe a proposition referring to a definite past experience of mine. One way of getting such a proposition is to take a situation in which the direction of fit is reversed, because, for example, I am asked about the shape of the window in my childhood bedroom. But in that case I would not say that my image felt familiar, still less that it struck me as familiar. Rather, it would feel right. So Russell should not have imported the definite past reference into the case described by Wittgenstein; and in the other case, which exhibits the reverse direction of fit, he should not have appealed to the feeling of familiarity. If my answer to a question feels familiar, that may be only because it is my usual error.

Although Russell marks the difference between an indefinite memory-claim and a definite one, his discussion of the transition from the first to the second shows that he is not aware of its importance. He illustrates the transition with an example which is peculiar in two different ways:[39] the object which sets

39. ibid., p. 176.

me going is not an image but a physical object, a wall with an array of pictures, and I feel that it is unfamiliar rather than familiar. The first of these two peculiarities tends to conceal the fact that there is any transition from the indefinite claim to the definite one, and the second introduces a complication which obscures the nature of the transition.

First, consider the second peculiarity, the fact that the arrangement of pictures strikes me as unfamiliar. If I made a memory-claim on the basis of this experience, it would be negative: 'This array of pictures is unlike anything that I have seen before.' No doubt, it is not likely that I would make this indefinite claim in this particular case. But it is easy to think of examples in which an indefinite claim would be natural. The important point is that such a claim is all that can be made on the basis of the unfamiliarity, and that it is negative. Similarly, if I went beyond the basis of felt unfamiliarity, and said what, in particular, the arrangement of pictures was unlike, that too would be a negative claim. This is a tiresome complication, and Russell might equally well have given an example of familiarity and a positive claim.

The other peculiarity of his example is more important. Why is it that in this case I do not have to think very hard before coming up with a definite reference to my past, *viz.*, to the wall when I last saw it? It is easier to answer this question for the positive case before considering the negative case. If the wall strikes me as familiar, no definite reference to the past can be based on that experience. It may be easy for me to provide a definite reference, but to do so would be to take a further step. But if it strikes me as unfamiliar, it would be absurd to try to take this further step, because when it strikes me as unlike anything that I have seen before, there is no particular thing which it will turn out to be unlike. So why do I not have to think very hard before coming up with a definite reference to my past in Russell's negative example? The search for such a reference in this case ought to be more than difficult; it ought to be an absurdity.

The answer to this question is obvious. In Russell's example the definite reference to my past does not lie close at hand, but, rather, is contained in the meaning of the original statement, that the wall strikes me as unfamiliar. He takes this to mean that it strikes me as unfamiliar-as-itself, or, to put this in plain English, that it strikes me that it has changed in some way (cf. the horse returning to its stable). Of course, this experience would still leave me with the residual question, 'In what way has it changed?' But it would not leave me with the residual problem of finding a definite past reference. For the definite past reference to the thing itself at an earlier point of time is already included in the meaning of the word 'unfamiliar' in the original statement. In that statement it means 'self-unfamiliar'. Similarly, if I had said that it struck me as familiar, I would probably have meant 'self-familiar'.

At first sight, these complications might appear to facilitate a smooth transition from the feeling of familiarity (or unfamiliarity) to Russell's past-oriented feeling of belief in a proposition with a definite past reference. But that would be an illusion. It is absurd to try to find a definite past reference after an experience of general unfamiliarity, and, though such a reference may be found after an experience of general familiarity, it is a further step to produce it. Moreover, when such a reference is already contained in the experience, that is only because it is a different experience. Self-familiarity is not the same thing as general familiarity. Here we tend to talk about the feeling of familiarity as if it were always the same feeling, whatever claim might be involved in its description. But this is to ignore the fact that the appropriateness of the claim is part of the criterion of identity of the feeling. If this mistake was made about the word 'strange', it would be more obvious. A person may look strange by looking unlike anyone else, or, more easily, by looking unlike himself. In these two cases, his strangeness is obviously not the same property.

In any case, most of Russell's examples in *The Analysis of Mind* involve the familiarity of images, and there is no concept of self-familiarity for images. For how would I identify the earlier manifestation of this image which I am now having? Of course, we could improvise a method of identification. But that has not yet been done, and there is no need to do it, whereas the method of identifying an earlier phase in the history of a material object has been settled, and it does answer to a need.

It may now be possible to explain Russell's insistence that the word 'this' refers both to the past experience and to the present image, with no distinction made between them.[40] He may have been trying to construe the general familiarity of an image in the typical situation described by Wittgenstein as a kind of self-familiarity. For when the specious present terminates, though the image detaches itself from the sensation and begins to lead a life of its own, they might both be regarded as phases in the history of a single entity, and this might suggest that a later phase – i.e. an image – might strike me as self-familiar, in much the same way that my childhood bedroom, if I returned to it, might strike me as self-familiar, or the horse's stable might strike it as self-familiar. However, this idea would be mistaken, because the horse and I have independent criteria for re-identifying the stable and the bedroom, but there are no such criteria for the entity which consists of a sensation followed by a long series of image-phases. The concept of 'the self-unfamiliarity of an image' breaks down in the same way.

It is worth observing that there is an analogy between Russell's theory of memory in *The Analysis of Mind* and the theory of desire that he develops in Chapter 3 of the same book. In the latter discomfort plays a role much like that of familiarity in the former. Discomfort is treated as an immediately recognisable causal property of a mental occurrence.[41] It is the property of initiating a behaviour-cycle which terminates with the attainment of an object which removes the discomfort and so produces quiescence. According to Russell, a desire is simply a mental occurrence with this property. 'A desire is called "conscious" when it is accompanied by a true belief as to the state of affairs that will bring quiescence; otherwise it is called "unconscious".'[42]

Now Russell rightly insists that a true paradigmatic memory-claim must be caused by the experience to which it refers.[43] It follows that any paradigmatic memory-claim will implicitly involve such a stipulation about its own causation. So suppose, as Russell does, that the claim is based on an image which strikes me as familiar (general familiarity). Then the implied stipulation will be that this image was caused by some experi-

40. ibid., p. 179, already quoted.
41. ibid., pp. 66, 75.
42. ibid, p. 76.
43. ibid., p. 82.

ence of mine that was like it (indefinite reference to my past).

Here we have a causal requirement about the past, which is analogous to Russell's causal requirement about the future in the case of desire. In order to exhibit the analogy, let us make the unrealistic assumption that any feeling of discomfort will suggest, and lead me to believe, the proposition that it will cause a behaviour-cycle terminating in the attainment of some object that will remove it. Then the felt general discomfort of a mental occurrence will be like Russell's felt general familiarity of an image, which suggests, and leads me to believe the proposition that the image was caused by some prototype in my past. Notice that this proposition could be true, without my realising that it was true, and even without its occurring to me that it might be true. In such a case it would be possible to say that the image was familiar, but did not strike me as familiar. Similarly, a person might want something and yet not be aware that he wanted anything. In such a case Russell would have to say that his awareness of his discomfort was totally suppressed (given our unrealistic assumption). Conversely, an image might strike me as familiar when it was not familiar. Similarly, I might suffer from false general discomfort (like false hunger, except for the fact that false hunger is specific). Moreover, an image might strike me as familiar when it was familiar, but not *because* it was familiar (if the normal causal requirement for memory was not met). Similarly, my discomfort might not be the cause of the behaviour-cycle which led to its removal.

This theory of desire is unrealistic in many ways, but most obviously so when Russell tries to answer the question how I know what I want. For he can hardly suppose that every kind of object is associated with a recognisable type of discomfort. But, to pursue the analogy, it would be equally implausible to suppose that, when I make a definite memory-claim, I base it on a specific kind of familiarity in my image. It is very obvious that at this point in his theory of desire he ought to have brought in his other idea, that desire is an attitude to propositions, to be treated like belief.[44] This criticism of his theory of desire is similar to the main criticism of Theory II that has been developed in this paper.

However, Theory II does not rely so heavily on immediately

44. 'The philosophy of logical atomism', pp. 218, 228.

felt causal properties of mental occurrences. For, though he uses examples of self-familiarity, he does not go so far as to claim that the general feeling of familiarity is divisible into species which can be recognised immediately as pointing towards particular prototypes. However, he does make the transition from the feeling of general familiarity to the past-oriented feeling of belief in singular propositions of remote memory in a way that blurs the distinction between data and symbols.

The development of Russell's ideas about memory illustrates a general feature of his philosophy. He sees the importance of propositions in the theory of knowledge, but he does not entirely emancipate himself from the point of view of his eighteenth-century predecessors, who were less aware of their importance. Consequently, he runs too closely together, even if he does not actually confuse, symbols and data, things that we do and things that happen to us, criteria and credentials, and other similarly related couples.

10 Russell's Theory of Desire

Russell's account of desire in *The Analysis of Mind* is an attempt to combine elements drawn from two different sources, behaviouristic theory and depth psychology. It is only a sketch, and his method of blending the disparate elements is too simple. But, characteristically, it introduces some central problems in a very direct way.

He begins with a view which, he says, he is going to reject. 'When we say: "I hope it will rain", or "I expect it will rain", we express, in the first case, a desire, and, in the second, a belief, with an identical content, namely, the image of rain. It would be easy to say that, just as belief is one kind of feeling in relation to this content, so desire is another kind.'[1] In fact, he himself had said this in 'The philosophy of logical atomism'.[2]

The view to be rejected is related to Hume's theory, that a desire is an impression of reflection excited by, and attached to, an idea.[3] But the relation is not identity. For though Russell in his description of the view says that the content is the image of rain, he means that the content is a proposition composed of images.[4] This is an improvement on Hume's view, that a desire is attached to a single idea, or image, because it allows for the articulateness and definiteness of typical reports of desires.

However, Russell does not regard it as an improvement, if it is offered as an account of the essence of desire. It is true that we can usually express our desires with an articulateness and definiteness that require propositions. But he rejects the suggestion that this form of expression reveals the deep structure of the concept of desire. 'According to this view, what comes first in

1. *The Analysis of Mind*, p. 58.
2. Reprinted in *Essays in Logic and Knowledge*, pp. 218, 228.
3. *Treatise of Human Nature*, Bk. II, pt. 1, § i; Bk. II, pt. 3, § ix.
4. See 'On propositions', reprinted in *Essays in Logic and Knowledge*, p. 309.

desire is something imagined, with a specific feeling related to it, namely the specific feeling which we call "desiring" it. The discomfort associated with unsatisfied desire, and the actions which aim at satisfying desire, are, in this view, both of them effects of the desire.' But this, he thinks, attributes too much importance to the thought of the end to be achieved. Even when this thought does produce action, it is never the prime mover. The prime mover is always a mental occurrence involving discomfort. So 'the primitive non-cognitive element in desire seems to be a push, not a pull, an impulsion away from the actual, rather than an attraction towards the ideal. Certain sensations and other mental occurrences have a property which we call discomfort; these cause such bodily movements as are likely to lead to their cessation'.[5] This, he thinks, is the essence of desire, and the overlay of beliefs about the objects that we desire merely differentiates conscious desire, which is only one species in the genus.

Most of his arguments for this account of the essence of desire are drawn from the two sources already mentioned, behaviouristic theory and depth psychology. It is, of course, intended to demonstrate a continuous development from animals to human beings. Psychoanalysis is represented as uncovering the primitive essence of desire, which persists in many animals without its characteristically human overlay of beliefs. It should be added that he also appeals to two further kinds of evidence: the occurrence of totally unreflective human actions, and the existence of preconscious motivation (which he does not sufficiently distinguish from unconscious motivation).

How behaviouristic is this account of the essence of desire? The passages so far quoted suggest that at least it avoids the extreme rejection of any events additional to stimulus and behaviour. In them he allows that there are extra events, namely sensations and other mental occurrences involving discomfort.

But if we look more closely at his exposition, the matter becomes less clear. His main concern is to demonstrate that desire does not essentially involve the thought of the end to be achieved, and his first argument is based on a denial that such thoughts occur in animals. But a close examination of his argument may well leave us uncertain whether he is denying more than this.

5. *The Analysis of Mind*, pp. 58, 68.

Speaking of animals, he says, 'They *may* have minds in which all sorts of things take place, but we can know nothing about their minds except by means of inferences from their actions; and the more such inferences are examined, the more dubious they appear. It would seem, therefore, that actions alone must be the test of the desires of animals. From this it is an easy step to the conclusion that an animal's desire is nothing but a characteristic of a certain series of actions, namely those that would commonly be regarded as inspired by the desire in question. And when it has been shown that this view affords a satisfactory account of animal desires, it is not difficult to see that the same explanation is applicable to the desires of human beings.' So, according to him, what is needed is 'a re-statement of what constitutes desire, exhibiting it as a causal law of our actions, not as something existing in our minds'.[6]

If he really took the 'easy step' to the reductive conclusion about animals' desires, his account of them would be faulty, and the fault would produce a different, but related, fault in his account of human desires. The fault in his account of animals' desires, which is pointed out by Kenny,[7] is that they would lack starting points. But particular desires must be timeable, and so their criterion of identity must involve some kind of starting point. Now the starting point need not be mental. The argument is more general: *viz.*, that, since it must be possible for a desire to antedate the stimulus which produces behaviour leading to satisfaction, the starting point must be some kind of event in the organism itself. A symmetrical criticism can be made of Russell's account of the termination of an animal's desire:[8] this too must involve an event in the organism which marks the difference between satisfaction and frustration after the behaviour has ceased, but which, like the initiating event, need not be mental.

The consequential fault in his account of human desire would be slightly different. He assumes that the essence of human desire involves nothing which does not occur in animals. If he did take the 'easy step' about animals, this assumption would produce a more subtle fault in his account of human desire. The

6. ibid., pp. 62, 60.
7. *Action, Emotion and Will*, p. 108.
8. ibid, pp. 106 ff.

trouble would not be that he denies that desires in human beings have mental accompaniments. He explicitly says that they are accompanied by sensations involving discomfort,[9] and for human beings he never accepts the kind of extreme behaviourism that would rule out such accompaniments.[10] The fault would be that, if he took the 'easy step', he could not regard the accompaniments as essential to human desire. Yet it is essential that our desires should have starting points and terminating points of some kind in ourselves. If their starting points and terminating points do not depend on the mental accompaniments, on what do they depend?

The requirement of timeability is entirely general, but he does not take advantage of its generality. For the only starting and terminating points that he considers are the onset and cessation of sensations involving discomfort. But he should have cast his net more widely. It is hardly likely that animals' desires always start and end with sensations. It is true that he allows that an organism need not be conscious of all its sensations. But he insists that they are the sort of thing of which it could be conscious.[11] Yet an animal's desire might be initiated and terminated by neural events which never produced any direct effect in its consciousness.

But, to return to interpretation, did Russell take the 'easy step' in his account of animals' desires? He certainly appears to take it, because he says that the 'detour through the animal's supposed mind is wholly unnecessary', and that he will apply a term like 'hunger' not to 'some possibly mythical, and certainly unverifiable, ingredient of the animal's mind', but to the appropriate 'observable trait in [its] bodily behaviour'.[12] He even crystallises this usage inexplicit definitions: 'The "purpose" of a behaviour-cycle is the result which brings it to an end, normally by a condition of temporary quiescence – provided there is no interruption. An animal is said to "desire" the purpose of a behaviour-cycle while the behaviour-cycle is in progress. I believe these definitions to be adequate to human

9. *The Analysis of Mind*, p. 67.

10. See *Human Knowledge*, London, 1948, p. 58, and *My Philosophical Development*, London, 1957, p. 138.

11. *The Analysis of Mind*, p. 288.

12. ibid., pp. 62, 63.

purposes and desires, but for the present I am only concerned with animals, and with what can be learned by external observation. I am very anxious that no ideas should be attached to the words "purpose" and "desire" beyond those included in the above definitions.'[13]

This seems as clear as crystal, and undoubtedly vulnerable to the criticisms sketched above. But in the next paragraph he says: 'We have not so far considered what is the initial stimulus to a behaviour-cycle', and then, *à propos* of birds building nests, etc., he says: 'We must suppose that the stimulus to the performance of each act is an impulsion from behind, and not an attraction from the future. The same considerations apply to other instincts. A hungry animal feels restless, and is led by instinctive impulse to perform the movements which give it nourishment; but the act of seeking food is not sufficient evidence to conclude that the animal has the thought of food in its mind.'[14] He is, of course, aware that this is incompatible with the extreme denial that there are any events in addition to external stimulus and behaviour. 'Abandoning momentarily the standpoint of behaviourism, we may presume that hungry animals experience sensations involving discomfort, and stimulating such movements as are likely to bring them to the food which is outside their cages. When they have reached the food and eaten it, their discomfort ceases, and their sensations become pleasurable. It *seems*, mistakenly, as if the animals had had this situation in mind throughout, when in fact they have been continually pushed by discomfort.'[15]

But what sort of momentary abandonment of the standpoint of behaviourism is this? Are we to conclude that his view about the hypothesis that there are additional events is only that it is unverifiable, and therefore hazardous? But that would leave unanswered the central question to which his account of animal behaviour was supposed to provide an answer: 'What is the essence of desire?' If it is uncertain whether desire in animals involves any additional events, he is not in a position to argue that such events are not essential because they are not involved in their case. So his definition of desire in animals stands in need

13. ibid., pp. 65–6.
14. ibid., pp. 66–7.
15. ibid., p. 68.

of some other support. But, instead of giving it, he immediately goes on to supplement it with a very necessary account of the 'initial stimulus to a behaviour-cycle'. So perhaps the most natural interpretation is that his definition of desire in animals was not intended to be complete. This involves attributing a confusion to him, since he explicitly offers it as a complete definition.

If this interpretation is correct, the explanation of the confusion may be that he sets out to exclude from the essence of desire a particular kind of initiating mental event, the thought of the end to be achieved, but goes on to exclude all kinds of initiating mental events. This would still not necessarily be a fault, because there might be non-mental initiating events. What finally produces the fault is his failure to consider this possibility, or to see the necessity for considering it. Apparently, his preoccupation with behaviourism diverted him from his quest for the essence of desire, and he did not inquire sufficiently closely into the scope of behaviourism's vague rejections.

In his discussion of human desires he never expresses the faintest doubt that they begin with discomfort. The only doubt that could be attributed to him is whether this type of internal initiating event (or some type) is essential, and even thisdoubt has to be deduced from the preceding discussion of animals' desires.

However, Kenny argues that, when discomfort is defined in Russell's way, its onset and cessation will not be events that are identifiable without reference to the behaviour-cycle that they initiate and terminate.[16] Russell's definition is as follows: 'Discomfort is a property of a sensation or other mental occurrence, consisting in the fact that the occurrence in question stimulates voluntary or reflex movements tending to produce some more or less definite change involving the cessation of the occurrence.' Now his main contention is that 'only experience can show what causes a discomfort to cease'.[17] Kenny's comment is that 'he means that only experience can show what causes the *feeling* of discomfort to cease. But he has no right to mean this when he has defined discomfort not as a feeling but as a causal characteristic.'[18] That is, the fact that the behaviour-

16. *Action, Emotion and Will*, p. 105.
17. *The Analysis of Mind*, pp. 71, 72.
18. *Action, Emotion and Will*, p. 105.

cycle is occurring is the logically necessary and sufficient condition of the existence of the characteristic, discomfort, which initiates it and is removed by its completion.

If this is all that Russell has a right to mean, then, as Kenny points out, he cannot explain the very possibility that his theory is designed to explain – the possibility that a person might refer to his desire, and then make a mistake in specifying its object. For the only available method of identifying it would be through what happens next, and the only possible mistake would lie in the description – or, more likely, prediction – of what happens next. The typal description of a desire through its object would then be impossible, because what was being described would lack any criterion of individual identity. Its onset would be an occult cause, and its cessation an occult effect, of behaviour. So we could not understand how it could antedate the behaviour, or, symmetrically, how it could persist frustrated after the behaviour had ceased.

The relation between this criticism and the one considered earlier is clear. The earlier criticism was that Russell excludes internal initiating events from the essence of desire. According to this one, he includes events which are really non-events. The effect is similar. But this criticism will not work in such an extreme form. For his account of discomfort is evidently a piece of moderate behaviourism, which allows for the immediate awareness of a mental entity with a criterial causal sequel. To feel discomfort is to be immediately aware of a causal characteristic of a sensation. Such a theory cannot be rejected on the general ground that it is incoherent.

But coherence is not truth, and what Russell offers is very far from being a universally true account of desire. The verb 'to want' applies to a scale of cases which runs from needing to the sort of wanting which does not have to be directly based on a specific need, and which is often called 'desiring'. When the two ends of this scale are distinguished, it is evident that, though Russell's theory is roughly appropriate to a certain kind of need, it is hardly appropriate to desire. The kind of need to which it applies is the kind that can, and presumably often does, produce behaviour that leads to satisfaction without the intervention of consciousness. When Russell claims that his description of this kind of need captures the essence of desire, he knows that this is a paradox. The point of the paradox is that, in his opinion, people are aware of what they desire less often than is popularly supposed. He even rejects the general presumption of such awareness in the absence of some block: '. . . the deeper the Freudians delve into the underground regions of instinct, the further they travel from anything resembling conscious desire, and the less possible it becomes to believe that only positive self-deception conceals from us that we really wish for things that are abhorrent to our explicit life.'[19]

Philosophical paradoxes of this kind are a mixture of insights and distortions. In this case the distortions have often been discussed, but less has been said on the other side. In fact, there are many different kinds of cases in which a person is unaware of what he wants, and it is worth asking which of them are explicable in Russell's way. Can Freudian theory really be rewritten in his moderately behaviouristic style? Are there not also ordinary, non-Freudian cases of this sort of lack of self-knowledge, and, if so, are they all to be interpreted in the way that he suggests? Presumably the familiar arguments against the universal applicability of his account would establish a negative answer to this question, unless it becomes impossible for people to be unaware of what they want at the very point at which his account begins to be inapplicable. But, if that is so, it would need to be explained. How would we make the transition from problematical needs to infallibly known desires?

To say that an organism wants something is to say that it is in a state. One difficult question for Russell to answer is, as Kenny shows, how such states are identified individually. Moreover, his assimilation of human desires to needs makes it difficult for him to answer the question how they are identified typally. Yet both questions must be answerable if the concept of 'a want' is a proper concept. One way of investigating them would be to examine the different kinds of cases in which people are unaware of what they want. I shall follow this method, hoping to find out whether the criteria of identity, typal and individual, that Russell suggests, provide the right kind of framework for these cases.

Russell's theory achieves its best fit with hunger, sex and similar needs. A need of this kind is a syndrome of connected

19. *The Analysis of Mind*, p. 60.

items, the first member of which does not have to be a sensation of discomfort. But in a hungry person such sensations often do occur fairly early. Suppose, then, that someone misinterprets the sensations that he is having. Either he does not realise that he is hungry, or he thinks that he is when he is not. In the first case he may, but will not necessarily think that his sensations signal some other need, and in the second case they may in fact signal some other need, but will not necessarily do so.

Let us look more closely at the role played by these characteristic sensations. According to Russell, a particular bout of hunger begins with their onset and ends with their cessation. But this, by itself, does not provide a complete criterion of individual identity. For a different need might take over the production of the sensations without interrupting the signal, and, if this happened, we would not want to back-date this need to the first onset of the sensations. It is, therefore, essential to Russell's theory that sensations of hunger should have a specific character additional to the discomfort which they share with items initiating syndromes that constitute other needs. It is also essential that this specific character should be additional to the specific behaviour that it causes. If these requirements were not met, the criterion of individual identity would be inadequate. But its adequacy does not require that the specific characters should belong to sensations, or that it should be recognised by the person or produce any direct effect in his consciousness. The initiating items might be mental but preconscious, or purely neural.

However, this last requirement is created by a second role which Russell assigns to the specific character of the sensations. He uses their character to explain the fact that a person is often able to identify a need of this kind in himself before it is satisfied. As has already been pointed out, the explanation of this fact might be minimal: the specific character of the initiating item might merely be that it belonged to the syndrome which constitutes a certain need, and that it caused him to recognise the onset of the syndrome before any of its other items occurred. For example, it might be a neural event, which without the intervention of any sensation produced the unmediated recognition of the syndrome and then produced the other items in it. However, it is clear that at least in this area, which is the home-ground of his theory, Russell assumes, too restrictively, that, if a person were not aware of the specific character of the initiating item, his early knowledge of his need would be inexplicable. So according to him, the specific character of the sensations plays its second role in the obvious way: the person is aware of it and treats it as a signal.

This theory provides a simple explanation, but presumably not the only explanation of the fact that a person may be hungry without realising it, or may think that he is hungry when he is not. Of course, not all sensations of discomfort signal needs. So if it is possible for someone to have a need without knowing what its object is, Russell's explanation would be that he recognises that his sensations have the specific character of some need, but does not know of which one.

There is one last point about this application of his theory which should be emphasised. His criterion for determining the object of a need is not the organism's behaviour, but the result that removes discomfort. But in the case of animals either the behaviour that achieves this result is instinctive, or else the capacity to learn it rapidly and successfully is innate. So the initial steps in an animal's behaviour-cycle are a good indication of its need. When he extends this theory to such needs in human beings, he modifies this feature of it, because he has to allow for the operations of the intellect. He takes the rather romantic view that, in order to determine what we want (at this end of the scale), we hardly require our intellects, and that, when we do use them, they tend to misinterpret the signals, and so to send our behaviour astray. 'While we are talking or reading we may eat in complete unconsciousness, but we perform the actions of eating just as we should if we were conscious, and they cease when our hunger is appeased. What we call "consciousness" seems to be a mere spectator of the process; even when it issues orders, they are usually, like those of a wise parent, just such as would have been obeyed even if they had not been given.'[20]

If we now move to the other end of the scale, we find a patently different situation. It is, of course, possible for a person to think that he wants (desires) to do one thing in a certain predicament, when he really wants to do another, or to make a

20. ibid., p. 67.

mistake about his motivation for an action. Such cases do not necessarily involve the repression of his real desire and its confinement to the unconscious. It may merely be preconscious until he becomes aware of it. So far, there is some resemblance with needs. The differences begin to appear when we inquire what criteria of identity, individual and typal, are appropriate to a person's desires in such cases. Certainly, the criteria suggested by Russell are not the right ones. This is not just because a person cannot use mental occurrences involving discomfort in order to distinguish between the various desires (to do this, to achieve that, etc.) which he may happen to have at a given moment. The reason is more general: nothing that does not involve a specification of the object of such a desire will serve as a criterion of its typal identity, and nothing that does not involve its typal identity will serve as a criterion of its individual identity. So, though he can refer to his desire in that predicament, or to the desire that motivated his action, and, though he can correct his mistake by assigning a different object to a desire described in either of these two ways, he will not be assigning a different object to the same desire. The desire to which he now refers will not be the one that he thought it was. This is simply a consequence of the criterion of individual identity that we use in everyday life.

A second difference is that mistakes about the objects of desires are rarely established by the mere fact that the alleged object would not satisfy the relevant need (if there is one), or, more generally, that it would leave the person unsatisfied. For though what he finally wants to do in a certain predicament is related to his needs, and, more generally, to what would satisfy him, the relation is not nearly so close as Russell suggests. Of course, it is usually difficult to isolate the relevant need, and the concept of satisfaction is exceedingly vague. So there are many cases in which we simply do not know how to answer the question whether a person really wants to do something from which he will not in fact get any satisfaction when that desire is satisfied. How would we set about answering it in unimportant cases? But in serious predicaments, when it can be answered, there is no doubt that what would give a person satisfaction in anything more than the trivial sense that it matches what he thought that he wanted, is determined in a way that allows it to diverge not only from what he thought that he wanted, but also from what he really wanted. On this score too Russell ought not to have equated desires with needs or with anything like needs.

How, then, do we establish that a person is mistaken about what he wants to do in a certain predicament, or about his motivation for a certain action? We mostly rely on his behaviour, supplemented, if possible, by his own later retraction, even if his behaviour does not produce substantial satisfaction. The details of this critique of sincere first-person statements of this kind are complex, but one simple point is clear: it is largely based on what the person does and says, both on this occasion and on other similar occasions, and we ignore, for the most part, the origin of his rationally integrated system of desires. We determine his desires through their behavioural effects rather than through their causes, and when the effect does not match the sincerely reported object, we impute a mistake if the mismatch cannot otherwise be explained. It is true that we sometimes impute a mistake on the ground suggested by Russell, that the sincerely reported object did not bring substantial satisfaction. But this style of criticism is more remote, and its basis is more obscure. It would involve a psychological investigation of a person's original constitution, with its basic needs, and this sort of consideration lies very much on the edge of the area within which our everyday critique operates.

These facts about desires are so familiar that it is hard to find them strange. Yet it is strange that desires should be identified by their effects, while needs are identified by what would satisfy them, which depends on the original constitution of the organism. What makes this strange is that desires are related to needs in such a way that we can sometimes infer real desires from needs, and, if the conclusion of such an inference is negative, it can sometimes be strong. So Russell's paradoxical equation of desires and needs is a simple version of what we might have expected if we were not so accustomed to human life. How did we acquire two such related concepts, one with forward-looking criteria and the other with backward-looking criteria? Why do the criteria of identity of a desire, typal and individual, involve the specification of an object which is not determined by what would give substantial satisfaction?

The answer to this question ought to be deducible from the function of the kind of thinking that involves the concept of a desire. The two main operations of thought which involve it are planning and explaining. Planning is the primary one, because the reason why we use the concept in explaining a person's actions is that he used it in planning them. Now when someone makes plans for his future, he moves around his desires and beliefs on the chessboard of his mind, combining them according to a simple rule: he must never change the specification of the object of a desire unless the change is warranted by his factual beliefs. The point of this notional rehearsal is to discover, or create the strongest convergence of desire on to a single possible action. In the course of his life there will be many such rehearsals in different but related predicaments, and through them he will gradually build up a rationally integrated system of desires. Whenever real performance fails to bring satisfaction in anything more than the trivial sense, he will be likely to revise the relevant part of the system. The problem, then, is this: if such systems are subject to improvement on the ground that substantial satisfaction has been missed, why do we build them up with a concept of desire whose connection with substantial satisfaction is much less close than that of a need? Why does the system of desires achieve the degree of autonomy that is reflected in their criteria of identity, both typal and individual?

One point, at least, hardly needs explanation. It is almost inevitable that a mind of any complexity should file its programme in the form which Russell refuses to regard as fundamental – i.e. as a set of desires directed on to objects. The difficult question is this: Why do we operate with a basic set of such desires below which we do not usually dig in deliberation? Part of the answer seems to be that human life is too variegated for us to operate in any other way. It may be possible to trace back these basic desires to needs of the kind that serve Russell as a paradigm, but it certainly cannot be done in any simple way. Freud's theory of instincts is a typical one. Instead of taking each basic desire and neatly identifying it with a primitive need, he tries to make the connections in a way that is far too complex for those who accept it to be able to use it as the starting-point of their deliberations. His theory, in its so-called 'economic' aspect, treats a human being as a device with an inbuilt tendency to a certain kind of equilibrium. But the environment is so variegated that brief and serviceable instructions have to be printed on it. This is the role of the system of desires specified through their objects. The system is not imprinted at birth, but appears gradually, and its development is controlled by the revenue of substantial satisfaction. But it could not play its role of handy guide unless it enjoyed a considerable degree of autonomy.

The natural response to a theory like Russell's is to point out how deeply entrenched this autonomy is. Even when a desire is directly based on a need, it may not be included in everybody's system, or at least its normal form may not be included. When it is included, its strength may not be proportionate to the importance of the need. When it is proportionate, the person may not identify himself with it. This autonomy is, of course, quite different from the Kantian autonomy of the will. The formation of the ego is not entirely under our control. The autonomy of the system of desires does not set the will above them, but them above needs. So when we think of deliberation as the creative process of making up our minds, we are on an entirely different track. The autonomy of the system of desires would still be preserved even if we regarded deliberation as a process of discovering on what possible action the system, in its present state, converges with maximum force. For this would be quite different from regarding it as the process of discovering what action would maximise substantial satisfaction.

But there is also something to be said on Russell's side. The system of desires must govern by consent, and it must aim at some satisfaction of the needs from which, directly or indirectly, it originated. If it provides too little satisfaction, the sanctions are obvious. But perhaps the requirement that it must aim at some satisfaction is, in the end, tautologically fulfilled. For if it aimed at none it is hard to see from what source it could derive its strength, although, of course, the derivation might be devious. But, in its stricter forms, the requirement is substantial, and it has to be met in the long run by a person's enduring desires for kinds of things. What Russell does is to impose it on a person's momentary desires for particular things. Of course, the latter are manifestations of the former, and so we do sometimes use Russell's test when we judge a person's real desire. But we use it less often, and with less confidence than the more direct behavioural test.

Somewhere in the middle of the scale of desires and needs Freud introduced the concept of an unconscious desire. Unconscious desires retain an affinity with conscious desires, but at the same time they achieve a closer connection with needs. They are the mediators between the two concepts that Russell equates. When Russell equates them, he simply treats conscious desires like needs. When Freud inserts these mediators between the two, he gives them criteria of identity which are similar to the everyday criteria of identity of conscious desires. This is clearly a move in the opposite direction to Russell's theory. But he also makes the revenue of substantial satisfaction produce its effect on them without the intervention of consciousness. This is a move in the same direction as Russell's theory, because it brings them closer to needs.

Russell says very little about Freud's theory of instincts. His main concern is with the theory of unconscious desires, which he uses to support his own account of the mistakes that people make about what they desire. At the same time he suggests a revision of this theory which would make it more behaviouristic. In the remainder of this paper I shall point out some features of the theory which are recalcitrant to this treatment.

The most striking difference between Freud's theory and Russell's re-writing of it is that the dynamism has been reduced. According to Russell, most of the mistakes that people make about their own desires are not motivated, but simply attributable to lack of experience or faulty education.[21] In such cases there is no emotional obstacle making it difficult for the person who has made such a mistake to correct it. Russell does allow that some mistakes about one's own desires are motivated, but he assigns much less force than Freud does to the motives at work. His examples involve motives, such as the desire to think well of oneself, whose work is not too difficult to undo, because it is done near the surface of the mind.[22] This kind of motive produces superficial self-deception, and, while the person is still unaware of his real desire, it will merely be pre-conscious,

21. ibid., p. 72.
22. ibid., pp. 57, 73.

and that is, by definition, a state from which he can recover it relatively easily by a process that is largely intellectual.

The view that Russell takes of all such mistakes is a rationalist's view, which exaggerates the power of the intellect: if its operations are disturbed by the emotions, it can easily reassert itself. The exaggeration is partly the result of his assimilation of unconscious desires to simple unrecognised needs. But it is also the result of his assimilation of unconscious desires to preconscious desires, which is an independent error. An unconscious desire, according to Freud's theory, is one which has been repressed by a powerful emotional force, operating without the intervention of consciousness, and which is, therefore, impossible for the person to recover unaided or by purely intellectual means.

The concept of a new kind of entity requires criteria of identity, both typal and individual. So what are the criteria for an unconscious desire? This question is being asked in the context of a second question, which has been shaping the discussion of Russell's theory: Can a person refer to his want, assign the wrong object to it, and then correct his mistake by assigning the right object to the same want? The second question was answered in the affirmative for needs, but in the negative for motives and for the kind of desire that an agent has, or forms in a given predicament. So, when we ask it about unconscious desires, there appears to be a dilemma. Either the answer is affirmative, in this case, or it is negative. If it is affirmative then, at least to this extent, but perhaps not to the extent required by Russell, their criterion of individual identity will be like that of needs. If, on the other hand, the answer is negative, their criterion of individual identity will be like that of conscious desires.

If unconscious desires are to serve as mediating entities, it looks as if a middle way must be found between these two alternatives. The middle way taken by Freud was to treat conscious desires as the terminal products of a long and complex sequence of mental transformations, which goes right back to the early needs of the infant, but which has a certain distant affinity with rational deliberation. One way to appreciate the character of this compromise is to contrast it with Russell's revised version of it. Russell connects a conscious desire with its earlier history by simply equating it with a need. Freud's move in this direction is more subtle. He traces back the desire to its origin as a member of a more primitive system, the unconscious, which develops from early needs. At the same time he maintains a close connection between the desire in its primitive form in the unconscious and the desire in its later conscious form by giving it a similar criterion of identity. An unconscious desire, like a conscious one, consists of an element of feeling directed on to an object and its criteria of typal and individual identity involve this object in the same familiar way. It is through this similarity that the affinity between the operations of the unconscious and rational deliberation is preserved.

This affinity with rational deliberation is another, striking difference between Freud's theory and Russell's revision of it. Freud starts from the fairly common view, held by Hume and by Russell himself in 'The philosophy of logical atomism', but rejected in the opening paragraphs of Chapter 3 of *The Analysis of Mind*, that a desire consists of an element of feeling directed on to an object. This view is often criticised on the ground that it does not fit cases of trivial objects or instant satisfaction. Such criticisms do not go very deep, and Russell's method of assessing it is better. For taken by itself, it has very little substance, and almost everything depends on how it is developed. What Russell does is to ask how far back in the history of a conscious desire it can be pushed. His answer is that it can scarcely be pushed any distance. He merely allows that, when a person misinterprets his 'primary desire', the misinterpretation will generate a 'secondary desire', which will not start with a problematical feeling of discomfort, because its object will be determined by the belief which generated it.[23] But this is a small and qualified concession to the view that he rejects. Freud's elaboration of the rejected view is the essence of his theory. He pushes it far back into the early history of a conscious desire, uncovering an analogue of rational deliberation in the unconscious.

There is one very obvious way of using the view rejected by Russell in order to produce a genetic account of a conscious desire. If someone wants to do a particular thing, this momen-

23. ibid., pp. 72–4.

tary desire may have been derived by rational deliberation from a long-standing desire for a certain kind of goal. If so, we might say that an element of feeling had been transmitted from that kind of goal, which would be one object, to the particular action, which would be another object. This requires the following criterion of identity for an element of feeling: any element which is a component of a desire produced by deliberation may be identified with any element which is a component of one of its ancestors in deliberation. Treated in this way, the identity of an element of feeling is like that of a family, or clone. The family multiplies when a person's desire for a general kind of goal fans out into a wide range of desires for more specific, and finally for individual objects. Here, of course, it is assumed that the various desires in a family of this kind are distinguished by the ordinary criterion of individual identity, which involves the specification of their objects. It is only the feeling that remains identical. But, once we have reached this point, it is a short further step to treating the desires themselves as identical.

These two steps seem to be harmless and free from difficulty, provided that they are restricted to simple pieces of deliberation which do not involve intermarriage between different families. We merely have to keep cool and avoid any confusion between the ordinary criterion of individual identity of a desire and the new genetic criterion of identity. However, these developments of the common, Humean view are of no great importance to Freud's theory of unconscious desires. What is important is what makes them possible: *viz.*, the fact that 'affect' is attached to one object because, and only because, it was attached to another. His really novel suggestion is concerned with the nature of this kind of ancestral relationship between desires identified individually by the ordinary criterion which involves their objects. He dropped the assumption that the process of generation must be rational deliberation which is conscious, or, at least, preconscious, and claimed to have found another, otherwise similar, but non-rational method of generation, governed by laws of its own in the unconscious. If this claim is correct, it will be possible to use the new genetic criterion of individual identity for desires. Indeed, it would be natural to make use of it, because Freud's 'affects' are often emotions with complex structures and slots for the insertion of suitably inter-related objects. But it would hardly matter whether we actually exploited this opportunity or not. Its existence would be the important thing.

It is notoriously difficult to keep doubts about the truth of Freud's claim separate from doubts about its intelligibility. For the latter are often expressed in an ambiguous way: 'How can desires, identified individually in the ordinary way, be generated out of one another by a non-rational process?' But if this is a question of intelligibility, we might as well say that we cannot understand that everyday miracle, rational deliberation, which regularly transmits an element of feeling from one object to another along a chain of factual beliefs.

A more profound doubt might be felt about the particular way in which Freud understands the theory. Certainly, he identifies unconscious desires by the ordinary criterion which involves their objects. But if they originate from infantile needs, is there any real difference between identifying them in this way and identifying them in something like Russell's way? The affinity between the operations of the unconscious and rational deliberation ought to amount to more than the adoption of a *façon de parler*. Why should not Russell's theory be applied to unconscious desires? The history of an unconscious desire would then be a series of unconscious interpretations of a need dictated by the revenue of substantial satisfaction.

But this revision of Freud's theory omits repression. If some unconscious desires have been forcibly repressed, because they were unbearable in consciousness, these at least could not be treated in Russell's way. But there are other theoretical reasons for treating all unconscious desires, including those that have not been repressed, in Freud's way. One is that the transmission of 'affect' from object to object is a more intelligible kind of unconscious mental event than the kind postulated by this version of Russell's revision. Another reason is that the stubbornness and rigidity of unconscious desires is more easily explicable if they have the autonomy that is characteristic of conscious desires than if they are based on unconscious intellectual errors. But the further back we go in the direction of infantile needs, the less difference there will be between the two conceptual schemes.

On the other borderline, which separates unconscious from pre-conscious desires, there are clear differences between the kinds of mistakes that can be made. In Russell's examples, whatever his theory about them, a desire is pre-conscious, and so the person makes a mistake about what he really wants to do, or about his motivation. What happens in these cases is that a desire drops into pre-consciousness, perhaps because it does not fit the person's image of himself. This lapse leaves other desires in control of the field of consciousness, and, as a result, his view of what he really wants to do, or of his motivation, is distorted. The matter is put straight when he realises that he wants to do something different from what he had thought that he wanted to do, or that his motive is not what he had thought it was. In either case, what happens is that he indicates the wrong desire, and the wrong desire is, by the ordinary criterion of individual identity, a different desire from the right one.

Now there is an obvious similarity between this kind of mistake and the kind of mistake that is made when an unconscious desire is involved. In both cases alike the person will be unaware of a desire that is relevant to his view of what he wants to do, or of his motivation for his action. But underneath this similarity there are several differences. The first is that an unconscious desire does not leave other desires in complete control of the field of consciousness. It promotes as its representative in consciousness a desire which, by the ordinary criterion of individual identity, is not the same one. Another difference is that when an unconscious desire is at work, the person really will be influenced by its representative, which will have taken over some of the power of its principal: whereas a pre-conscious desire does not have a representative in consciousness, and so, if we choose to say that it is masked by a conscious desire, this will be a different relationship, and there is no general presumption that the conscious desire will have any real power – it may even have been fabricated for the occasion.

It is a consequence of these two differences that a mistake caused by the fact that a desire is unconscious will not be complete. This may seem surprising, since a mistake of this kind may lead a person to think that he wants to do something which in fact he does not want to do, and that mistake, judged by the ordinary criterion of individual identity of a desire, really would be a complete one. But the paradox vanishes on closer inspection. What a person wants to do, or his motive for doing it, may be a function of many components, and the mistake that is not complete is a mistake about one of these components. The reason why it is not complete is that this component has taken over some of the power of the unconscious desire which produced it. Here, as at so many points in this theory, the genetic analysis of desires is essential.

So why should the theory not include the genetic criterion of individual identity of desires which was sketched earlier in this paper? Certainly, the comment 'Your desire is not really for this' (the object in consciousness) 'but for that' (the object in the unconscious) loses its paradoxical character when its meaning and the underlying theory are properly understood. Of course, no such comment can be made when 'affect' is transmitted by rational deliberation. But that is no mystery. However, the applicability of the genetic criterion of individual identity would be limited. For the pattern of generation is often complicated by intermarriage between different families, and when this happens, the appropriate analogue is a set of genes rather than a family.

But the genetic criterion of individual identity is an optional superstructure which hardly matters to the theory. If the theory is true, it will anyway be possible to refer to desires by specifying their causes rather than their effects or their objects. This is somewhat like the possibility of referring to a desire by specifying its initiating item, which Russell's theory allows. Of course, the two theories are not exactly alike at this point. For Russell bases the criterion of individual identity on the initiating item. But in Freud's theory the criterion of individual identity would be genetic, and its adoption is less important than what makes it possible to adopt it.

Finally, if Russell's revision of Freud's theory implies that every event in the unconscious has a separate behavioural correlate, he is really putting forward a different theory. For Freud's reconstructions of the histories of desires in the unconscious are more daring than this, and they are certainly offered in the spirit of scientific realism. From this it does not follow that the events in such histories are mental. But it is essential to his theory that they are connected through their contents, and this does make them mental, whatever else they are.

11 Wittgenstein's Treatment of Solipsism in the *Tractatus*

It would be difficult to feel confident in the completeness of an interpretation of *Tractatus* 5.6–5.641. For Wittgenstein's remarks in this enigmatic passage have a certain richness, which gives them the possibility of development in more than one direction. Their connections with Schopenhauer's ideas about solipsism, explored by P. M. S. Hacker in *Insight and Illusion*,[1] do not always make them easier to understand. How much does Wittgenstein's use of Schopenhauer's words commit him to acceptance of his ideas? Does the critique of solipsism in the *Tractatus* depend on the treatment of the will, which comes later in the book? These are difficult questions of interpretation, and I shall not attempt a full answer to them in this paper. Instead, I shall select a series of connected points which Wittgenstein makes prominently. There may well be other, equally interesting points in the background of his discussion, especially when it is read together with the remarks in the *Notebooks* that were not repeated in the *Tractatus*. I make no claim to the completeness of my interpretation, but I hope to show that there is a strong, independent and original argument linking the points that I select.

First, a rough classification of the various types of solipsism is needed. In general, the solipsist says that the things that exist are all related to his own experience. This, of course, is dogmatic solipsism, and there are weaker versions of the thesis. There are also two further dimensions of possible variation. One variant is the reference-point that is chosen: 'experience' is a vague word, and the reference-point might be the solipsist's immediate field of consciousness, or, alternatively, it might be the ego to which that field is supposed to be presented. The second variant is the relation between the reference-point and the only things to which the solipsist concedes existence: the relation might be identity – i.e. the thesis might be that the only things that exist

1. Oxford, 1972. See Ch. 3.

are the contents of the immediate field, identified in either of the two ways that have just been distinguished – or, alternatively, the relation might be more remote, so that the basis would be broader – e.g. things recollected might also be allowed to have existed, or perhaps the thesis might be even more liberal and let in things which could be recollected. There is, however, an absolute limit to the liberalisation of the theory: the privileged basis cannot include any things which would not be accessible in any direct way. All these versions of solipsism face an inconspicuous but formidable problem: How is the reference-point itself identified?

There is one more dimension of variation that needs to be mentioned before Wittgenstein's remarks are examined. The restriction put by the solipsist on the things that exist has two distinct consequences. It limits knowledge of truths, and it limits understanding of meanings. Traditional solipsism emphasises the first of these two consequences, and so-called 'linguistic solipsism' emphasises the second.

Wittgenstein's treatment of this topic in the *Tractatus* has four striking features:

i. It is an investigation of the subject-self, or ego.

ii. It explores the consequences of the fact that the ego is not an object of experience.

iii. It is especially concerned with the consequences for linguistic solipsism.

iv. The outcome of the investigation is that the linguistic solipsist is making a good point, but making it in the wrong way, because he is trying to say what can only be shown.

It can hardly be an accident that the last three points can be read as a criticism of the account of the ego which Russell gave in 'On the nature of acquaintance'. This work of Russell's was published as three articles in the *Monist* in 1914 and 1915, and they have been reprinted by R. C. Marsh in *Essays in Logic and Knowledge*. But the articles are, in fact, the opening chapters of a book, *Theory of Knowledge*, which Wittgenstein is known to have read and criticised severely in 1913, and which Russell never published in its entirety. So it might be useful to sketch in Russell's 1913 theory of the ego as part of the background of the *Tractatus*, without, of course, implying that there is no debt to Schopenhauer. Hacker makes the plausible conjecture that

Wittgenstein re-read Schopenhauer's *The World as Will and Idea* while he was writing the last of the three surviving notebooks.[2] What I am adding is that Russell's 1913 ideas were still vivid in his mind, the latest and one of the clearest examples of what he took to be a crucial error.

Russell's treatment of self-knowledge in 'On the nature of acquaintance' is entirely concerned with the ego. He points out that the theory of the ego has nothing to do with the problem of personal identity.[3] For this problem can be solved only through an examination of the contents of a mind,[4] and the ego is not among the contents of a mind. Here he is retracting his earlier view, maintained with some hesitation, that the ego is an object of acquaintance.[5] He has become convinced by Hume's criticisms of that kind of theory.

So far Wittgenstein's discussion runs roughly parallel. In the *Tractatus* there is the same focus on to the problem of the ego, and the same insistence that it is not an object of experience.[6] This Humean point is, of course, entirely compatible with the empirical accessibility of the composite self studied by psychology.[7] But Wittgenstein disagrees with what Russell says next. For Russell's next step is to argue that the ego is known only by description,[8] and, according to Wittgenstein, this is based on a misunderstanding of the consequences of the fact that the ego is not an object of experience.

It might be useful to look at the difficulties into which Russell's next step takes him. If the ego is known only by description, then, by the principles of Russell's empiricism, it ought to be either a logical construction out of things of some other type, or else sufficiently similar to some other type of thing with which we do have acquaintance. But Russell did not treat it in the first of these two ways until 1918,[9] and the ego hardly meets

2. ibid., p. 64.
3. 'On the nature of acquaintance', reprinted in *Essays in Logic and Knowledge*, p. 163.
4. ibid., p. 164.
5. *The Problems of Philosophy*, p. 50.
6. *Tractatus*, 5.631 ff.
7. ibid., 5.5421, 5.631, 5.641; see Hacker, *Insight and Illusion*, pp. 62–3.
8. 'On the nature of acquaintance', pp. 162–3.
9. See 'The philosophy of logical atomism', reprinted in *Essays in Logic and Knowledge*, p. 276.

the requirement of sufficient similarity to any other type of object of acquaintance, even when this requirement is interpreted loosely.

This leads to another, related, difficulty. If the concept of an ego is connected with experience in such a remote way, how was Russell to identify particular egos? In 'Knowledge by acquaintance and knowledge by description' he had suggested that 'I' means the subject-term in awareness of which *I* am aware. 'But', he observes, 'as a definition this cannot be regarded as a happy effort.'[10] For, of course, it is circular. In 'On the nature of acquaintance' he tries to improve the theory by eliminating the second occurrence of 'I', and so avoiding the circularity. The improvement is to take the experience, which is, in fact, my present experience, as given, and to refer to it with a pure demonstrative lacking any connotation. 'The subject attending to "this" is called "I", and the time of the things which have to "I" the relation of presence is called "the present time". "This" is the point from which the whole process starts, and "this" itself is not defined, but simply given. The confusions and difficulties arise from regarding "this" as *defined by the fact of being given*, rather than simply as given.'[11]

This solution avoids the circularity, but the price that it pays is that any ego will be identifiable only in a way that makes its ownership of experiences necessary ownership. It is here that Wittgenstein attacks it, when he explores the consequences of the fact that the ego is not an object of experience (stage ii in his treatment of solipsism in the *Tractatus*).

As for stage iii, it is interesting to observe that, in 'On the nature of acquaintance', Russell anticipates the linguistic version of solipsism that Wittgenstein uses in the *Tractatus*. He says: 'Every word that we now understand must have a meaning which falls within our present experience; we can never point to an object and say: "*This* lies outside my present experience." We cannot know any particular thing unless it is part of present experience . . .' (at this point he reverts to traditional solipsism, which restricts knowledge of truths rather than understanding of meaning).[12] This is the precursor of *Tractatus* 5.61: 'We can-

10. Reprinted in *Mysticism and Logic*, London, 1917; pp. 211–12.
11. 'On the nature of acquaintance', p. 168.
12. ibid., p. 134.

not say in logic, "The world has this in it, and this, but not that". For that would appear to presuppose that we were excluding certain possibilities, and this cannot be the case, since it would require that logic should go beyond the limits of the world.'

But Russell formulates linguistic solipsism only to reject it, whereas stage iv of Wittgenstein's treatment is qualified acceptance of it. This is the final and most important difference between the two philosophers in this area. Russell argues for the existence of his own ego as if he were arguing for the existence of an object which he merely happened not to know by acquaintance.[13] This is a clear example of a metaphysical hypothesis masquerading as a scientific hypothesis. Similarly, he tries to refute solipsism by arguing that, as a matter of scientific fact, 'there are particular things which lie outside present experience'.[14] Wittgenstein's treatment is entirely opposed to this procedure: neither the existence of the ego nor the truth of solipsism is an empirical matter for him. These are metaphysical questions which lie beyond the limit of what can be said, and, with this qualification, he accepts linguistic solipsism, unlike Russell, precisely because he takes a different view of the existence of the ego.

So Wittgenstein's treatment of solipsism may be regarded as (among other things) a critical continuation of Russell's investigation of this topic. It begins with the same narrow focus on to the problem of the ego, uses the same linguistic version of solipsism and endorses Hume's argument against 'an impression of the self' in the same way. Divergence and criticism begin at the point where Russell fails to see the consequences of the validity of Hume's argument.

The details of Wittgenstein's critical argument are notoriously difficult to interpret. Part of what he says is clear, and part is obscure. The clear part, which will be examined first, is the inference from the fact that the ego is not an object of experience, to the conclusion that it is a reference-point which is not identifiable independently of whatever field of objects is being considered, and the further inference that, therefore, the apparently fierce restriction that solipsism puts on the things that

13. ibid., pp. 163 ff.
14. ibid., pp. 134–5.

exist is mere pretence. The obscure part is the implied specification of the field of objects that is being considered. Are they the objects that have been in, and are in, the field of consciousness of a particular person? Or is this restriction removed when the ego is revealed as an unusable reference-point?

First, some account of the supposedly restrictive force of linguistic solipsism is needed. If Russell had developed his version of the theory, he would have done so in two stages. First, he would have said that the limit of the propositions that I can understand is fixed by my acquaintance with things. Here 'acquaintance' is narrower than 'experience', but not so narrow that it will not reach into my past, at least when its objects are qualities and relations. In fact, the theory must be liberalised to this extent, because my understanding of meanings could hardly be based exclusively on my contemporary objects of acquaintance. His second step in the development of the theory would have been to add that propositions which I cannot understand cannot be understood. The linguistic solipsist's justification of this step would be that nothing exists outside the circle of my acquaintance, so that the basis of all understandable propositions must be situated within that circle. The first of these two steps is simply an appeal to Russell's empiricist theory of meaning, but the second step, which is the fiercely restrictive one, uses an argument which he did not regard as valid. In 'On the nature of acquaintance' he develops solipsism only to reject it on quasi-scientific grounds.

In this version of linguistic solipsism the restrictive mechanism clearly requires for its working a previous identification of a particular ego through the objects with which that ego is acquainted. The same is true of the version discussed by Wittgenstein in the *Tractatus*. However, there are differences between the two versions, because they are developed in the setting of two different theories of language, and two different ontologies. To ignore the differences between the two versions might discredit the suggestion that in the *Tractatus* Wittgenstein really has Russell's 1913 theory of the ego in mind. For if the similarity between the two versions of linguistic solipsism were exaggerated, a natural reaction would be to discount it altogether. The truth is that the features shared by the two versions are all that is required for the continuity of the two philosophers' discussions of solipsism.

The strongest objections to this claim would be that Wittgenstein's objects are not objects of experience. This is true, and point ii in the analysis of his discussion of solipsism in the *Tractatus* would be more accurately stated, 'The ego is not an object'. However, the reason why the objects of the *Tractatus* are not objects of experience needs to be explained. The reason is not that our cognitive relation with objects would not be acquaintance.[15] Nor is it that objects would turn out to be things of a kind that empiricists would not normally treat as basic (the tentative examples used by Wittgenstein in the *Notebooks*, in the *Tractatus* and in his later comments on the theory make this quite clear). The reason is that, when he compiled the *Tractatus* he had not pushed the analysis of factual propositions far enough to be able to identify objects. Of course, he never did succeed in carrying out this programme. But this failure was hardly essential to his theory, and, while he still thought that he would succeed, he took over the apparatus of empiricism and set it up in a very speculative way at a level of analysis that he had not yet reached.

The result was not an empiricist theory of meaning. For the basis of that kind of theory has to be a familiar type of thing, or, at least, one that is already identified, and all factual propositions have to be constructed on that basis. But the first movement of Wittgenstein's thought was in the opposite direction, from ordinary factual propositions to a totally unfamiliar basis, established by a transcendental linguistic argument.[16] Nevertheless, he was confident that the objects of the *Tractatus* are suitable objects for acquaintance and the second movement of his thought was to use them as a basis for constructing all factual propositions. So the range of objects fixes the limit of understandable propositions,[17] and this is all that is required for the continuity of the discussions of solipsism in 'On the nature of acquaintance' and the *Tractatus*.

When Wittgenstein endorses Hume's argument and deduces the first consequence that undermines Russell's theory, he borrows a striking analogy from Schopenhauer.[18] 'The subject

15. See *Tractatus*, 2.0123.
16. ibid., 5.562–3.
17. ibid, 5,5561.
18. Hacker, *Insight and Illusion*, pp. 64–5.

does not belong to the world; rather, it is a limit of the world. Where *in* the world is a metaphysical subject to be found? You will say that this is exactly like the case of the eye and the visual field. But really you do *not* see the eye.'[19] This is Hume's argument. The first point against Russell's 1913 theory of the ego is made in the next sentence. 'And nothing in the visual field allows you to infer that it is seen by an eye.' This point is less obvious, and Wittgenstein argues for it in the immediate sequel. 'For the form of the visual field is surely not like this' – here he draws a picture of the visual field with an eye in its tapering root – 'This is connected with the fact that no part of our experience is at the same time *a priori*. Whatever we see could be other than it is. Whatever we can describe at all could be other than it is. There is no *a priori* order of things.'[20]

Taken as a point against Russell's 1913 theory of the ego this is clear enough. But it becomes less clear when it is taken as an indication that 'solipsism, when its implications are followed out strictly, coincides with pure realism', and that 'the self of solipsism shrinks to a point without extension, and there remains the reality co-ordinated with it'.[21]

The point against Russell must be that in his theory the ego can be defined *only* through the field of its objects. It would have been all right if he had first identified it in that way, and then given a description of it which might be used as an independent method of identifying it. For in that case we would not have been forced to treat the statement that a certain field of objects is presented to a particular ego as the statement of an *a priori* truth. We could have extracted an independent method of identifying the ego from the further description of it, and so made the statement contingent. But there is no such possibility in Russell's theory. That door is closed when he says that the ego can be identified *only* through the field of its objects, and so can be known only by a description of the form 'The ego acquainted with . . .'.[22] In effect, Wittgenstein is reminding Russell of a common feature of their two theories of language. If a type of

19. *Tractatus*, 5.632–3.
20. ibid., 5.6331 and 5.634.
21. ibid., 5.64.
22. 'On the nature of acquaintance', pp. 162 ff.

thing is introduced in the way that Russell introduces egos, then the correlation of egos with fields of objects cannot be established empirically.

It is important to see exactly how the analogy between ego and eye is supposed to work. Wittgenstein must be assuming that I start by defininining my eye as whatever takes in my visual field. But then I can discover by experiment which part of my body satisfies this definition. I cover the upper half of my face with my hands, and my visual field is switched off. So it is a contingent fact that my eye, identified as a particular part of my body, is the point of intake. Therefore, Wittgenstein must be excluding the possibility of this experiment from the analogy, and in fact the exclusion is justified. For when I carry out the experiment, I make certain assumptions about the identity and relative position of various parts of my body, and about the propagation of light-rays and the dependence of seeing on light-rays, and his thesis is only that nothing in my visual field allows me to infer that it is taken in by an eye. Against Russell's 1913 theory it is enough to establish this thesis. For in that theory egos are tied by definition to fields of acquaintance, without any possibility of supplementary descriptions of them. So when Wittgenstein uses my present visual field as an analogue, it is perfectly fair for him to insist that, for the purposes of the analogy, I am not allowed to use anything outside my present visual field. Thus the analogy explains how Russell's inference forfeits its empirical character.

This brings me to the end of the interpretation of the clear part of what Wittgenstein says. Before I attempt to interpret the obscure transition to solipsism, there are two points that need to be emphasised. First, the suggestion that Wittgenstein's target was Russell's 1913 theory of the ego does not imply that he had no knowledge of other similar theories put forward by earlier philosophers. The point is only that Russell's theory was the latest example to hand, and that he is known to have read and disapproved of the book that contained it. The second point is that even in his argument against Russell he may well have other issues in mind. In the sequel I shall try to show that his transition to solipsism is made in the light of the difference between his theory of representation and Schopenhauer's. In fact, solipsism is the dominant issue in the *Tractatus*, and he pronounces on it first, and it is only his argument for his verdict on solipsism that begins with the theory of the ego.

The first step towards understanding the connection between Wittgenstein's treatment of the ego and his critique of solipsism is to establish what the *a priori* truth alluded to in 5.6331 and 5.634 is. How exactly is the fact that the visual field is not as he sketches it connected with the fact that no part of our experience is at the same time *a priori*? I have suggested that he is thinking of the statement that a certain field of objects is related to a particular ego in a potentially cognitive way (in Russell's simpler theory the relation would be actual presentation, which is the converse of acquaintance). This would be true *a priori* if the ego were identifiable only through its relation to this field. This interpretation is obviously required by the thesis that his main target was Russell's 1913 theory of the ego. But that, of course, is not enough to establish it. It needs to be established by an independent argument.

There are, in fact, two rival interpretations, and one way of arguing for mine would be to try to eliminate them. Both the rival interpretations are latent in Hacker's preliminary paraphrase of 5.634. 'Whatever we see could be otherwise. But, by implication, that our experience belongs to us and could not belong to another is *a priori*. It could not happen that we should need to employ some principle of differentiation to distinguish within the flow of experience those experiences that belong to us from those that belong to others.'[23] I am not sure how the word 'experience' is being used here, but I think that it is a collective noun for sense-data, images, etc. So the *a priori* statement, that your sense-data belong to you and could not belong to another, would be based on the criteria of numerical identity of such phenomenal objects. Since yours cannot be shared by me, or transferred to me, I have no direct access to them, and this yields a familiar argument for solipsism.

I am not attributing this interpretation to Hacker, although he does claim to see a closer connection between the solipsism approved by Wittgenstein in the *Tractatus* and phenomenally based solipsism than I can see. I mention the interpretation because it is natural to read this kind of solipsism into the *Tractatus*. But it is quite wrong. There are several objections to

23. Hacker, *Insight and Illusion*, p. 63.

it, cumulatively conclusive. First and perhaps most weighty, is the evident fact that in the *Tractatus* Wittgenstein does not commit himself to the view that objects are phenomenal (or that they are not). Second, even if the treatment of solipsism were an isolated passage presupposing that they are phenomenal, there is no indication in the *Tractatus* of any route from phenomenally based solipsism to realism, although 5.64 shows that there ought to be. Of course, an itinerary of this kind is given in some of the writings of his middle period, but there does not seem to be sufficient evidence for reading it between the lines of the *Tractatus*, as Hacker does.[24] Third, the *a priori* statement suggested by this interpretation is not particularly closely connected with the theory of the ego. It is equally relevant to a theory which treats the self as a logical construction without any residual subject. Fourth, this interpretation misses the relevance of Wittgenstein's theory of representation – a point which I shall expand later.

The second interpretation implicit in Hacker's paraphrase of 5.634 is much closer to the one for which I am arguing, but not quite the same. According to it, the *a priori* statement would be that if I experience any object, then the experiencing of it is mine. It is a corollary of this that my ownership of the experiencing is not established by any feature of what I experience. This interpretation, unlike the other, is compatible with the thesis that the objects of the *Tractatus* are not phenomenal. It also fits Wittgenstein's remark that 'whatever we see could be other than it is'.[25] However, it is still not quite right. No doubt, it is an *a priori* truth that, if I experience an object, then the experiencing of it is mine, and, if solipsism is to be genuinely restrictive, I must be identifiable in some way that does not depend on what I experience. This creates a general difficulty for any formulation of solipsism, and to this extent the interpretation is correct. But it omits the fact that Wittgenstein is concerned only with a formulation of solipsism which treats me as an ego, and that in this case the difficulty takes on the special form that my ego is identifiable only through its field of objects.

Wittgenstein's remark is directed explicitly against this form-

24. ibid., pp. 187 ff.; pp. 80–1.
25. *Tractatus*, 5.634.

ulation of solipsism, and he does not generalise the problem in this period of his philosophy. The generalisation came later. In the *Tractatus* (5.64) he says that 'the self of solipsism shrinks to a point without extension', and that it is because this happens that solipsism, when its implications are followed out strictly, 'coincides with pure realism'. The same narrow focus is maintained in his explanation of this remark, which closes the discussion of solipsism in the *Tractatus*. 'Thus there really is a sense in which philosophy can talk about the self in a non-psychological way. What brings the self into philosophy is the fact that "the world is my world". The philosophical self is not the human being, not the human body, nor the human soul with which psychology deals, but rather the metaphysical subject, the limit of the world – not a part of it'.[26] But the interpretation under scrutiny, unlike the one for which I am arguing, ignores this narrow focus. Therefore, the latter is preferable.

This argument by elimination needs to be reinforced. It is not enough that my interpretation reflects a feature of Wittgenstein's discussion which he evidently felt to be important. We need to understand why it was important for him to keep it focussed on to the theory of the ego, and the only way to understand this is to establish how he supposed the theory of the ego to be connected with solipsism.

Earlier in this paper I posed the question, how he intended the field of objects that 'make up the substance of the world'[27] to be specified. I asked whether they are the objects that have been in, or are in, the field of consciousness of a particular person, or whether this restriction is removed when the ego is revealed as an unusable reference-point. This question may be reformulated in the light of some points already discussed. Are they the objects whose range fixes the limit of the propositions that are understandable to a particular person? Or is this restriction removed when the ego is discredited as a reference-point? In this formulation the question is about linguistic solipsism rather than traditional solipsism, and it does not presuppose that the person is actually acquainted with the objects that underpin his language.

One step towards answering this question has already been

26. ibid., 5.641.
27. ibid., 2.021.

taken. If Wittgenstein is not committed to the view that his objects are phenomenal, then he cannot mean to restrict the basic range of objects in any way that presupposes that view. In fact, the only way of restricting it that is envisaged in the *Tractatus* is quite different. The basic objects are the objects of 'my world'. Now this specification of them will be genuinely restrictive only if it is accompanied by an identification of me. But in the *Tractatus* the self to which the solipsist appeals is always 'the philosophical self' or ego, which 'does not belong to the world'.[28] So surely Wittgenstein's thesis must be that solipsism is not genuinely restrictive, because it uses the ego as a reference-point, and the ego cannot be used in this way. In his later writings he generalises this criticism of solipsism by detaching it from the theory of the ego. e.g. he says in the *Blue Book*: 'When I made my solipsist statement, I pointed, but I robbed the pointing of its sense by inseparably connecting that which points and that to which it points. I constructed a clock with all its wheels, etc., and in the end fastened the dial to the pointer and made it go round with it. And in this way the solipsist's "Only this is seen" reminds us of a tautology.'[29]

This interpretation is confirmed by the *Notebooks*, which contain no suggestion of any other method of specifying the solipsist's objects. So it is not the case that Wittgenstein had several ways of developing the solipsist's case, and then selected one version of it for discussion in the *Tractatus*. It is particularly important that never in this period does he use the idea that the solipsist's objects are restricted in range because objects are a private type of thing. The whole treatment is compatible with realism.

At this point it might be useful to relate his discussion of solipsism to the more general aims of the *Tractatus*. Stage iv in my preliminary analysis was that, according to him, the linguistic solipsist is making a good point, but making it in the wrong way, because he tries to say what can only be shown. What exactly is this thing that can only be shown? And why is it that it can only be shown? Answers to these questions might put his treatment of solipsism in its place in his system, and, when that has been done, the final details of the interpretation may be completed.

28. ibid., 5.6; 5.641; 5.632.

29. In *The Blue and Brown Books*, ed. Rush Rhees, Oxford, 1958, p. 71.

Several commentators have drawn attention to the importance of the context of the discussion of solipsism in the *Tractatus*. In 5.55 ff. Wittgenstein argues that we are unable 'to answer *a priori* the question about all the possible forms of elementary propositions'. But since their forms depend on objects, this means that we are unable to determine the range of objects *a priori*. The only thing that 'we know on purely logical grounds' is 'that there must be elementary propositions',[30] and so that there must be objects. Is it, then, an empirical matter that there are such and such objects in the world? We might be inclined to think so, because 'empirical reality is limited by the totality of objects'. [31] However, we would be wrong to regard the limitation as empirical, because the range of objects fixes the limit of understandable propositions, which is also the limit of the world.[32] I can say that a matchbox contains this match and this one, but not that one. But this is because the limits of the receptacle are not fixed by its contents. If the world is a receptacle, it is not one that satisfies this condition. 'So we cannot say in logic "The world has this in it, and this, but not that". For that would appear to presuppose that we were excluding certain possibilities, and this cannot be the case, since it would require that logic should go beyond the limits of the world; for only in that way could it view those limits from the other side as well. We cannot think what we cannot think; so what we cannot think we cannot *say* either.'[33]

This crucial passage answers both my general questions of interpretation. The thing that can only be shown is that there are such and such objects. The reason why it can only be shown is that it is not an empirical statement. It is presupposed by the existence of language. If it is a metaphysical conclusion, it is neither a quasi-scientific one nor an *a priori* one. Both these denials are directed at Russell.

Immediately after this crucial passage Wittgenstein says, 'This remark provides the key to the problem, how much truth there is in solipsism.'[34] But what exactly is the key? In the whole

30. *Tractatus*, 5.5562.
31. ibid., 5.5561.
32. ibid, 5.61.
33. ibid., 5.61.
34. ibid., 5.62.

passage from 5.55 down to the end of 5.61 there has been only one, possibly restrictive, reference to 'me'. 5.6, on which 5.61 is a comment, says that '*The limits of my language* mean the limits of my world', and the phrase 'This remark' must refer back to 5.6. For the key must be something that applies to language, and to my language in particular, and the only thing in the text preceding 5.62 which it could possibly be is the thesis, that the contents of a receptacle can only be shown, when it is impossible to give them empirically because they fix the limits of the receptacle. This thesis, which is stated in 5.61, applies to the relation between any set of objects and the world that it delimits. So it applies both to the relation between my objects and my world and to the relation between 'the totality of objects'[35] and the world. Equally, it applies both to the relation between my objects and the only language that I understand, and to the relation between 'the totality of objects' and language in general. This last application is based on the common features of Russell's and Wittgenstein's theories of language.

In the interpretation of this passage it is an extremely important fact that the key works only if my world is a receptacle with limits fixed by its contents. Now Wittgenstein considers only one alternative to regarding my world in this way, and that is regarding it as a world specified through an ego. However, at this point the stream of his reflections on Russell's 1913 theory of the ego joins the main stream of his discussion of solipsism, and he argues that the ego cannot be used as a reference-point. The details of that argument have already been examined. Since it demolishes the only alternative way of specifying my world that Wittgenstein considers, it follows that for him my world is a receptacle with limits fixed by its contents.

So 'the key to the problem, how much truth there is in solipsism' is the fact that both my world and the world are receptacles with limits fixed by their contents. From this it follows that their contents cannot be given empirically. Therefore, what they are can only be shown, and what is shown is not an *a priori* truth. But this is only the first step towards understanding solipsism. The second step is to see that there is more than a similarity between my world and the world. The world

35. ibid., 5.5561.

is my world. This follows from the fact that both worlds consist of objects, together with the fact that the apparently fierce restriction that solipsism puts on the range of objects is not really a restriction at all, because the ego cannot be used as a reference-point.

So how much truth *is* there in solipsism? Now Wittgenstein is only concerned with solipsism based on the ego. His assessment of it is that it makes the good point that the limit of the world and of language is fixed by a certain range of objects. But by what range of objects? Here, according to him, the solipsist spoils his good point by trying to say what can only be shown. Now the realm of what can be said is the realm of contingent propositions. So the solipsist's error is to try to transfer his good point to the realm of contingent propositions. The way in which he tries to effect this transference is subtle. First he says that the world is his world. Then he treats his world as a receptacle with limits fixed not by its contents but by their relation to his ego. If this treatment of his world were possible, his original statement really would be contingently true, if true at all. For it would identify the macrocosm with an empirically specified microcosm. But, even if this reductive identification were intelligible in other ways, it fails because it is impossible to specify the microcosm empirically. The solipsist has the illusion of success in this impossible enterprise only because he supposes his ego to be a usable reference-point. When he realises that it is not a usable reference-point, he can still go on saying that the world is his world, but he must now mean this not as an identity-statement which reduces the macrocosm to a specified microcosm, but rather as one which expands the microcosm to an unspecified macrocosm.

These are long words. The simple point on which Wittgenstein's assessment of solipsism rests is that the word 'ego' is not the name of an identifiable object, but something more like a variable. It is not exactly like a variable, because it cannot even take names as values. It is something more withdrawn, 'a limit of the world – not a part of it'.[36] If this point is to have the effect that he evidently thinks that it has – the expansion of the limit of 'my world' until it coincides with the limit of the world – he cannot be identifying objects with any private type of thing,

36. ibid., 5.641.

or, at least, if he does, he cannot be treating their privacy as absolute. It is essential to my interpretation that he should not be primarily concerned with phenomenally based solipsism, and that if his discussion happens to apply to that type of solipsism, that will not be because the solipsist makes any use of the fact that his objects are phenomenal, but because he relies on the ego as a reference-point. In fact, both the *Notebooks* and the *Tractatus* provide my interpretation with all the support that it needs at this point, and the evidence has been ignored by many commentators not because it is tenuous, but because Wittgenstein's grounds for solipsism are unusual.

It is a corollary of my interpretation that Wittgenstein was not any kind of restrictive solipsist. Of course, he was a solipsist, but only because he took the theory in an unrestrictive way. On the other hand, he sympathised with the solipsist's tendency to transfer his thesis to the realm of contingent propositions. But he did not agree with it. There is a passage in the *Notebooks* in which he gives his own solipsistic tendency full rein: 'What has history to do with me? Mine is the first and only world! I want to report how *I* found the world' etc.[37] But he immediately notes down the corrective: 'The philosophical self is not the human being . . .'[38]

It is, perhaps, not enough to argue that in the *Notebooks* and the *Tractatus* the only kind of solipsism considered by Wittgenstein is solipsism based on the ego, which, he maintains, can be reduced to a version of solipsism which treats 'my world' as a receptacle with limits fixed by its contents. This is certainly a fact. But we need to know why he confined his attention to this type of solipsism, and whether there is any plausibility and interest in the movement of his thought from the critique of Russell's 1913 theory of the ego to his own theory about the limit of language.

Let us start from the thesis that the word 'ego' is not the name of an identifiable object, but something more like a variable. Suppose that we tried to rewrite this thesis in the material mode.

37. *Notebooks* 1914–1916, ed. G. H. von Wright and G. E. M. Anscombe, with an English translation by G. E. M. Anscombe, Oxford, 1958; 2 September 1916.

38. This is the early version of the last paragraph of 5.641, but with a difference, which I shall mention later.

It would come out as a thesis about the nature of egos, or 'subjects that think and entertain ideas'.[39] Or rather, since the word 'ego' cannot even take names as values, it would come out as a thesis about the phenomenon of subjectivity – something like this: 'There really is only one world soul, which I for preference call *my* soul and as which alone I conceive what I call the souls of others.'[40]

The next entry for this day is: 'The above remark gives the key for deciding the way in which solipsism is a truth.' It might be thought that the phrase 'the above remark' does not have the same reference that the phrase 'this remark' has in *Tractatus* 5.62, and that the key is not the one that is mentioned there. But the first entry for the day, which immediately precedes the statement that 'there really is only one world soul', is: '*The limits of my language* mean the limits of my world', and this entry must be the reference of the phrase 'the above remark', as it must also be the reference of the phrase 'this remark' in the *Tractatus*. So the key is the same in the *Notebooks* and in the *Tractatus*: both the world and my world are receptacles with limits fixed by their contents. My world may appear to be an empirically limited receptacle. But this is an illusion, because my world cannot be individuated through an ego. There really is only one world soul.

When Wittgenstein's thesis about the ego is expressed in this way in the material mode, it may be called 'idealism'. He himself calls it that in the passage in the *Notebooks* in which he recapitulates his remarks about solipsism and the ego: 'This is the way I have travelled: Idealism singles men out from the world as unique, solipsism singles me alone out, and at last I see that I too belong with the rest of the world, and so on the one side *nothing* is left over, and on the other side, as unique, *the world*. In this way idealism leads to realism if it is strictly thought out.'[41] In the *Tractatus* he omits the first stage in his account of this journey, and makes it start from solipsism.[42]

Nevertheless, it is worth asking what kind of idealism he meant when he called the thesis, that there is only one world soul, 'idealism'. The answer to this question ought to throw light

39. *Tractatus*, 5.631.
40. *Notebooks*, 23 May 1915.
41. ibid, 15 October 1916.
42. *Tractatus*, 5.64.

on his unusual version of solipsism. For according to him, the two doctrines originate in the same kind of way.

We might conjecture that he meant some kind of Cartesian theory. But this cannot be right. For never in the *Notebooks* or in the *Tractatus* does he express even qualified agreement with the kind of idealism that restricts or tends to restrict the mind to knowledge of its own contents. It is true that he uses the language of 19th century idealism, and, in particular, the language of Schopenhauer. But he is putting new wine into old bottles, and he is characteristically reticent about its effect on them. His theory of representation is essentially realist. The mind consists of picturing facts,[43] but its knowledge is not restricted to them. If its knowledge did not reach beyond them, it could not have constructed them.

It is, at first, difficult to see how any kind of idealism could have developed out of this theory. But there is a clue to the development, and it is contained in the doctrine that 'The world is all that is the case'.[44] If all facts belong to the world, they are all on the same level. But some are pictured facts and some are picturing facts, and when a mind, which is a series of picturing facts, tries to picture itself, it is likely to suffer from a persistent illusion. It will seem that behind the mirror of this mind's language there must be an individual focal point, the ego. This is not entirely wrong, because thinking requires a thinker. The illusion begins when the thinker is treated as an individual and yet not identified with the series of facts that constitute his physical and mental life. The way to dispel the illusion is to realise that on the one hand the ego does not belong to the world, and that, on the other, all facts, including those that constitute the thinker, do belong to it and are on the same level. So the world contains my picturing facts and yours, and an elephant's, if it has any. If we wish to bring in the ego, we should not show favouritism. There is no privileged set of picturing facts. Any set has a focal point, but no focal point can be individuated empirically. They all merge into the single focal point behind 'the great mirror'.[45] Idealism is mistaken

43. ibid, 5.541–5.5421, and letter to Russell dated 19 August 1919, *Notebooks*, p. 129.

44. *Tractatus*, 1.

45. ibid., 5.511.

when it 'singles men out from the world as unique', and solipsism is equally mistaken when it 'singles me alone out'.[46]

One reason for accepting this interpretation of Wittgenstein's treatment of solipsism and realism in the *Tractatus* is that it is the only one that makes his connections of thought intelligible. Why else would he say that 'the self of solipsism shrinks to a point without extension'?[47] But there is also some supporting evidence in the *Notebooks*. As has already been mentioned, the early version of the last paragraph of 5.641 occurs on 2 September 1916. But it is a slightly longer and more explicit version: 'The philosophical self is not the human being, not the human body or the human soul with the psychological properties, but the metaphysical subject, the boundary (not a part) of the world. The human body, however, my body in particular, is a part of the world among others, among animals, plants, stones, etc., etc.' The extra point about the human body is picked up in the next two entries: 'Whoever realises this will not want to procure a pre-eminent place for his own body or for the human body. He will regard humans and animals quite naively as objects which are similar and belong together.' This must mean that anyone who realises that he, body and body-based mind, belongs to the world of facts, like any other identifiable thing, will no longer want to show solipsistic favouritism to himself, or idealistic favouritism to all human beings. The piece of favouritism that Wittgenstein has in mind is the attempt to associate 'the metaphysical subject' with one's own body, or with human bodies rather than with animals' bodies, or, more generally, with any restricted type of thing.

This interpretation receives some further confirmation from an obscure discussion of psycho-physical parallelism a few days later. 'Now of course the question is why I have given a snake just this spirit. And the answer to this can only lie in the psycho-physical parallelism. If I were to look like the snake and to do what it does then I should be such-and-such. The same with the elephant, with the fly, with the wasp.'[48] So far, the word 'spirit' signifies something empirically discoverable, which includes character and intellect. But in the next three entries the concept

46. *Notebooks*, 15 October 1916.
47. *Tractatus*, 5.64.
48. *Notebooks*, 15 October 1916.

of 'spirit' detaches itself from its empirical basis and becomes the transcendental concept of 'the metaphysical subject'. 'But the question arises whether even here my body is not on the same level as that of the wasp and of the snake (and surely it is so), so that I have neither inferred from that of the wasp to mine [*sc.* spirit] nor from mine to that of the wasp. Is this the solution of the puzzle why men have always believed that there was *one* spirit common to the whole world? And in that case it would, of course, also be common to lifeless things too. This is the way I have travelled . . .' (already quoted).

The *Tractatus* omits this part of his itinerary. Perhaps the reason is that the interpretation of idealism is too far-fetched. Or perhaps it is that it does not attribute sufficient importance to the mind. But the excursion in the *Notebooks* does throw some light on his treatment of solipsism. It corroborates the suggestion that the solipsism of the *Tractatus* is based on the ego. For the idealism of the *Notebooks* is based on the ego, and it is a parallel formation.

The solipsism of the *Tractatus*, based on an ego treated in the way that Wittgenstein treats it, is genuinely transcendental. A solipsism based on the assumption that all my objects are private would not have this character at all. In his later writings Wittgenstein generalised his criticism of solipsism by detaching it from the theory of the ego, and he explored the consequences of identifying objects with sense-data. The solipsism that he envisaged then acquired a different character.

It would require another paper to trace that development and assess the relative importance of the two routes to solipsism. All that I hope to have achieved in this one is a demonstration of the coherence and power of Wittgenstein's critique of solipsism based on the ego. Certainly, he borrows the terminology and imagery of Schopenhauer. But the result is not a patchwork, because the ideas are his own, and a strong line of argument runs through them and connects them. In presenting the argument I started from Russell's 1913 theory of the ego. If this seemed to put the emphasis in the wrong place, I hope that that has now been corrected. Russell's theory was clearly vulnerable to objections derived from Kant through Schopenhauer. The most striking element in Wittgenstein's discussion of that old controversy is the way in which he connects it with his own theory of language.

Index

ability:
  conditional, 152–5, 158
  dispositional analysis of, 142, 157, 168–92
acquaintance, 223–33, 277, 281
action, 13, 18, 30, 97–141
Anscombe, G. E. M., 28 n, 29 n, 41 n, 42, 49–53, 58, 62, 154 n, 288 n
Aristotle, 236
atomism:
  logical, 194
  psychological, 194
Aune, B., 169, 177 n
Austin, J. L., 142–92
aversion, 122, 131
  see also desire
Ayer, A. J., 193, 203
Ayers, M. R., 145 n, 148 n, 153 n, 180, 187 n

behaviour-cycle, 253–6
behaviourism, 251, 254, 257
belief, 237, 239, 244, 249
Bergson, H., 225
Berkeley, G., 235 n
Berofsky, B., 144, 153 n, 155 n

Canfield, J. V., 80 n
capacity, *see* ability
causal, 56, 58–60, 72, 73, 76, 98, 131, 250
causation, 60, 63, 99, 127, 211
  see also necessity, causal
cause, 38, 61–5, 71, 79, 97, 106, 107, 111
  requirement of logical isolation of, 100–7, 123
  see also effect
Chisholm, R., 144 n, 155 n, 169 n
choice, 17, 19
choosing, 143, 144, 147, 149, 151, 160–4, 167–72, 179
commands, 26, 28, 37, 39–55
conditionals, 142–92
  contrapositive test of, 143–50, 157–61
  non-detachment test of, 143–8, 158–61
  pseudo-, 143–92
  integrated, 161, 166
  non-integrated, 161, 168
  subordinate, 148, 150, 156
corrigibility, 56, 57, 60, 74
  see also mistake, immunity from

Dahl, N., 147 n
Davidson, D., 46
deception, 80–96
decision, 13–38, 99
deliberation, 13, 36–8, 99, 117, 135, 269
depth psychology, 251
  see also psychoanalysis
desire, 16–38, 97, 99, 108, 121–4, 129, 131, 135, 248, 251–71
  change of, 20, 24, 108
  degree of, 38, 114, 132
  preconscious, 261, 265, 269, 270
  unconscious, 95, 265, 266
  see also want
discomfort, 248, 252–7

dispositions, 25, 132, 133
see also ability, dispositional analysis of

effect, requirement of logical isolation of, 104–6
see also cause
ego, 227, 228, 234, 273–89, 292
error, *see* mistake
existence, 197–9

familiarity, 238–50
general, 246, 247
self-, 246, 247
Fann, K. T., 164 n
feelings, 56–79
Fingarette, H., 80 n, 89
fit, direction of, 28, 29, 50, 51, 241
Foot, P. R., 173 n
foreknowledge, immediate, 98, 103, 116
inductive, *see* prediction
Freud, S., 263–71
Freudian, 94, 95, 258

Gauthier, D., 45, 46
Grice, H. P., 150 n, 164, 166 n
Gustafson, D. F., 80 n

Hacker, P. M. S., 272–4, 278 n, 281, 282
Hampshire, S. N., 13 n, 80 n
Hare, R. M., 39–49
Hart, H., 13 n
Honoré, A. M., 164 n
Hume, D., 56, 59, 63, 76, 126, 193–223, 237, 244, 251, 267, 274–9
Humean, 57, 58, 65, 268, 274
hypotheticals, 142–92

idealism, 206, 289–92
identity of material objects, 217, 218
of persons, 207–23, 274
images, 223, 226, 229, 235, 236, 240, 241
imperative mood, 40, 44–8, 53, 55
implicature, conversational, 164, 179 n
impossibility, 110, 130
incorrigibility, 57, 73, 74
see also mistake, immunity from
infallibility, *see* mistake, immunity from
inference, 202
a priori, 205, 206
initiating factor, 157, 167, 170–9, 182–6
insincerity, 26, 27, 31, 32, 41, 109, 129
see also sincerity
intention, 22, 26–9, 33, 38–55, 81–3
conditional, 149
irrationality, 86, 87

James, W., 209, 211, 221
judgment, Russell's theories of, 232–6

Kant, I., 198
Kantian, 264, 292
Kenny, A., 26 n, 28 n, 40–54, 154 n, 253–8
knowledge:
by description, 274
immediate, 24, 57, 97–9, 113–15, 126
practical, 116

Lehrer, K., 143, 147, 151 n, 169, 170, 173–9
Locke, D., 148 n
lying, 88–93

Mackay, D. M., 13 n
Mackie, J. L., 119

MacNabb, D. G. C., 193 n, 208 n
Malpas, R. M., 145 n
Marsh, R. C., 195 n, 223 n, 273
Marx, G., 165
Meinong, A., 228
memory, 24, 34–7, 114–16, 197, 211, 212, 224–50
  habit, 225, 236
  immediate, 225
  quasi-, 219
  remote, 225
mistake, 31, 32, 50–2, 56–60, 63–6, 70, 73, 111, 127, 129, 261
  immunity from, 61, 70, 72, 75, 79, 127, 137–9, 232
  see also incorrigibility
Moore, G. E., 169–71, 173–9
motivation:
  experience of, 134
  impression of, 127–38
  preconscious, 140, 141
motive, 91, 133
  see also reason for action
Myro, G., 174 n

names, logically proper, 201
necessity, causal, 195, 214
  see also causation
need, 98, 99, 104, 257, 260, 262, 266
neurology, 104, 116
Newton, I., 111
Nowell-Smith, P., 153 n, 179, 187, 192

objects of feelings, etc., 59–79, 100, 101, 114
  flexibility of the concept of, 67–70, 112

perception, 230–3
performance-specifying factor, 149–52, 160, 167–79
Perkins, R. K., 228 n
possibility:
  physical, 109
  psychological, 109
power, *see* ability
preconscious belief, 95
  desire, *see* desire
  motivation, 140, 141
prediction, inductive, 13–38, 113
propositions, 234–50
pseudo-conditionals, *see* conditionals
psychoanalysis, 252
  see also depth psychology
psychoanalyst, 94
psychoanalytic, 65, 66
purposive self-deception, 95

Quine, W. V. O., 201

reason for action, 97, 117–41
  see also motive
  falsification of statement of, 118–41
Rhees, R., 284
Roxbee Cox, J. W., 17 n
Russell, B., 194, 198–201, 224–81, 285, 286, 290 n
Ryle, G., 121

Sartre, J.-P., 81, 86–91, 94, 95
Schopenhauer, A., 272, 274, 278, 280, 290, 292
self-deception, 67–9, 80–96, 129, 265
self-exhortation, 27, 42, 44, 49, 52
sense-data, 230–3
Shoemaker, S., 219
sincerity, 108, 127, 262
  see also insincerity
solipsism, 271–92
  linguistic, 273, 275–7, 283
specious present, 226
subjunctive mood, 155
substance, 208, 219, 283

Thalberg, I., 164 n, 179 n, 181 n
trying, 173, 179, 191

unconscious, belief, 80
  see also preconscious belief
  desire, *see* desire
  mind, 261
Urmson, J. O., 228 n

verification, 189
Von Wright, G. H., 215 n, 288 n

want, 39, 45, 48
  see also desire *and* need
will, freedom of the, 143
wanting, 97–141, 108, 113, 151
Williams, B., 59, 71–3
wishes, 49, 53, 83–5, 93, 109
wishful thinking, 80, 83–5, 90, 95
Wittgenstein, L., 59, 206, 234,
    240–5, 248, 271–92

Yalden-Thomson, D. C., 193 n

Zeno, 82